THE CONSTRUCTIVIST LEADER
2ND EDITION

The Constructivist Leader

2ND EDITION

LINDA LAMBERT

DEBORAH WALKER

DIANE P. ZIMMERMAN

JOANNE E. COOPER

MORGAN DALE LAMBERT

MARY E. GARDNER

MARGARET SZABO

foreword by

MAXINE GREENE

Teachers College
Columbia University
New York and London

National Staff
Development Council
Oxford, Ohio

Published simultaneously by Teachers College Press, 1234 Amsterdam Avenue, New York, NY 10027, and by the National Staff Development Council, P.O. Box 240, Oxford, OH 45056

Library of Congress Cataloging-in-Publication Data

The constructivist leader / by Linda Lambert ... [et al.] ; foreword by Maxine Greene.—
2nd ed.
    p. cm.
    Includes bibliographical references and index.
    ISBN 0-8077-4254-6 (alk. paper) — ISBN 0-8077-4253-8 (pbk. : alk. paper)
    1. Educational leadership—United States. 2. School management and
    organization—United States. 3. School administrators—United States. 4. Educational
    change—United States. I. Lambert, Linda.
    LB2805 .C634 2002
    371.2'00973—dc21   2002024576

ISBN 0-8077-4253-8 (paper)
ISBN 0-8077-4254-6 (cloth)

Printed on acid-free paper
Manufactured in the United States of America

09 08 07 06 05 04 03 02   8 7 6 5 4 3 2 1

Contents

Foreword by Maxine Greene   *vii*

Acknowledgments   *xi*

Introduction by Linda Lambert   *xv*

CHAPTER 1   Constructivist Leadership: Standards, Equity, and Learning—Weaving Whole Cloth from Multiple Strands   1
DEBORAH WALKER

CHAPTER 2   Toward a Deepened Theory of Constructivist Leadership   34
LINDA LAMBERT

CHAPTER 3   Leading the Conversations   63
LINDA LAMBERT

CHAPTER 4   The Linguistics of Leadership   89
DIANE P. ZIMMERMAN

CHAPTER 5   Constructivist Leadership: Its Evolving Narrative   112
JOANNE E. COOPER

CHAPTER 6   Constructing School Change—School Stories   127
LINDA LAMBERT
DEBORAH WALKER

CHAPTER 7   The School District as Interdependent Learning Community   164
MORGAN DALE LAMBERT
MARY E. GARDNER

CHAPTER 8   The Preparation of New Constructivist   204
              Leaders
              MARGARET SZABO
              LINDA LAMBERT

Epilogue by Linda Lambert   239

Appendix   245

References   257

Index   269

About the Authors   283

Foreword

In the view of public schooling still widely taken for granted, images of hierarchy and management dominate the scene. The young are expected to learn what is doled out to them in texts or classrooms. They are to acknowledge and accept objective realities defined by people in authority; they are to master whatever skills are required to meet market demand. This, after all, is the way of conservatism. Traditions and social realities are not subject to interpretation, nor are they contingent on point of view. Neither the young nor their teachers are expected to say how, from their own situated perspectives, they make sense of the complex world around them. They are not asked to explain how events impinge on their lived experience or what those events mean from their vantage point. The meanings, after all, are considered inherent in what occurs; they are "given" to the same degree that the classroom chairs are given, the bells that mark off the periods, the principal's office door. They are, simply and objectively, *there*.

The last decade, however, has been marked by remarkable challenges to all this, and the domains of educational discourse have been alight with new visions of possibility. Pondering numerous educators' changing views, we find it hard not to be reminded of Albert Camus' writing (in *The Myth of Sisyphus*) about the feeling that stage sets are collapsing. "One day," he says, "the 'why' arises and everything begins in that weariness tinged with amazement. 'Begins'—this is important." Against the background of "Goals 2000," "world class standards," predefined outcome, and the rest, new ideas are finding articulation. There is a coming together of newly honed "progressive" approaches, qualitative research, and an awareness of multiple realities in the worlds of schooling.

For many (including the writers of *The Constructivist Leader*) these modes of sense-making bring with them what Camus calls "the definitive awakening." They cannot imagine a retreat to outmoded behaviorisms or to conceptions of truth as a correspondence with an objectively existent reality. Crucial to their contemporary orientation is the recognition that reality is socially constructed, and that a great number of once silenced people (including students, teachers, and parents) participate in that construction.

In schools and district offices, where right answers were determined by administrators alone, this represents a breaking of many frames. It argues strongly, therefore, for a theory of constructivist leadership.

There is something in the nature of a breakthrough as well in the realization that reciprocal processes within complex educational communities must now take the place of imposed agreements and totalities. Handed down as they so often have been through bureaucratic structures, they have frequently affected people as the consequences of what Hannah Arendt calls "rule by nobody." The anonymity of decision making, like the impersonality of so much of what has been handed down, is exposed and challenged in this book. As its arguments develop, all sorts of meanings radiate from such exposures and challenges. They are meanings that have been achieved (and are in the process of being achieved) by diverse thinkers and practitioners in a variety of contexts. Readers will be familiar with such notions as shared inquiry and shared decision making, as they will with the idea of a community of learners pervaded by critical questioning. The names and work of such predecessors as John Dewey, Jean Piaget, Lev Vygotsky, Jerome Bruner, Gregory Bateson, Howard Gardner, and others will be familiar as well. The interesting thing, however, is that they now appear in a novel configuration due in part to the writers' consulting a rich variety of contemporary psychologists, anthropologists, linguists, narratologists, and practitioners in many dimensions of existing schools. The book is enlivened and strengthened by concrete examples of efforts to reconceive leadership in a school and a school district, both marked by interdependent learning communities. The ideas derived from social and human scientists lose their abstractness and take on new meanings as we find ourselves attending to dialogic conversation and to what Linda Lambert calls "partnering" and "sustaining" conversations—each of them interacting with or infusing "inquiring" conversations geared to problem finding and problem resolution, or with conversations seeking shared intentions and opportunities for reflections on experiences that are open to common understandings.

Constructivist leadership is conceived as "the reciprocal processes that enable participants in an educational community to construct meanings that lead toward a common purpose about schooling." Dr. Lambert and her colleagues go far beyond both the management ideal and the monological norm. The very notion of reciprocity summons up not only interactions of many kinds but the kinds of imaginative activities that enable people to recognize how those with whom they are involved perceive the common world. Clifford Geertz writes about the importance of "regarding the community as the shop in which thoughts are constructed and deconstructed" and about how cognition, perception, imagination, and memory must be conceived "as themselves, and directly, social affairs." It is with such an approach that Linda Lambert and her exciting co-workers go at the exploration of "constructivist leadership." Like Geertz, they hope to make it "possible for people inhabiting different worlds to have a genuine and reciprocal impact upon one another." What is fascinating about what they say is the vision of educators, as they strive to render their practice meaningful, defining (yes, and redefining) a common purpose when it comes to schooling. Leadership then becomes an act of release as well as transformation. Persons are freed to envisage what might be and what should be, even as they are supported in their efforts to devise their projects in an always ambiguous world.

Storytelling, focused conversation, mentoring, humor, metaphor: all these may lead to new modes of discourse, to new ways of risking a breaking of the frames. Yes, difference must be affirmed as well as coherence, plurality as well as community. This book takes its readers on a remarkable journey through the landscapes of our culture, even as it moves us to see ourselves as collaborators working toward a "sea change" in public education. The book is scholarly, inclusive, and oddly energizing. It asks its readers to interpret what they find. It asks that marvelous "why" to arise with the hope that we who choose constructivist leadership can definitely begin.

Maxine Greene
Teachers College
Columbia University

Acknowledgments

In the 7 years that have elapsed since we constructed the first text together, we have had continuing opportunities to work with communities of learners and with each other—relationships that have served to deepen our understandings. This version of our work has been made meaningful by the educational leaders who have gone forth and done the work, reshaping the dailiness of their professional lives and creating larger images and possibilities.

We are honored that some of those leaders have written their stories for this text. These principals and professors tell stories of constructivist leadership in practice in real schools in the United States and Canada. We especially thank these principals: Theresa Jensen, Engelhard Elementary School in Louisville, Kentucky; Donna Burlow, Glenlawn High School in Winnipeg, Manitoba; Peggy Bryan, Sherman Oaks School in San Jose, California; Jan Huls, Garfield School in San Leandro, California; Del Bouck, Winterburn School in Edmonton, Canada; and Walt Thompson, Wyandotte High School in Kansas City, Kansas. Rosemary Foster, Assistant Professor at the University of Manitoba; Gus Jacobs, Director of the Kauffman Principals Institute and Assistant Professor at the University of Missouri, Kansas City; and Linda Starnes of Seattle, former high school administrator and Adjunct Professor at California State University, Hayward (CSUH) also wrote stories and conversations that brought life to their unique experiences in schools. Rosemary and Gus wrote the stories of Glenlawn and Wyandotte. Without these co-authors, this book could not have been written.

Interviews with superintendents also elicited fascinating stories about the challenges and satisfactions in the work of educational system leadership. We thank the following for their insights and encouraging examples: Les Adelson, South Pasadena, California; Daniel Callahan, Martinez, California; Ray Daniels, Kansas City, Kansas; Donna Michaels, Brandon, Manitoba.

Linda Lambert has had an opportunity to work with many outstanding practitioners and theorists and continues to delve deeply into the well of experience and insights gained from her relationships with Del

Della Dora, Art Costa, Mary Gardner, Linda Starnes, and Morgan Lambert—friend, mentor, colleague, editor, and husband. She is particularly thankful for having been a member of a unique university learning community, the Department of Educational Leadership, at CSUH.

Deborah Walker would like to acknowledge her Kentucky colleagues who have demonstrated the difference educators can make in the lives of young people, when they commit to constructivist principles. These include Clarice Cochran, Cindy Butterfield, and Sue Levy, teachers at Norton Elementary School; district-level colleagues, in particular Lennie Hay and Rita Peterson; and Linda Hargan and the staff of the Collaborative for Teaching and Learning. In addition, she would like to acknowledge her children, Nate and Savannah, for giving her firsthand evidence of the impact of constructivist learning.

Diane P. Zimmerman takes energy and inspiration from associations with several communities of conversation. Special thanks go to Arthur Costa and Robert Garmston for their vision in creating this community of learners found in the cognitive coaching network. Influential in this work have been conversations with William Baker, Linda Lambert, Morgan Lambert, William Sommers, Laura Lipton, Bruce Wellman, Mark Cary, and many other educators in the Davis Joint Unified School District. Intellectual pursuits require support and encouragement and for this Diane thanks her family, especially her mother, Margaret Power, and her husband, Richard Zimmerman.

Joanne Cooper acknowledges the early influence of Pat and Richard Schmuck, Pat in the study of women and leadership and understanding of organizational development in schools. Joanne's work with Maenette Benham and with Jane Strachan of New Zealand has sharpened her understanding of both women and indigenous peoples in educational leadership roles. In addition, Joanne's work on school leadership could not exist without the voices of her colleagues and students in Hawaii. Finally, she is grateful to four powerful women: to Eleanor Roosevelt, for her very early generosity and hospitality; to her mother, Marion May, who taught her courage and perseverance; and to her daughters, Kimberly and Katherine, who have helped her to stay sane and grounded in the world.

Morgan Dale Lambert's intellectual twig was bent by interaction with professors at the University of California, Berkeley. More recent influences have included Art Costa, Bob Garmston, Bruce Joyce, Del Della Dora, Bob Blackburn, and chapter co-author Mary Gardner. Experience in three California school districts (Castro Valley, Novato, Lagunitas) helped powerfully in the construction of meaning about change and renewal. Later work as facilitator with two networks of restructuring schools and observations and interviews with superintendents and other school leaders around North America have added to his learnings. Most significant has been an inspirational 25-year co-mentoring relationship with his wife, Linda Lambert.

Mary E. Gardner thanks Linda and Morgan Lambert for their friendship and stimulating conversations. She also thanks the Saratoga Union School District team—teachers, administration, school board, support staff, parents, and students—for the opportunity to practice constructivist leadership, and her five grandchildren for providing the opportunity to witness the power of constructivist learning. Last but not least, she thanks the many educators, friends, and her daughters, who have been critical friends in the evolution of her view of learning, leadership, and life.

Maggie Szabo draws courage and energy from participants in the university leadership preparation program—folks whose struggles, joys, and accomplishments help her stay real. Her colleagues are another source of intellectual challenge, practical know-how, and caring personal support. Key among many have been Linda Lambert, Linda Leader-Picone, Joel Baum, Kathleen Osta, Glenn Singleton, and Richard Valle, who have helped her "make the familiar strange" in sometimes unsettling but always fruitful ways.

Introduction

LINDA LAMBERT

Since *The Constructivist Leader* was first published in 1995, the response to the text has been nothing short of surprising. It became a best seller as a textbook at major universities in the United States and Canada. It found its way into conversation circles among K–12 educators, staff developers, and school reformers. We believe this response to be an acknowledgment of the need for meaning, clarity, and congruence in an educational world responding to increased calls for reform, accountability, and results. A number of these changes have taken the form of legislation that removes from teachers and principals the primary authority to assess needs and develop initiatives to respond to their individual contexts. Within the framework of constructivist leadership, faculties must have the ability to make sense of their unique situation and to develop strategies that fit.

At the same time, educators and noneducators alike are frustrated by the seeming inability of schools to solve their most intractable problems, especially those related to educating minority and poor students. There are no easy solutions, but the standards movement, if it is applied in a way that assures all students a rich, high-quality learning experience, and if it provides safety nets for students to reach those high standards, does hold promise. This new edition of *The Constructivist Leader* strives to advance a framework for standards and accountability consistent with the basic assumptions articulated in the book. In doing so, the authors hope to persuade educators and those who influence educational policy to choose integrity over urgency, autonomy and discretion over control, complexity over simplicity. In responding to the standards movement, the book asks the question, How do we make sense of it, respond to it intelligently, and not lose sight of our best wisdom and knowledge about learning and leading?

As we have worked with schools and districts over the past several years, we have focused our attention on practicing leaders and their stories. There are those who surface with a lightness of spirit, who tackle the intractable problems and don't turn away. Most of the stories involve courageous principals devoted to the belief that all adults can lead—just as all children can learn. It is from these sagas that we draw hope, hope that schools can become places of deep learning for children and adults. We share some of those stories with you in this book.

Once again, we ask that you imagine leading as the facilitation of constructivist reciprocal learning processes among participants in an educational community. Such learning draws from our knowledge of constructivism as evoking mental maps of the world, engaging with others to learn new knowledge and make sense of it, and reordering or deepening understandings. Our challenge to traditional conceptions and metaphors will deepen and expand our original work. Our reconceptualization of "leadership" will travel farther down the road to shared understanding because now we have new stories to tell—stories of schools and districts engaging in this work.

KEY IDEAS IN *THE CONSTRUCTIVIST LEADER*

The key ideas in this book remain the following, although we will sharpen the clarity and meaning of each:

1. *The lives of children and adults are inextricably intertwined.* The lives and needs of adults and children are closely tied together. It is important that we come to understand and interpret the learning needs of children and adults as patterns that recur in complex ways—the learning patterns of all humans. If something is worthy for children, it is also worthy for adults. Democracy must be experienced by both children and adults, as must trust and positive regard. Authentic work must be experienced by adults as well as children, as must authentic relationships and possibilities. These patterns of learning must repeat themselves throughout the lives of individuals if our personal, professional, and community endeavors are to make sense to us, to have coherence and meaning.

2. *Constructivism is the primary basis of learning for children, adults, and organizations.* The patterns of learning at the heart of this work lie in constructivism, an epistomological concept underlying theories of how children, adults, and even organizations learn. Individuals and organizations bring past experiences and beliefs, as well as their cultural histories and world views, into the process of learning; all of these influence how we interact with and interpret our encounters with new ideas and events. As our personal perspectives are mediated with the world through inquiry,

we construct and attribute meaning to these encounters, building new knowledge in the process. This constructive, interpretative work is facilitated and deepened when it is undertaken with others and with reflection.

Our chief understandings of constructivism have arisen from early childhood development and student curriculum. It has become more deeply understood during the past 5 years as a guiding principle in professional development and leadership. This text situates constructivism in leadership, identifying the reciprocal learning processes that enable individuals to construct meaning and knowledge together in community. Shared purpose emerges from this process, enabling individuals and their organizations to find heightened possibilities for growth.

3. Communities that encourage the growth of human potential are based on the principles of ecology. Social and biological systems share certain principles that capture the meaning of community. These principles of interdependence, sustainability, cycles, partnership, flexibility, diversity, energy flow, and coevolution are constructivist in nature. We believe that the energy that drives both communities and development is constructivist learning. As participants construct meaning and knowledge together, the professional culture becomes more coherent and focused on emerging shared purposes for teaching and learning. It becomes a community.

4. Patterns of relationships form the primary bases for human growth and development. Communities are generated from the patterns of learning and the patterns of relationships that grow within them. The principles of community place relationships at the heart of successful, self-renewing schools and districts. These patterns are the connecting nodes of the educational community through which meaning and knowledge are constructed and shared.

The connections form the basis for reflecting on and making sense of who we are and how we work. Relationships may well be the most important factor in our past, present, and future possibilities.

5. Diversity provides complexity, depth, multiple perspectives, and equity to relationships, thereby extending human and societal possibilities. Working and learning from diversity requires essential prerequisites of understanding. Among these is that diversity is a fundamental complexity in relationships and perceptions. Vital to such diversity is the presence of reciprocal, mutual, equitable relationships. If we do not understand each other as equal—in the sense of having something of value to bring to the learning process—we cannot form relationships that contribute to growth and purpose. The ecology of our systems will be out of balance. Power and authority, rather than learning, will drive the culture.

Diversity grows from increased consciousness, for its roots are in multiple frames, perceptions, perspectives, and interpretations (Bruner, 1994). Constructivism, by evoking multiple interpretations, perceptions, and reciprocity, promotes diversity. When the multiplicities of our own thoughts and those of participants working in equitable relationships are liberated, embracing diversity can be a natural understanding we meet on the road to learning and leading.

This text will now deepen our views and discussion of diversity and equity.

The intractable problems of American schools in failing to educate all children require that we strengthen this theme and offer practical means for reaching essential goals while holding fast to a constructivist vision of learning and leading.

6. *Leadership as critical social and intellectual transformation is achieved through reciprocal, purposeful learning in community* Leadership is about transformation of self, others, organizations, and society. Such changes are embedded in reciprocal, equitable relationships that enable participants in community to find purpose together. This is the essence of social and intellectual growth and development; this is the essence of leadership—a concept that has found a new home within communities.

It is shared purpose, a commitment to deep core values, that situates constructivist leadership in a social constructivist pattern. Constructivist learning and leading enables its participants to alter the worlds around them, fostering the hope that the larger society can indeed be reconstructed.

ABOUT THE CHAPTERS

In Chapter 1, Deborah Walker explores the dynamic history of learning and leading in this century, ending with a survey of constructivist learning. New scholarship from practice and literature will be added in the areas of cognition; brain research; and social, cultural, and emotional learning. The challenge to schools to educate all children well will sharpen our emphasis on equity and diversity.

In Chapter 2, Linda Lambert advances and deepens the theory of constructivist leadership. This definition draws from new scholarship and experiences to strengthen our commitment to equity and social action and the implications for schools and districts. Constructivist leadership is related to the work in spiritual leadership and its application to leadership capacity.

In Chapter 3, Linda Lambert suggests that a primary role of the constructivist leader is as a leader of conversations. A framework for understanding conversations is described with emphasis on reconstructing relationships through reciprocal conversations, especially with parents. The learning agenda for leaders will describe what we need to know and be able to do in order to lead the conversation.

In Chapter 4, Diane Zimmerman describes how leaders can apply language tools and maps that frame and sharpen our thinking in order to explore meaning and make language choices that further a group's shared understanding and clarity. This linguistic approach will be closely articulated with Chapter 5.

In Chapter 5, Joanne Cooper builds upon Chapters 3 and 4 to more fully engage narrative, stories, and reflection as a framework for meaning construction. Stories draw more explicitly from the ethnicity and gender of storytellers and describe identity formation across cultural contexts.

In Chapter 6, Linda Lambert and Deborah Walker present stories of six schools from the United States and Canada that are engaged in this work. These success stories will frame the challenge and promise of constructivist leadership and draw forth major learnings from each.

In Chapter 7, Morgan Lambert and Mary Gardner refocus the district's roles in sustainable educational improvement. They also present stories or cases from the field that portray school districts that are using constructivist leadership strategies that show great promise—in urban as well as suburban sites in the United States and Canada.

In Chapter 8, Maggie Szabo and Linda Lambert suggest further approaches for preparing constructivist leaders by describing successful university, regional, and district programs in leadership preparation. Further, they forecast the future of leadership preparation in our society.

In the Epilogue, Linda Lambert reflects on the patterns of meaning within the text and advances possibilities for the future of this new work in leadership. This new work will frame the new iteration of leadership development as reciprocal, purposeful, and situated within learning communities.

These authors join with a growing body of professionals who are challenging historical and traditional thought about leadership. This community of professionals has come to understand that unless leadership stretches itself beyond role, person, and position, it will cease to invite others into its work. This text represents pioneering work in the field and opens possibilities for a new century of leaders.

CONSTRUCTIVIST LEADERSHIP: STANDARDS, EQUITY, AND LEARNING— WEAVING WHOLE CLOTH FROM MULTIPLE STRANDS

DEBORAH WALKER

INTRODUCTION

When *The Constructivist Leader* was first published in 1995, it described in broad terms the antecedents of constructivism—constructivism defined as the theory of learners constructing meaning based upon their previous knowledge, beliefs, and experiences—and their application to schools. In order to convey a sense of history, the book also advanced ideas that were timeless, that would apply across settings and yet stay fresh and new. That is why Chapter 1 opened with a quote from John Dewey: "It is a cardinal precept of the newer school of education that the beginning of instruction shall be made with the experience learners already have" (1938, p. 74). Woven throughout were citations from early researchers in the fields of learning theory and cognitive development, leading to a definition of constructive leadership as the "reciprocal processes that enable participants in a community to construct meanings that lead toward a shared purpose of schooling."

But this is not 1995, and the context for education has changed—again. On educators' minds is the persistent achievement gap between minority and majority students that challenges our long-held beliefs about education as a social equalizer. In addition, the standards movement has generated great controversy, with standards viewed as a tool for achieving equity, or a means of standardizing and simplifying that which can be neither standard nor simple. No discussion of school leadership would be complete without addressing these two issues as well as a related one: the culture of accountability and its implications for learning and leading. So

Chapter 1 of *The Constructivist Leader, 2nd Edition,* presents a different way of looking at learning, and leading, through the lenses of culture and equity. The definition of constructivist leadership does not change but rather is reconciled with changing conditions and priorities for education.

As the chapter title indicates, the central metaphor for constructivist leadership is that of weaving whole cloth from threads of different textures, colors, and lengths. These threads are the concepts that, when woven together, result in a new understanding of leadership. The cloth has repeating patterns, just as the field of education engages in reform cycles that do not solve its problems but instead set the stage for further reforms. The colors and textures suggest the cultural diversity that is a reality in our country and in our schools. Moreover, the cloth as art calls for each person seeing it to interpret its meaning, to engage in the process of making sense that is essential to constructivist leadership.

CHANGING CONTEXT FOR LEADERSHIP

STANDARDS, ACCOUNTABILITY, AND THE ACHIEVEMENT GAP

The standards and accountability movement, just emerging when the first edition of *The Constructivist Leader* was written, has widened in influence and deepened in impact. Theories of leadership that have served school administrators in the past pale in the face of demands that all students achieve at high levels and that schools and their leaders be accountable for that achievement. As more states adopt standards for student learning and testing systems to assess progress, the conversation about leadership changes from an emphasis on the process of improvement to a results orientation. This is an important distinction and reflects a growing impatience with schools that are always in the process of improving without significantly changing conditions for students most at risk.

Kentucky, Texas, Maryland, California, and other states have invested significant resources in testing as a way of enhancing student achievement. Newly elected President George W. Bush has advanced an educational reform package that relies heavily on annual student testing in reading and math to ensure that students are learning. The culture of accountability presents thoughtful school leaders with a problem: Do they reduce teaching and learning to simple preparation for the state tests? Or is there a way for them to place student learning in a broader context that has students learn at deep levels *and* perform well on state assessments? This problem presents a central challenge to school leaders in the new century, one of creating a larger meaning and larger purposes in a sometimes reductionist milieu.

As school leaders examine their test data and strive to foster higher levels of student achievement, they cannot ignore what has been labeled the "achievement gap," that is, the disparity in performance between minority and majority, affluent and poor students. This gap has persisted even in settings where overall progress has been made in student achievement. Since race remains an unresolved issue in this country and, in particular, a legacy of slavery undermines the education and advancement of African American students, even middle-class minority students often underperform in school (Miller, 1995). National conferences and educational literature suggest strategies for closing the achievement gap (Hale, 1994; Delpit, 1995; Williams, 1996), yet the problem remains unresolved. In a high-stakes context, school leaders must search for ways to create a culture of high expectations and support for all students and a set of norms around teacher growth that enables teachers to teach all students well.

The work of the Education Trust points to some lessons that can help schools move toward results, especially in light of data that point to a widening of the achievement gap and reports from students in urban settings that they are not challenged by their courses or teachers. These lessons, summarized by director Katie Haycock (2001), serve to extend the conversation regarding why constructivist principles are essential to reach increased levels of student learning. The lessons are simple ones:

1. Standards are key if we are going to ask more of students and have agreement about what constitutes good performance.
2. Students must all have a challenging curriculum.
3. Students need extra help to meet increased standards.
4. Teachers matter, so both the preparation and ongoing development of teachers are critical to students' learning. (pp. 8–11)

Throughout this second edition, issues related to creating meaning-centered learning environments and promoting equity will be explored. While the lessons Haycock shares are simple, the actions required are not. New frameworks and structures are needed to substantially change the ways we think about schooling and its impact on students.

INTERNATIONAL COMPARISONS

The Third International Math and Science Study (TIMSS) pointed out gaps in teaching and learning for America's students as compared with students in other countries, primarily Germany and Japan. Authors Stigler and Hiebert, in the companion research study that examines classroom practices for secondary mathematics in the United States, Germany, and Japan, conclude that differences in classrooms within our country are much smaller than differences between American classrooms and their counterparts in other parts of the world. The authors describe how the national culture of each country influences the design of curriculum and instruction, as well as the roles that teachers and students play. While these differences will be explored later in the chapter, it is important to note here that during an era of increased standards, American schools have done little to change their basic structures and approaches in order to help all students reach those higher standards. Instead, the curriculum continues to be wide ranging and shallow; the teaching emphasizes practice without deep understanding; and the role of the student is to function as passive recipient of teacher knowledge that has little application to real-world settings (Stigler & Hiebert, 1999). In contrast, rather than covering so many topics superficially without assuring student mastery, teachers in Japan cover a few key concepts well, making sure that students understand them and can apply them.

The TIMSS study makes a case for leadership based on the construction of knowledge and the making of meaning within the school in two ways. First, in the comparison countries, instruction is designed in such a way that students take responsibility for inventing problem-solving strategies and for teaching each other. Second, teachers, especially in Japan, engage collaboratively in sustained development and refinement of lessons, called "lesson study," so that they grow in their understanding of how students learn. Looking at differences in student and teacher roles causes us to think about different conceptions of leadership as well. What kind of leadership among principals and teachers must exist in order to give students a more active role in their own learning? and to give teachers the opportunity to grow with their colleagues in their craft, so that teacher knowledge is viewed as dynamic rather than static? This chapter will introduce constructivist leadership, that is, leading for meaning, which will be developed throughout the book.

DEFINITIONS AND DILEMMAS

STANDARDS AND CONSTRUCTIVIST LEADERSHIP

Standards are defined in starkly different ways in school districts, in statehouses, and in the professional literature. In part, this is because the emergence of standards as a key component of education reform is based on several factors. A critical factor is the need to assure educational equity for all students. Standards themselves are not new. As Ruth Mitchell of the Education Trust explains in *Front-End Alignment* (1996), we have always had standards for some students. The difference is the requirement of high standards for all students, so that all achieve and all, regardless of background, have access to a rich, rigorous curriculum. Implied also in the view of standards as equity is the idea that schools and school leaders will put in place supports to ensure that those students who struggle in school for whatever reason will now succeed. Mitchell uses the analogy that in the past disadvantaged students have run blindfolded in a race where some can see the finish line. She posits that "Standards should remove the blindfold and make the tape clear to everyone, because standards are public statements of what all students know and should be able to do" (p. 3).

It is important to note here that the standards movement has evolved from an earlier trend toward emphasizing student outcomes rather than just content coverage. For years educators have searched for a way not only to teach important content but to ensure that students learn that content at a deep level and can apply it. Outcomes-based education— that is, focusing on what students have learned rather than what teachers have taught—is an earlier iteration of standards. Both outcomes and standards have at their core the recognition that learning is more than recitation; it is instead the process of making sense of new knowledge.

Legislators have defined standards as a way of raising the bar for student achievement and enabling states to enforce measurement systems based on those standards so student progress can be tracked. Ideally standards describe in broad terms the knowledge and skills expected of students (content standards) or the levels of performance students must reach (performance standards) to demonstrate they have met the standards (Mitchell, 1996, p. 4). In some states, however, the list of standards in fact describes discrete skills students must master and are not really standards. Multiple definitions lead to confusion, and political needs for accountability tied to funding can drive the standards movement in a different direction. Researcher and educational critic Alfie Kohn (1999) criticizes the implementation of standards—the reality versus the ideal—as a move toward uniformity and standardization, which hinders the creativity of teachers and the imagination of students. When standards are misapplied, they limit the ability of students and teachers to engage in meaningful learning.

The professional literature describes the need for standards to provide coherence to principals, teachers, students, and parents about what is important to teach (Schmoker & Marzano, 1999). The consensus in the literature is that standards are useful when they provide guidance about commonly agreed-upon goals without robbing teachers and schools of the autonomy needed to help their particular students. Benchmarks that accompany the standards—that is, examples of what good student work looks like so teachers can assess if students are meeting the standards—are another critical piece (Graham & Fahey, 1999). The process of benchmarking itself, where teachers engage in dialogue regarding what level of student performance is good enough, reflects constructivist theory of how teachers grow in their understanding of teaching and learning (see Chapter 3 for more on the role of dialogue in constructing meaning).

Constructivist leadership must navigate this debate about the definition and role of standards while at the same time staying true to constructivist principles. These include (1) making sense of different conceptions of schooling held by educators, policy-makers, and researchers; (2) imagining schools where students are engaged in authentic learning, which is part of the larger equity issue; and (3) making multiple meanings that reflect the cultural diversity of the student population. Here is where constructivist theory comes into play. If we define standards as a set of discrete skills to be taught uniformly, then we will not have gained for students a more meaningful and effective learning environment. If, on the other hand, we define standards as broad learning goals that represent important knowledge, and teachers and principals have the latitude to design authentic instruction for students, then we will have gained something valuable for the students in our schools. Returning a moment to the central metaphor of this chapter, weaving whole cloth from multiple strands, the standards debate and the impact of standards on the schooling of disadvantaged and minority students is a central design feature. Constructivist leadership calls for school leaders to weave together these different threads so the fabric of education is strengthened rather than weakened, and so the cloth has both aesthetic value and functionality.

CONSTRUCTIVISM AS LEARNING AND KNOWING

The debate over standards, accountability, and the seeming intractability of the achievement gap, while grounded in the 1990s, did not start there. Rarely has there been agreement around educational philosophy and practice. More than 50 years before John Dewey challenged prevailing views of learning by suggesting that education is an internal process in which the learner uses prior knowledge and experience to shape meaning and to construct new knowledge. The debate was not new to Dewey's time, but rather reflected a continuing struggle to understand how students learn and how schools are capable of fostering that learning. The purpose of this book is to advance a theory of learning and leading and, in doing so, to enter the debate in which Dewey was a significant voice. Using the theory of constructivism, this book suggests new directions for the structure of schooling and new roles for those who lead schools.

Constructivism has become a theory of learning that has emerged from a theory of knowing. It is an epistemological concept that draws from a variety of fields, including philosophy, psychology, and science. Fosnot (1992) points out that constructivism "is at once a theory of 'knowing' and a theory of 'coming to know'" (p. 167). The theory of knowing, as first articulated by Piaget, is essentially biological in nature; that is, an organism encounters new experiences and events and seeks to *assimilate* these into existing cognitive structures or to adjust the structures to *accommodate* the new information. The cognitive structures, or schemas, are formed and re-formed based on experiences, beliefs, values, sociocultural histories, and prior perceptions. Piaget noted that schemas are "under construction," meaning that the cognitive structures evolve as individuals interpret, understand, and come to know (Piaget, 1971, in Duffy & Jonassen, 1992, p. 140).

The "what" and "why" of knowing render the process both a psychological and a philosophical one. Individuals do more than assimilate and accommodate as described in biology; they reformulate their schemas to make sense of dissonant information and experience. Growth and development are prompted by discrepancy or "disequilibrium" between what is believed to be true and what is now revealing itself in experience. The reformulation of personal schemas has coherence and purpose: It is shaped by the values that contribute to an individual's being able to make meaning. Thus individuals assign meaning to experience and at the same time construct knowledge from experience.

The processes of "coming to know" are influenced and shaped by reflection, mediation, and social interactions. Both Bruner (Bruner & Haste, 1987) and Vygotsky framed current understandings about the social construction of knowledge. Bruner (1966) described the role of language and prior experience in creating mutual representations for interpretation. Vygotsky (1962, 1978) described the "zone of proximal development" through which knowing is mediated and negotiated. In recent decades, Reuven Feuerstein's work (Feuerstein, 1990; Feuerstein, Klein, & Tannenbaum, 1991) has added significantly to our understandings of the mediated construction of the self, or self-modification. In the process of encountering new experience and applying reflective interpretation within social contexts, the individual learns and comes to know.

This psychological process is also a developmental one; it is a process in motion. Kegan (1982) advanced the idea that "meaning is, in its origins, a physical activity (grasping and seeing), a social activity (it requires another), a survival activity (in doing it, we live). Meaning understood in this way, is the primary human motion, irreducible" (pp. 18–19). Meaning, by its very nature, is developmental; that is, it propels us and causes us to evolve. It is motion.

More recent work in cognition builds on Kegan by noting that "learning is highly tuned to the situation in which it takes place" (Resnick, 1989, as cited in Furtwengler, 1999/2000, p. 4). The concept of situated learning has meaning for both students and teachers. For students, it can mean learning outside the classroom, in other settings, where the knowledge and experiences are authentic and not mediated by the rules and processes of the classroom. For teachers and principals, it means learning that is embedded in the classroom and school, not taken out of context and culture as in a lecture hall or professional development activity separate from the work of the school. In this instance, the process of coming to know is "anchored in a meaningful context" (Furtwengler, 1999/2000, p. 4).

Understandings of how individuals come to know have been translated into theories of constructivist learning and classroom practices. In this text we apply these same understandings to adults in educational communities, in their roles as learners and leaders.

THE EVOLUTION OF CONTEMPORARY EDUCATIONAL THOUGHT

As educators we struggle to define the purposes, processes, and structures of education. This is not an easy task. Education serves not only students and their families but also the social, political, and economic needs of our nation, and so it is influenced by many sources outside the educational sphere. A historical compact has enlisted us all to varying degrees into an agreement that public education prepares our children for citizenship in a democracy, but a closer look at schooling reveals that this commitment is not the dominant agenda. The prevailing winds of history, often those perceived of as threatening democracy, cast a long shadow into our schools. During the last century, the schools served a nation in populist reform, at war, in depression, in international competition, and in civil upheaval. Each of these forces has advanced different themes and concerns. For example, the 1950s were concerned with national security and the race to establish dominance in outer space. The resulting educational policy emphasized science, foreign language instruction, and new approaches to mathematics. The women's movement, fueled by the factories of World War II, merged with other civil rights movements and exploded in the 1960s, bringing efforts to achieve educational equality and choice. In turn, the 1970s were characterized by a return to the "basics" in curriculum, the use of behavioral models of instruction and teacher supervision, and a focus on standardized measures of student achievement, all with the alleged purpose of creating a more uniformly educated workforce for a faltering economy. *A Nation at Risk* (National Commission on Excellence in Education, 1983), issued in the mid-1980s, portrayed our educational system as weakening our stamina and abilities to fight the Cold War. By the mid-1990s, *America 2000* (U.S. Department of Education, 1991) had merged into Goals 2000 (1994) in a call for systemic reform, and the driving force was still the economy.

Even within education, there is wide variation as to philosophy, beliefs, and professional knowledge regarding how students learn and achieve. While educators are influenced by social, political, and economic trends, and sometimes the funding attached to these priorities, they tend to formulate their notions about education according to those theories and styles of instruction that fit their own learning patterns and experiences and their own world views. Educators can be socialized by district and school norms: for example, to be inclusive in their attitudes toward student differences and parent expectations or to be exclusive, expecting student behavior and parent expectations to conform to institutional norms rather than accommodating differences. Recent efforts at teacher, and now administrator, induction are aimed at creating a socialization process that enables beginning educators to understand and apply common insights regarding teaching and learning. In spite of these efforts, educators continue to subscribe to a wide range of theories and beliefs regarding the education of students and their own roles in the learning-leading process.

This chapter provides a brief retrospective survey of the evolution of educational theories of learning and leading within the context of recent history. The historical context provides a vehicle for understanding how educational theories are influenced by their times and by the dynamic between and among theories. It is important to note that even as new ideas about learning and leading develop and are tested, traditional theories continue to exert their influence, and in some instances they remain dominant. They are based on past practice, convention, and what is often referred to as teacher and community lore; that is, believing educational tenets to be true because they have been repeated so often.

As we progress through the twentieth century, we will begin to converge with a powerful stream of influence that began with Dewey, Bruner, Piaget, and Vygotsky and has joined with new understandings of intelligence and the brain and the impact of culture on student achievement to form constructivist learning. As we reveal the roots of constructivism, this chapter will set the scene for the description of the next new edge of leadership theory: Constructivist Leadership.

LEARNING AND LEADING: PARALLEL DEVELOPMENT

Educational literature abounds with the influences of learning theory on school leadership. For example, behavioral principles, when applied to learning, result in a system emphasizing skill development based on task analysis and rewards for progress made. When applied to leading, behaviorist principles result in school leaders' emphasizing external targets for teacher growth supported by a system of rewards. This example vividly reminds us that education typically has derived its theoretical principles from fields outside of education, such as psychology and sociology. Educational administration, as a subset of education, has also looked to business and industry for theories of how leaders lead and how organizations develop. The influence of the social, political, and economic forces referred to above and the evolving theories from other disciplines have given rise to parallel themes or movements that attempt to define both learning and leading in our schools.

These parallel and mutually influential themes or movements constitute dominant eras in learning and leading: traditional, behavioral, grouping/tracking and contingency/situational, effectiveness and instructional leadership, community of learners and community of leaders, and constructivist. Figure 1.1 offers a description of each of them and highlights of the prevailing assumptions and key theorists. Such attempts at categorization must be accompanied by several caveats. Each era experienced forces from multiple schools of thought. Each theorist's ideas are complex and evolved over time; notably, key theorists of one era often led the transition to the next.

The various movements in learning and leading dominated during specific eras, yet each world view continues to exert some influence on our institutions today. Learning and leading theories, as we shall see, have

FIGURE 1.1
Learning and Leading: A Framework of Parallel Development

LEARNING	THEORISTS	LEADING	THEORISTS
TRADITIONAL Students learn a prescribed body of knowledge through memorization, with knowledge viewed as true and unchanging. Strategies for learning focus on the teacher as the source of knowledge and students as recipients, with knowledge existing outside the learner. Emphasis is on obedience to authority. While an important learning goal is preparation for participation in a democracy, the classroom does not mirror or give students experience with democratic processes.	Jefferson Rush Mann Swett	TRADITIONAL The leader serves to maintain tradition and direct efforts of the teaching staff. Teachers have little authority over decision making related to goals, curriculum, or student progress. Leadership does not reflect democratic processes and is autocratic in nature. Notions of leadership are influenced by scientific management theory, with emphasis on efficiency and quality control.	Moore Schenk Taylor Bobbitt Fayol Gulick Urwick
BEHAVIORAL Learning takes place when knowledge is broken down into smaller pieces and students are rewarded for successful performance. Direct teaching strategies dominate, based on the belief that student behavior can be measured, diagnosed, and predicted. The aim in the classroom is to calibrate behavior to achieve set learning objectives and goals.	Mager Thorndike Popham Skinner Hunter	BEHAVIORAL The role of the leader is to shape human behavior to match organizational aims. Leaders, such as principals, reward desired teacher behavior and use sanctions when teachers do not cooperate. Leadership is viewed as being "transactional" in nature, that is, there is an exchange between leader and worker to achieve established goals.	Burns Halpin Barnard Simon Bundel

(continued)

FIGURE 1.1 (CONTINUED)

LEARNING	THEORISTS	LEADING	THEORISTS
GROUPING/TRACKING Based on assumptions from behavioral theory, students are characterized as differing widely in ability, necessitating homogeneous grouping strategies where similar students are given the same learning "treatment." Teaching efforts are directed at moving students to higher level groups, although in practice group placement generally remains fixed. Variations in teaching strategies and learning activities are based on the perceived ability level of students.	Thorndike Binet Dunn & Dunn Gregoric	CONTINGENCY/SITUATIONAL Originating in the business literature, leadership is differentiated based upon the maturity level or work style of the employee. Teacher supervision by principals has as its aim moving teachers to higher levels of functioning. Leaders are either more or less directive with those they lead so that organizational goals are met.	Fiedler Bogardus Hersey & Blanchard Vroom-Yetton & Jago Glickman Glatthorn Pigors
LEARNING/SCHOOL EFFECTIVENESS Students learn when the curricular goals are clearly delineated and when teaching and assessment methods are aligned with the curriculum. Time spent engaged in active learning is correlated with achievement. The underlying assumptions draw again from behavioral theory, in that a combination of teaching behaviors or or school factors can predict learning. Student esteem is believed to be enhanced by academic outcomes. Students evidence growth when teachers hold high expectations and when there	Lezotte Edmonds Brookover Good Brophy Weinstein Murphy Weil Hunter	INSTRUCTIONAL LEADERSHIP/TRAIT THEORY School-level factors contribute to student success, especially instructional leadership by the principal. The principal carries out key instructional functions, including monitoring student progress and serving as a visible presence on campus. Time spent observing in classrooms, participating in staff development, and providing resources for teachers influence both teacher and student growth as well as	Edmonds Murphy Hallinger Little Bird Smith & Andrews Leithwood Burns Bennis Nanus

is "press" for academic performance. A core belief is that all students can learn.

COMMUNITIES OF LEARNERS

Student learning is enhanced when students work cooperatively and share knowledge. Classroom reward structures are designed to encourage cooperative learning and assessment methods are adapted to determine group and individual progress. The process for learning is valued as highly as the content. Students and their teachers learn together, with group skills and interdependence emphasized.

The teacher's role changes from presenter to facilitator of knowledge; classroom processes tend to be more democratic. The role of the educational environment or "ecology" is also seen as interrelated with how students learn and how teachers teach. Student ability or intelligence is believed not to be an innate quality but part of the educational context.

The professional community of the school takes on added meaning and importance. Teachers and principals must be part of an effective learning community to affect positively student learning.

Johnson &
 Johnson
Slavin
Cohen
Goodlad
Oakes
Costa
Eisner
Della Dora
Egan
Bowers
Flinders
Sternberg
Joyce
Resnick
Newman
Whelage
Krovetz

overall school improvement. Business literature offers parallel traits of effective leaders who achieve organizational goals.

Peters
Waterman
Deal
Meier

COMMUNITIES OF LEADERS

Leadership is viewed as a shared process among educators—principals and teachers. The principal is seen as a "leader among leaders" who facilitates the growth of others. Thus, the organizational structure is flattened and integrated, and participants share common values and purposes.

The interactive nature of a community promotes continuous improvement, with assessment integral to the work of the community. Again, democratic processes are emphasized. This view of leadership has its roots in a number of theoretical constructs, including human relations and systems theory and ecological thought.

Lieberman
Little
Sarason
Barth
Vygotsky
Sergiovanni
J. Gardner
Follett
Getzels & Guba
Garmston
Bowers
Flinders
Glickman
Seashore Louis
Kellerman

(continued)

13

FIGURE 1.1 (CONTINUED)

LEARNING	THEORISTS	LEADING	THEORISTS
CONSTRUCTIVIST LEARNING	Dewey	CONSTRUCTIVIST LEADING	Greene
Based on assumptions from the community of learners/leaders theory, students construct meaning from personal values, beliefs, and experiences. The development of personal schema and the ability to reflect upon one's experiences are key theoretical principles. Unlike traditional thought, it is believed that knowledge exists within the learner. The social nature of learning is emphasized: shared inquiry is a central activity. Multiple outcomes are expected and encouraged, with assessment being integral to the process.	Bruner Piaget Vygotsky Feuerstein Tyler Resnick H. Gardner Scinto Duckworth Brooks & Brooks Leinhardt	Leadership is viewed as a reciprocal process among the adults in the school. Purposes and goals develop from among the participants, based upon values, beliefs, and individual and shared experiences. The school functions as a community that is self-motivating and that views the growth of its members as fundamental. There is an emphasis on language as a means for shaping the school culture, conveying commonality of experience, and articulating a joint vision. Shared	Senge Zohar Wheatley Foster Kegan Barnett Carlsen Garmston & Lipton Walker Lambert
Human growth is a moral imperative. New understandings of the brain and implications for teaching and learning support constructivism. The role of culture and the push for equity become a central focus for applying constructivist principles.	Perkins Marzano Jensen Lowery Ladson-Billings Hale	inquiry is an important activity in problem identification and resolution; participants conduct action research and share findings as a way of improving practice.	Siddle Walker Delpit Miller

Source: Lambert, L., Walker, D., Zimmerman, D., Cooper, J., Lambert, M., Gardner, M., & Ford Slack, P. J. (1995). *The constructivist leader.* New York: Teachers College Press.

exercised a dynamic influence on each other. Teachers and leaders, separate actors through most of our history, have been cast as parallel characters, each as authority figures possessing formal knowledge and practical know-how as well as charged with carrying out the mission of the school and the larger society.

HISTORICAL ANTECEDENTS TO CONSTRUCTIVIST THEORY

TRADITIONAL APPROACHES TO LEARNING AND LEADING

We entered this century with thousands of years of convention behind our notions of traditionalism. It is not surprising that this impulse remains strong. In communities in which parents make contributions to the design and purposes of schools, traditional school formats tend to be adopted at both the elementary and secondary levels, characterized by a uniform curriculum, an emphasis on basic skills, strict discipline, and in some instances dress codes and student uniforms. Traditional schools provide for continuity and assure parents an education for their children that is similar to the one they themselves experienced in school. While innovative teaching may take place, program innovation is not central to the traditional school philosophy. Whole-group instruction, lecture and drill, and a focus on standardized measures of student achievement are typical of traditional schools. This approach embodies the view that learning is externally motivated and determined and that students do not possess within themselves the necessary knowledge and experience to take a more active role in constructing knowledge and shaping meaning. The teacher, depository of classical curricula, is seen as the sole source of knowledge and learning. Thus classroom structures tend to be teacher centered and hierarchical, fostering adherence to a single set of standards.

In 1927, at a major conference on leadership, Steward defined leadership as "the ability to impress the will of the leader on those led and induce obedience, respect, loyalty, and cooperation" (quoted in Moore, 1927, p. 124, as cited in Rost, 1991, p. 47). Obedience, respect, loyalty, and cooperation were, and often still are, most highly valued for teachers as well as students. In traditional schools, lines of authority are usually clear, with the principal or headmaster functioning as the decision maker, policy setter, and taskmaster. Since it is assumed that the values of a traditional school are closely aligned with those of the community, teachers are expected to conform to those standards and to maintain the status quo, as directed by the principal (Mitchell & Tucker, 1992). Teacher supervision may follow one of several patterns. Teachers may be closely supervised, with the principal setting job targets and fulfilling a quality control function; or supervision may be perfunctory, based on the assumption that everyone understands the standards and expectations and that teachers will perform their role as expected. In either instance, the principal is not seen as a facilitator of teacher growth, nor does the purpose of teacher supervision seem to be the professional development of the teaching staff.

While a central purpose of the first schools was to ensure continuance of our democracy, the theme of the dominance of administrator authority in traditionalism obscured this purpose. Glickman (1993), in his writings about empowerment and school change, notes that schools are perhaps the least democratic of institutions and that attempts to democratize them and share authority in them are often met with disdain from colleagues at other schools and from the central office. Likewise, traditional schools have not promoted shared leadership with teachers, nor have they involved students in making decisions about their curriculum or in evaluating their own progress. In this sense, traditionalism is at the opposite end of the learning-leading continuum from constructivism, especially as envisioned by Dewey in *Democracy and Education* (1916) and his other writings.

BEHAVIORAL APPROACHES TO LEARNING AND LEADING

Behavioral theories of learning and leading draw from a confluence of thought regarding the nature of the world and the extent to which human phenomena can be measured and predicted. Newtonian science, social theories, and religious dogma advanced the view that the world and the universe are predictable, static, and clocklike. Quantitative research, which to a large extent has shaped education's knowledge base, also derived many of its approaches from a similar set of assumptions: that behavior can be predicted; that intelligence is fixed and innate; that differences in intelligence can be accurately measured; and that based on these measurements, learning "treatments" can be prescribed.

In the classroom, behavioral psychology translates into teachers breaking down large concepts into component parts and discrete skills, often taught in isolation, with drill and practice and large-group instruction favored. Behavioral approaches include increased dependence on standardized measures of achievement, offering rewards for learning as a way of shaping student behavior. The development of the "behavioral objective" concept by Mager (1962), and the more narrow definition given to the idea by Baker and Popham (1973), ushered in a whole generation of educators who learned how to write and apply behavioral objectives. Behavioral approaches are very much alive, especially in special education classes and most forms of remedial programs.

Behavioral psychology's influence extends beyond the classroom to how we in education—and others in business and industry—view organizational behavior. The input/output model favored by behavioral psychologists suggests a direct relationship between resources fed in and results produced: learning, teaching, and leading are based on information, materials, or funds fed in, and they result in outputs, such as test scores achieved, professional credentials granted, or organizational goals accomplished. Millstein and Belasco (1973), in a comprehensive text about systems theory, organized the chapters into input, throughput, and output concepts, which at that time were drawn from behavioral assumptions. This input-output model as a behavioral framework has formed the basis for school funding formulas and traditional approaches to change, and takes shape most recently in the accountability measures implemented by many states. When states set targets for progress and improved scores, based on implementing a set of reforms, and apply rewards and sanctions for performance and lack of performance, they are operating on behavioral principles of learning.

In the behavioral construct for school leadership, the principal is viewed as being responsible for the quality of teacher performance and for using rewards and sanctions to ensure that teachers maintain standards. This view of leadership is not unlike Burns's (1978) conception of "transactional leadership," in which the principal transacts or exchanges rewards for desired behavior that is clearly specified and understood. The principal's role is to "shape" teacher behavior, in much the same way as the classroom teacher shapes student behavior. It seems to be a natural outgrowth of behaviorism to seek to cluster people into manageable and "treatable" groups, based on identifiable and measurable behaviors.

GROUPING/TRACKING AND CONTINGENCY/SITUATIONAL APPROACHES TO LEARNING AND LEADING

During the Industrial Revolution in this country, the need to sort people emerged as a societal imperative for two reasons: Unprecedented numbers of immigrants were entering the country who were unfamiliar with the principles of democracy and who often needed to acquire facility in

English; and the growth of factories introduced the need for large numbers of production-line workers. The children of the more affluent Americans, who were considered to be superior to the immigrants, attended school to prepare themselves for higher education or to run the businesses and factories; the children of immigrants completed courses to enable them to work in the factories and to function as citizens in a democracy. This early sorting was bolstered by the formulation of statistical analysis as a way of determining intelligence and academic performance. Fueled by a societal belief in racial and ethnic superiority, educators such as Elwood Cubberly used research techniques to justify the sorting of students in preparation for their life's work (Oakes, 1985).

Though we are long past the Industrial Revolution and many believe in a new revolution sparked by the information age, we continue to sort students in school as early as kindergarten, often on bases that reflect socioeconomic status, language, gender, and race. Elementary-age students are grouped by ability for reading and math as well as for other subjects, and secondary students are tracked by ability and placed in academic or nonacademic courses of study. While the last decade has brought increased pressure to revise and eliminate grouping and tracking practices, they still persist, based on educators' beliefs regarding students' capacity to learn or access learning through a second language—and also because teachers often lack the tools to teach in heterogeneous settings. An underlying premise of grouping and tracking remains the belief that student ability is fixed and can be accurately assessed at a young age.

Another prevailing myth related to grouping and tracking is that if students are placed in low-ability groups or in remedial classes, they will eventually acquire the necessary skills and catch up with their peers. Remedial efforts tend to cover the same ground repeatedly; they also teach discrete skills in a sequential manner without providing opportunities for students to put these skills together in a coherent way. The reality is that these students never catch up; in fact, they fall farther behind as they progress through the grades (Braddock & McPartland, 1990). The process of grouping and tracking assigns students to fixed tracks throughout their schooling and limits their opportunities beyond school.

The movement that resulted in the grouping and tracking of students also shaped conceptions of leadership and of the formal leader's relationship to teachers in the school. In their training, principals were presented with a variety of contingencies or situations to which they must adapt their leadership style. These situations share common assumptions with the grouping/tracking of students: that teacher capacity is fixed; that the leader's role is to learn to deal with the different abilities of teachers and manage them successfully; and that teachers will naturally sort themselves into high-, average-, and low-performing groups, much like students. Hershey and Blanchard's (1972) situational leadership suggests that leaders need to be flexible in their approach to employee supervision, but it also suggests that employees can be easily categorized and that an appropriate "treatment" exists for each category of behavior. It is important to remember that no theme or movement in learning and leading exists alone, but rather is connected to previous, concurrent, and countervailing movements—in these instances the behavioral movement.

The work on differentiated supervision and teacher development also categorizes teacher behavior, although the goals are more laudable. According to Glatthorn (1984), Glickman (1990), and Robbins and Alvy (1995), supervisors can, by varying their approaches, move teachers to higher levels of performance and development. Glickman advances a continuum of leader behavior, from directed to nondirected, correlated with particular levels of teacher development. His work forms a transition from the situational approach to leadership, which has its roots in turn-of-the-century conceptions of fixed ability, to developmental approaches with the belief in teachers' capacity for growth.

EFFECTIVENESS AND INSTRUCTIONAL LEADERSHIP APPROACHES TO LEARNING AND LEADING

The school effectiveness movement was sparked by the conclusions of the Coleman Report, *Equality of Educational Opportunity* (Coleman et al., 1966). This report attributed student achievement to factors largely beyond the control of the school, namely, parent income and education level. In response, educational researchers identified schools—mostly in the inner cities, with students who were from lower socioeconomic groups and were often minorities—that had produced high levels of student achievement on standard measures in reading and math. These researchers studied these schools, looking for patterns to which they could attribute increases in achievement and from which other schools could learn. They found that the mission of the school was generally narrow and focused on basic skill acquisition as measured by achievement tests; there was alignment among the curriculum, teaching methods, and assessment; there was sufficient opportunity to learn in terms of engaged time and success rate; and a "safe and orderly" environment existed (Brookover et al., 1982; Edmonds, 1979).

From these initial findings grew a related body of research known as learning or teaching effectiveness, which focused on classroom practices related to student achievement. Direct instruction (Brophy & Good, 1986;

Hunter, quoted in Brandt, 1985) emerged as a style of teaching especially appropriate to basic skill acquisition. It drew from behavioral theory— for example, learning is broken down into small pieces, expectations are made very clear, and approximations of desired behavior are rewarded. While learning/school effectiveness did not necessarily promote active learning and student construction of knowledge, it did establish two basic tenets that still underscore reform movements today: the belief that all children can learn (argued much earlier by Bruner) and the recognition that when teachers hold high expectations for student achievement and press for academic performance, students tend to meet those expectations.

Another important finding drawn from the effectiveness literature that contributes to the knowledge bases of learning and leading links instructional leadership, particularly on the part of the principal, to student achievement. While the effectiveness research is correlational and not causal, there is corroborating evidence that instructional leadership by the principal can increase the achievement of those students most at risk (Andrews, quoted in Brandt, 1987). A substantial body of literature exists on "instructional leadership," which proposes that formal leaders pay attention to what goes on in the classroom through direct observation and focused discussion, participate in staff development, be visible on campus, and make instructional resources available to teachers (Hallinger & Murphy, 1987; Little & Bird, 1987). More recent work by practitioners such as Deborah Meier (1995), considered to be an architect of the small school movement, describes a leader-colleague role for the principal that empowers not only teachers to shape the culture of the school but students to function as active participants in their own learning and in developing a school culture that supports them.

Parallel to the development of the effectiveness theories of learning and leading was the emergence of the "excellence" literature in business. There are many similarities and one large difference in these approaches. The similarities lie in the emphasis on a well-defined vision or mission (that of the leader), processes aligned with the vision, the importance of training and staff development, expectations for high performance, and involved leaders. Both education and business advanced a "trait" theory of what makes an effective leader: articulating a sense of purpose, keeping people focused on goals, and working collaboratively within the organization. The assumption was that if we could observe what highly successful leaders did and teach it to others, they, too, could be highly successful. Some of this thinking had grown out of notions of "charismatic" leadership, such as in the work of Weber (1947, 1968). The major difference is that the business literature promoted excellence as a way of achieving greater profits, while the education literature promoted equity as a means of increasing opportunities for those students typically underserved by schools.

The theory of effectiveness as applied to both learning and leading was seen as a template that one could superimpose on schools, their leader, and classroom teachers to promote equity and increased achievement. The theoretical principles embedded in the research contributed to focused efforts at school improvement, resulting in some statewide initiatives in California, Michigan, Connecticut, Kentucky, Texas, and other states. Application of the template without recognition of the complexity of school improvement, the importance of context, and efforts to change existing practice, however, revealed the limitations of the effectiveness theory. Because effectiveness literature drew heavily on the behavioral movement, it focused on direct teaching and learning and did not adequately address the issues of school culture and established patterns of interactions that dramatically influence both learning and leading.

THE COMMUNITY OF LEARNERS AND COMMUNITY OF LEADERS: APPROACHES TO LEARNING AND LEADING

Over the years, schools have struggled with various metaphors to describe their central enterprise. A metaphor that dominated from the turn of the century was that of the school as factory, emphasizing assembly-line production, compliance, and uniformity. During the 1980s the metaphor of the school as a community of learners emerged, calling forth new images of learning. In a community of learners, both individual and collective growth is valued, as are the processes for achieving that growth.

The shift in consciousness ushered in a new synthesis of educational thought and a new set of assumptions. It was a coming together of major countervailing themes from throughout the century: the work of Bruner and Vygotsky in the social construction of knowledge, of Dewey and Combs in democracy in schooling, changing conceptions about the fluidity and scope of intelligences, quantum theory, women in leadership and research, brain research, the emergence into respectability of qualitative research, critical theory, and postmodern thought.

This new "enlightenment" advanced some challenging assumptions, among which were: (1) the capacity to learn is not fixed or innate; (2) the social construction of knowledge actually changes "intelligence"; therefore, learning must be an active and interactive process; (3) student and adult learning are both fluid and linked; (4) achievement is increased when the culture of the school supports learning for both students and adults; and (5) new norms need to be developed that foster collaboration and shared inquiry. This was the first movement to place a high value on teacher growth and to link teacher and student learning. Collaborative teaching methods that promote learning for all students are applied to the organizational processes that characterize the school, so that the school becomes a learning organization (a continually renewing place to live and work).

The community of learners' movement reshapes classroom interactions from student as passive listener and teacher as source of knowledge to learning as an interactive process entered into by both students and teachers. Students take greater responsibility for designing their work, setting deadlines, and evaluating progress in terms of individual and group outcomes. Interdependence and group skills are emphasized, along with mastery of content, sharing knowledge, and gaining multiple perspectives (Johnson & Johnson, 1988; Slavin, 1986). Cooperative learning approaches provide a forum for the social construction of knowledge as well as the promotion of democratic practices.

The research done by Newmann, Secada, and Wehlage (1995) points to a set of standards or criteria for authentic instruction beyond the processes of cooperative learning and hands-on projects. These criteria aim to increase the intellectual complexity of schoolwork and promote teaching for understanding. Newmann and his colleagues group the criteria into these categories: construction of knowledge, disciplined inquiry, and value beyond school. The actual criteria denote a learning environment where constructing meaning is paramount: higher order thinking, deep knowledge, substantive conversation, and connections to the world beyond the classroom (pp. 28–29).

Parallel research in the field of resiliency provides a deep source of knowledge as to how classrooms and schools can create a sense of community that supports students at risk. Krovetz (1999) notes that schools must move from a problem focus where the goal is "fixing" students to a focus on strengthening the environment in which students learn. In his analysis of research he notes that schools need to develop the resiliency of students by helping them develop social competence, problem-solving skills, autonomy, and a sense of purpose and future. In addition, the school community needs to provide these protective factors: a caring environment where at least one adult knows the child; positive, high expectations and support; and participation, that is, opportunities for meaningful involvement and for assuming responsibility. Moreover, to create an environment that promotes student resiliency, teachers and principals need time together to know each other and their work.

At the school level, this sense of community is evidenced in a commitment to the growth of the faculty as a whole and to activities such as seminar groups, reflective writing, team research, and discussion. In addition, Karen Seashore Louis's (1995) work on professional community shows schools that change norms by providing for differentiated roles for teachers, including teachers learning from each other and playing both lead and secondary roles in the classroom. Her rubric, developed to assess the degree of community that exists in a school, is tied to the overall effectiveness of the school as a learning organization for students and teachers.

Community refers not just to a sense of cohesion among students and teachers but also to the notion that the educational environment or "ecology" plays an important role in how students learn and teachers teach (Bateson, 1972; Bowers & Flinders, 1990; Eisner, 1988; Goodlad, 1987; B. Joyce, personal communication, 1976). The concept of the school as an "ecology" was thought to comprise the norms of the school, expectations, patterns of behavior, processes, and human and material resources. This integrative view of schooling suggests that ecology is a complex and interrelated system that influences and supports intellectual growth (see Chapter 2 for a more in-depth discussion). Further, student ability or intelligence is viewed not as predominantly innate but as a function of the educational context (Egan, 1979; Resnick, 1989, cited in Furtwengler, 1999/2000).

The roots of the concept of community of leaders run as deep as the roots of community of learners. Mary Follett's (1924) work in the human relations movement in business led to democratic ways of relating in the workplace, and to Burns's (1978) transformational leadership. This humane and participatory philosophy also influenced Total Quality notions and Senge's "learning organization" in *The Fifth Discipline* (Senge, 1990). Max Weber's systems theory (1947) contributed to our early understanding of the influence of the social and organizational context, and Getzels and Guba's (1957) adaptations of this theory described the relationship of systems theory to roles and personalities.

The community of leaders language was introduced into education by Roland Barth (1988) as an interactive process of shared leadership. Leadership is shared among the professional staff, with the principal seen as a leader of leaders (Barth, 1988; Glickman, 1993; Schlechty, 1990). The hierarchical structure is replaced by shared responsibility for school governance, professional growth, and achievement of agreed-on goals. Because a community is characterized by shared values and hopes, many of the control functions associated with school leadership become less important and even counterproductive. In a community of leaders, it is assumed that all teachers can lead and contribute to accomplishing the work of the school. Like classroom processes, school-level processes emphasize participation, interaction, and collective growth (Palmer, 1998). Recently, renewed attention has been paid to how school culture incorporates and reflects democratic process, and what role leadership plays in assuring that the democracy we prepare our students for is alive and well within the schools (Glickman, 1998; Kellerman, 1999). These ideas are developed more extensively in Chapter 2.

CONSTRUCTIVIST APPROACHES TO LEARNING AND LEADING

Interest in constructivist theory as a school of thought in education has grown in response to a variety of factors, including increased expectations for all students to successfully complete secondary school and most to enter college; student boredom and dissatisfaction with traditional, teacher-centered modes of instruction; the impact of technology on student learning independent of school; and research on learning and the brain. Conversations about education often take the form of absolutes: textbook learning versus constructed learning; seat work versus hands-on, experiential learning. The same debate plays out between constructivist learning in comparison with more traditional views of school and classroom practices, although what would be more productive is a way of seeing how each view of learning can positively influence the other.

Constructivist learning derives from the field of epistemological psychology and describes how people construct their reality and make sense of their world. Its application to the field of education suggests that students make their own meaning and is based in part on Plato's contention that knowledge is formed within the learner and is brought to the surface by a skilled teacher through processes of inquiry and Socratic dialogue. In some ways, it is easier to define constructivist learning by what it is not, rather than what it is. For years, education and learning have been viewed as an external process. Students, whether they are children or adult learners, are "empty vessels" into which knowledge and even wisdom are poured. Meaning is considered to be inherent in ideas, events, experience, and knowledge; and students are to learn about the meanings that others have interpreted. The teacher possesses this knowledge and wisdom, which is shared with students through strategies such as telling, recitation, and drill.

Research on the Brain, Culture, and Learning

During the last years of the twentieth century, brain research established principles of learning in counterpoint to much of what had been accepted as the way teachers teach and students learn. Howard Gardner's (1983) work on multiple intelligences certainly led the way by advancing the notion that students had preferred ways of thinking and processing information, and that what were perceived as typical patterns for students to acquire knowledge were effective for only a small percentage. Harvey Silver (2000) developed a framework for teaching and learning that incorporated Gardner's work as well as Marzano's (1988) formulation of learning styles. Eric Jensen (1998), Pat Wolfe (2001), and others have applied research on the brain to the design of curriculum and instruction in the classroom. What these researchers attempted to do was to illustrate how the brain operates to take in new learning and how students' "natural way" of learning enables them to process, store, and retrieve information so they can demonstrate what they have learned.

In addition to a deeper understanding of how the brain develops and how learning occurs is the recognition that students of color may construct meaning in different ways from their white peers. This line of research and professional writing is critical to constructivist leadership because it points to a more expansive, inclusive view of leadership than may have existed previously. If schools are to do a more effective job of educating minority students, then those who assume leadership for schools must understand their students, the culture they bring with them, and the traditions of their schooling in past generations. Vanessa Siddle Walker's study (1996, 1998) of a segregated school in the South during the middle of the past century points out not only the inequities of blacks-only schools but also a leadership dimension long forgotten or ignored. The principals of such schools were intentional about giving students experiences they would not otherwise have and about inspiring the staff to prepare students for life in and out of school. In her book *The Dreamkeepers* (1996), Gloria Ladson-Billings describes those educators who would not let students fail and who gave them a positive sense of themselves. The belief in teaching as a calling and school leadership as a spiritual mission was integral to life in the segregated South. This belief may have existed during previous eras of education and education change, but it is most essential to the notion of constructivist leadership, where values and meaning form the core.

Typically the experiences and practical knowledge that students bring with them are not woven into the curriculum or classroom learning activities. For instance, students write about classroom topics primarily in expository form, and even narrative writing is largely based on classroom materials rather than parallel experiences that students have had. According to this theory of learning, students acquire "school knowledge" (Schön, 1987) that is separate from and unrelated to the practical knowledge they have gained at home and in the community. This view

of teaching and learning has remained fairly constant since colonial times
and persists today in many quarters.

Principles of Constructivism

In the opening of this chapter, we described some of the origins of the
concept of constructivism in conceptualizing the epistemological processes
of "knowing and coming to know." When translated into constructivist
learning within the framework of the educative process known as schooling, constructivist learning theory can be distinguished from other theories by the following principles and brief descriptors.

Knowledge and beliefs are formed within the learner. Rather than considering learners as "empty vessels," constructivist learning theory assumes
that learners bring experience and understanding to the classroom. Thus
they do not encounter new information out of context but rather apply
what they know to assimilating this information, or they accommodate
or reframe what they know to match new understandings they have gained.
Either way, the process of coming to know is an interactive one.

Learners personally imbue experiences with meaning. Teachers typically explain meaning for learners—what a poem means, what events in
history signify, what theme a painting conveys—instead of allowing learners themselves to suggest possible meanings. The values and beliefs they
have already formed help learners to interpret and assign meaning, as do
their interactions with other students. Meaning is constructed and is
shaded by the students' previous experiences. Thus two students may
read a poem and hear the same images summoned by the language of the
poet, yet the meaning of the images is determined first by each student's
personal schemas and second by the interaction with the perspectives
being formed by other students' schemas.

*Learning activities should cause learners to gain access to their expe-
riences, knowledge, and beliefs.* Constructivist approaches to learning
include those that allow learners to use what they know to interpret new
information and construct new knowledge. Teachers often complain that
learners have little to write about and, when they do find subjects to
address, that their writing is devoid of rich detail or insight. Constructivist
learning theory suggests that the questions posed to students must prompt
their writing to connect with what they know and believe. When these
connections are made, learners draw on what they know and reshape it
in new and newly meaningful ways.

Culture, race, and economic status affect student learning individually and collectively. Who they are and where they come from affect students' experiences both in and out of school. While it is important to incorporate these experiences into the learning, it is even more important to help students understand how their race and economic status affect them in school and beyond. Helping students make sense of the "hidden curriculum" in schools, that which is not taught and not recognized, can give poor and minority students tools they need to construct meaning for themselves and in collaboration with peers. For poor and minority students, the hidden curriculum is often the message that they have not contributed to the history, literature, arts, or economics of the society because their experiences and accomplishments are not reflected in the formal curriculum. By situating their learning within the context where they learn and live, students can draw important lessons for their success in school and beyond.

Learning is a social activity that is enhanced by shared inquiry. Learners learn with more depth and understanding when they are able to share ideas with others, engage in the dynamic and synergistic process of thinking together, consider other points of view, and broaden their own perspectives. Constructivism advances the idea that learning is a social endeavor requiring engagement with others in order to gain a growing understanding of the world and one's relationship to it.

Reflection and metacognition are essential aspects of constructing knowledge and meaning. Learners clarify their understandings when they are able to reflect on their learning and analyze the ways they construct knowledge and meaning. Constructivism suggests a more complex and dynamic process for learning than is traditionally described (in which students are thought to absorb information like sponges and feed it back at test time): Students develop as learners when they are aware of the processes they engage in as they "come to know." This awareness enhances their ability to learn and make sense of new information.

Learners play a critical role in assessing their own learning. Traditionally teachers establish learning goals and criteria for success, and they evaluate student progress. A constructivist approach suggests that students can help to determine how much they have learned as well as the processes by which they have come to know. Student self-assessment makes the processes for learning explicit to students, shaping their personal schemas and enabling them to actively engage with new learning in the future. This kind of "authentic assessment" also provides insight for the teacher into how students develop and view their own growth (See Chapter 7, Figure 7.1).

The outcomes of the learning process are varied and often unpredictable. Constructivist approaches allow the students to direct the learning and to generate both understanding and meaning. In a sense, the teacher gives up a degree of control over both the process and outcomes. Student interpretations and perspectives may be richer than the teacher imagined and may take a different path than anticipated. Constructivist learning theory holds promise for broadening current definitions of learning to take into account the way knowledge is constructed and to consider the subtleties and nuances that emerge when students, working together, create meaning from what they know, value, and believe.

Based on these principles, a constructivist theory of learning is the antithesis of the factory model that has dominated in education. Learning is not uniform and cannot be specified in advance; it is not assembled like parts of a machine but rather evolves in nonlinear ways from the experiences and attitudes of the learners.

THEORETICAL ROOTS OF CONSTRUCTIVISM

Dewey and Constructivism

Each era or theme in education is built on preceding themes and is an outgrowth of social, political, and economic forces. Because each era is complex in its prevailing attitudes and growing understandings, notions of learning and leading from early in the century continue to influence current thought. Nowhere is this connection to the past more vivid than in the case for constructivism.

While John Dewey did not use the term *constructivism,* certainly his ideas contributed to the formulation of constructivist theories of learning and leading. Dewey (1916) first gave voice to this view of learning, noting that students must learn and make sense of new knowledge together, based on their individual and collective experiences. He perceived learning as a social endeavor, and his ideas about instruction can be found in current models of cooperative learning that emphasize the social construction of knowledge. He questioned the prevailing wisdom that education was preparation for life, holding instead that education should allow students to experience life, that authentic experience was essential to learning. He believed that the development of the self into a self-directing, inquiring, and reasoning human being was central to education. He invited us to understand that democracy is the chief purpose of education and that the structures of education should model this purpose. Even though he never used the term *constructivism*, Dewey's ideas regarding the centrality of student experience to the learning process have informed the evolution of the theory of constructivist learning.

Moreover, Dewey was eloquent in his plea for teachers to assume a decision-making role in regard to curriculum, instruction, and the assessment of student progress. He believed that teachers should have a determining role in the structure of a school. His early notions of shared decision making shaped evolving notions of schools as communities of learners and leaders and also contributed to the emerging theory of constructivist leadership. His visionary ideas, dating from the turn of the century, planted the seeds that, watered by other theorists and educators, created a soil favorable to the growth of constructivist theory.

Constructivist Approaches to Learning

If Dewey set the stage for the emergence of constructivist thought, we can credit Jean Piaget with expanding our understanding of learning in ways that support and contribute to constructivism. Piaget understood that knowledge is not a static body of information that is passed on to learners but rather a process. He viewed this process as one of continual construction and reorganization of knowledge, with the learner taking responsibility for constructing and reorganizing (Piaget, 1971, cited in Brooks & Brooks, 1993; Piaget, 1985). According to Piaget, learners move through stages of cognitive development—from concrete to abstract—prompted by a discrepancy or "disequilibrium" between what they previously believed to be true and their new insights and experiences. As learners mature, they develop new cognitive structures, or schemas, that are more sophisticated, allowing them to make sense of increasingly more complex knowledge. Piaget saw the child as an "active scientist, constructing hypotheses about the world, reflecting upon experience, interacting with the physical environment and formulating increasingly complex structures of thought" (quoted in Bruner & Haste, 1987, p. x). During the 1980s and 1990s the work of Piaget has come under close scrutiny for his approaches to the study of the learner and his observations and assumptions about stages of development. He viewed, and therefore studied, the learner from a primarily individualistic perspective, rather than seeking opportunities to view learning in social or multiple contexts.

His explanations of the stages of development are now viewed as too linear, sequential, and compartmentalized. These criticisms, however, do not detract from the powerful influence of Piaget's work on the public dialogue about the nature of knowing and learning.

De Vries and Kohlberg (1987, 1990) pointed out that the first major paradigm shift in learning theory in this country began in the mid-1960s in the field of early childhood education, based on the work of Piaget. Piaget "fundamentally altered our views of the child and the nature of mental development. The central theme of this paradigm is the view of the child as active in constructing not only knowledge but intelligence itself" (1987, p. xi). Piaget's contribution to constructivist thought cannot be understated. His theory of learning, translated by others into new approaches to teaching and learning in the primary grades with very young children, gave rise to a reconsideration of how students create knowledge.

As is often the case with new or different conceptions of learning, a number of educators developed converging theories of learning. Like Dewey and Piaget, Bruner emphasized the learner as constructor of knowledge and the role of prior experience in enriching the learning experience. In addition, Bruner altered Piaget's stage theory, suggesting that simple maturation alone does not account for the development of new cognitive structures or schemas (cited in Brooks & Brooks, 1993). He determined that other factors, including the development and complexity of language in use and prior experiences, contribute to cognitive growth (Bruner, 1966). In *Making Sense,* Bruner reflected on "a quiet revolution" recently taking place in developmental psychology in which the child is once again seen "as a social being. . . . 'Making sense' is a social process; it is an activity that is always situated within a cultural and historical context" (Bruner & Haste, 1987, p. i).

Like Dewey, Piaget, and Bruner, Lev Vygotsky (1962, 1978) assumed a major role as a co-creator of constructivist thought. Earlier we noted the significant role played by the notion of the "zone of proximal development," the space or field among learners and teachers in which individuals negotiate meaning and create knowledge and intelligence. Further, he persuaded us that learning could not be viewed without context, as if independent of cultural or historical influences or significance. Learning is a cumulative experience derived and informed by an individual's and a group's cultural and historical experiences. Bruner, in introducing Vygotsky to educational thinkers in America, understood that this view of learning was vital to the understanding that knowledge and intelligence are socially constructed. Social interaction in the moment could not adequately explain the social processes of learning.

Following World War II, Reuven Feuerstein began to work in Israel with children who had been in concentration camps. In his assessment of these children, he detected major cognitive gaps undoubtedly arising from limited and distorted experiences. He developed a means through which he assessed, taught, and reassessed learning, noting significant changes in cognitive complexity. His teaching approaches involve mediation during learning by teachers and other students so that children can "self-modify" or self-construct themselves as learners. Today, Feuerstein (1990; Feuerstein et al., 1991) is considered one of the most insightful and influential constructivists of our time, the "modern day Piaget" (A. Costa, personal communication, 1994).

As the preceding discussion demonstrates, constructivism has evolved based on the contributions of educational theorists and practitioners whose work influences what we know about teaching and learning. Dewey, Piaget, Bruner, and Vygotsky laid the foundation of important ideas that set the stage for the emergence of constructivist learning.

Constructivism, Culture, and Learning

The theories of constructed learning described in the preceding sections begin to build a foundation for understanding how and why our schools function as they do. Looking at the cultural norms that shape our schools in this country and contrasting them with norms in other countries deepens this understanding. The work of Stigler and Hiebert on TIMSS, cited earlier and captured in their book entitled *The Teaching Gap*, suggests that our values as a country shape our school systems and cause a kind of homogeneity across state boundaries, economic and racial lines, and in urban, suburban, and rural settings.

American classrooms, the authors conclude, are not in general characterized by constructivist approaches to teaching and learning. Instead, students work independently and in interaction with the teacher to cover content and learn a great deal of subject area at a superficial level. The pattern in the secondary classes they observed was some variation of the teacher presenting a math problem, the students working through a practice set of problems, the teacher reviewing the definitions, rules, and procedures for the problems, and quizzes and tests on the definitions and rules. In contrast, Japanese classrooms spent long periods of time on one concept, with the teacher posing a question that groups of students endeavored to answer, often generating a formula or strategy

for solution and then explaining it to their classmates. The teacher facilitated the discussion of the strategy, pressed for other approaches, and
encouraged students to invent and solve their own problems. Conceptual
understanding, rather than learning the rules, was the focus in Japanese
classrooms.

The authors suggest that while there is much to learn from classrooms
in other countries, the real key to change is in rethinking cultural norms
and values. For school leaders, the message is clear: They must find ways
to encourage their colleagues to engage in processes that will further their
thinking, adapt their beliefs, and foster a desire to teach differently.
Moreover, without firsthand experience in new processes for teaching, it
will be difficult for teachers to change their practice, because they will
lack the experience base to do so. Some of these processes are explored
in subsequent chapters of this book as a way of setting the stage for
changes that are needed to our current system of schooling.

THE CENTRAL CHALLENGE FOR CONSTRUCTIVISM

The first edition of this book made a case that constructivist theory should
inform our conceptions of classroom learning and shared, reciprocal leadership. This sequel sharpens our focus on issues of learning and leading
by raising the question, What purpose is constructivist leadership designed
to achieve? Many educational reforms have invested in processes designed
to improve the lives of those in schools, but have not been sufficiently
outcomes-based to provide for real or lasting change. While the process
to achieve change is important as a reflection of our values, it is not
enough if as a result students do not learn more than they are learning
now, particularly students who have not been well served by schools in
the past. The case studies presented in Chapter 6 detail both the processes
of change and its impact on teacher practice and student learning.

A second, related question this book will address is, Can this new
framework for leadership, based on constructivist theory, help schools do
what they have not done so far, that is, help all students achieve at high
levels? Ron Edmonds, one of the researchers cited above in the section on
school effectiveness, lamented that as a nation we had not evidenced the
will needed to educate poor and minority students well. The central challenge for constructivist leadership, then, is to achieve equity for students
who have been running the race blindfolded, to use Ruth Mitchell's analogy. What is interesting and compelling about this challenge is that it is

the same one issued by Benjamin Rusk at the formation of our nation, that a country cannot prosper when only some have advantage. This was the impetus for the creation of the common school. More than 200 years later, after many movements aimed at improving education, we still have not accomplished this one seminal goal of equity.

CHAPTER **2**

TOWARD A DEEPENED THEORY OF CONSTRUCTIVIST LEADERSHIP

LINDA LAMBERT

... man grows beyond his work, walks up the stairs of his concepts, emerges ahead of his accomplishments ...

John Steinbeck
Sea of Cortez, *1941*

As we have seen, during this past century concepts about learning and leading have been influenced by similar historical, philosophical, and cultural ideas. Learning and leading are intertwined because these conceptions arise from our understandings of what it is to be human. To be human is to learn, and to learn is to construct meaning and knowledge about the world. Constructivism, therefore, has emerged as an important educational perspective that is changing how educational researchers, writers, professional developers, and leaders view the world. This learning perspective has given rise to the recognition that constructivism is critical to adult and organizational learning. This perspective has also required a reexamination of the concept of leadership, and a new definition has taken form—a definition that we have called "constructivist leadership." This book will once again examine the relationship between learning and leading and deepen the theory of constructivist leadership.

At the beginning of this new century, we can declare with some certainty that all humans bring to the process of learning personal schemas that have been formed by prior experiences, beliefs, values, sociocultural histories, and perceptions. When new experiences are encountered and mediated by reflection, inquiry, and social interaction, meaning and knowledge are constructed. Learning takes place, as does adult development. When actively engaged in reflective dialogue, adults become more complex in their thinking about the world, more tolerant of diverse perspectives, more flexible and open toward new experiences. Personal and professional learning require an interactive professional culture if adults are to engage with one another in the processes of growth and development.

Despite this linkage between learning and leading, it is uncommon for adults to be members of coherent, dynamic educational communities in which they develop collective meaning together. This is perhaps more true today for teachers than it was a decade ago. Bound by rules, schedules, accountability policies, hierarchical roles, and timeworn practices, educators still experience cultures that limit interaction and mitigate against professional growth. They have few opportunities to engage in the reciprocal processes that would call forth their ideas and successful experiences and enable them to make sense of their world together. Nor are they experiencing the supported encounters with discrepant information about teaching and learning that are essential for moving toward significant change. While there is more emphasis today being placed on data, these data tend to be of a singular nature and the accompanying dialogue is often superficial. Any possibility for thoughtful conversation that would tease out underlying complexities is sabotaged by the desperate hunt for a solution, the quick fix. Hurried interactions of the sort that often characterize faculty room encounters and faculty meetings tend to draw on the sameness of teaching, reaffirming and reiterating familiar educational practices. Hurried solutions shield us from differences and therefore from challenges to our old ways of thinking while it "protects" us from growth.

Leadership that would change our schools and our communities must be cognizant of the essential actions needed to alter the lives of teachers in schools. Constructivist leadership addresses the need for sense-making, for coherence, and for seeing educational communities as growth-producing entities. Leadership that is formed around the principles of constructivist learning for adults capture these possibilities for learning. Leadership is being redefined. It is time to deepen the theory and attend it with examples of successful practices in schools and districts.

The concept of constructivist leadership is based on the same ideas that underlie constructivist learning: Adults, as well as children, learn through the processes of meaning and knowledge construction, inquiry, participation, and reflection. The function of leadership must be to engage people in the processes that create the conditions for learning and form common ground about teaching and learning. Schooling must be organized and led in such a way that these learning processes provide direction and momentum to human and educational development. This chapter will further describe the influence that the constructivist perspective is having on our notions about leadership. We refer to constructivist leadership as

> the reciprocal processes that enable participants in an educational community to construct meanings that lead toward a shared purpose of schooling.

In this text, *leadership* is defined as a concept transcending individuals, roles, and behaviors. Therefore, anyone in the educational community—teachers, administrators, parents, students—can engage in leadership actions. As we deepen this theory of leadership, we combine and interpret assumptions regarding reciprocal processes, participation in educational communities, construction of meaning, and shared purpose of schooling that lead us toward an explanation of constructivist leadership. Further, we will expand our conception of reciprocity and community to examine the role that equity and spirituality hold in our expression of leadership.

Constructivist leadership continues to distinguish itself from prevailing notions of leadership that are influencing education and business in a number of ways, particularly in reference to who leads, the role of constructivist learning, and the need for community. However, our new definition no longer stands alone, as others have joined in the journey to frame leadership as a vital construct for human endeavor.

NOTIONS OF LEADERSHIP

Rost (1991), in an extensive analysis of influential writers from 1900 through 1990, found a consistent picture of the conceptions of leadership:

> Leadership is good management. . . . Leadership is great men and women with certain preferred traits influencing followers to do what the leaders wish in order to achieve group/organizational goals that reflect excellence defined as some kind of higher-level effectiveness. (p. 180)

Rost refers to this composite definition as the "industrial leadership paradigm," which is hierarchical, individualistic, reductionistic, linear, and mechanical—ideas that are worlds away from the ideas in this book and the needs of today's schools and society. At the beginning of this new century, it would be difficult to find anyone writing in this vein. Leadership has entered a new dimension (although there are charges that many leadership preparation programs are still based on those outdated ideas). The conversation about leadership is broader, with a wider range of possibilities, than ever before.

Four sets of reactions to the concept of leadership are emerging. First, a call for the abandonment of the word and idea altogether in favor of another word and idea. Second, reframing leadership by changing its defined personal qualities within a larger, but constant, definition. Third, puzzlement about the meaning of the term . . . puzzlement from thinkers who were heretofore more sure. Fourth, redefining the concept, allowing leadership to take on new meanings and suppositions.

First, there is a call for the abandonment of the word and idea of leadership. In the winter of 1997, at a conference of the California Staff Development Council, Tom Sergiovanni asked if I would give up the word *leadership*. At the time, I replied that I might if he would consider giving up the word *followership*. Neither of us responded definitively to those challenges by abandoning our fondness for the concepts, but the request has lingered. Peter Block (1996) did abandon *leadership* in favor of *stewardship,* which he says "can be most simply defined as giving order to the dispersion of power. It requires us to systematically move choice and resources closer and closer to the bottom and edges of the organization. Leadership, in contrast, gives order to the centralization of power."

In his recent reflections on leadership, Warren Bennis (2000) includes a chapter entitled "The End of Leadership." Bennis calls for an abandonment of the archaic baggage that has situated leadership in top-down hierarchical models, sensing that this core metaphor may be so burdened with old meanings that it cannot be saved.

Second, there is a move to reframe leadership by changing its defined qualities within a larger, but constant, definition. Although Bennis calls for an end to leadership, he proceeds to reframe leadership by changing the defined qualities of the leader in these ways:

1. The New Leader understands and practices the power of appreciation.
2. They are connoisseurs of talent, more curators than creators.
3. The New Leader keeps reminding people of what is important.
4. The New Leader generates and sustains trust.
5. The New Leader and the Led are intimate allies. (2000, pp. 153–157)

Thus Bennis remains in the second category of responses to leadership. According to this way of thinking, leadership is something that leaders do with or to others (followers, the "Led"). Most writers, however, continue to use *leadership* and *leader* as interchangeable. "The problem with the organization is leadership," an analyst might claim when referring to a specific person, the leader. "The absence of leadership (a person in that role) resulted in confusion and continuing conflict." Leadership means the sets of skills or actions held by a person in a particular role or position. What continues to change, however, is the collaborative, engaging language being used to describe the actions of the leader. Values of human endeavor are more explicit; control and manipulation are minimized.

These definitions play out in persistent patterns of process that characterize what leaders do or what leadership is. Whether a writer is describing leadership or leader, definitions inevitably fall into three parts: (1) what the leader does, (2) for or with whom the action is taken, and (3) toward what end the actions are taken. A few additional illustrative definitions from the work of these authors will clarify this three-dimensional analysis:

Carl Glickman (1998): Leaders engage others in the development of schools as democratic communities, thereby invoking broad scale participation and learning.

Ronald Heifetz (1994): Leaders mobilize people to tackle tough problems. Leadership is solving tough problems (p. 15). (This definition will fall under two categories.)

Parker Palmer (1998): Leaders "lead from the same model we have been exploring for teaching itself, creating a space centered on the great thing called teaching and learning around which a community of truth can gather" (p. 160).

Thomas Sergiovanni (2000): Leaders bring diverse people into a common cause by making the school a covenantal community. He also describes and uses the concept of constructivist leadership and Palmer's (1998) ideas of spirituality as congruent with his own writings on moral leadership.

Barbara Kellerman (1999): "Leadership is the effort of leaders—who may hold, but do not necessarily hold, formal positions of authority—to engage followers in the joint pursuit of mutually agreed-on goals. These goals represent significant, rather than merely incremental, change" (p. 10).

Bruce J. Avolio (1999): Transformational leadership involves the process whereby leaders develop followers into leaders . . . the leader has a development plan in her or his head for each follower (p. 34).

Stoll and Fink (1996): Invitational Leadership is "about communicating invitational messages to individuals and groups with whom leaders interact in order to build and act on a shared and evolving vision of enhanced educational experiences for students" (p. 109).

Gene Hall (personal communication, 2001): Leadership is facilitating change so that all members of the organization become confident and competent users of the innovation. Confident means that they have resolved concerns for self and task, along with the arousal of concern about the impact on students the innovation is having. Competent means moving beyond the mechanical use of an innovation to include routine use and refinement, and the configuration of the innovation being used is seen as acceptable to ideal.

John Gardner (1990): Leadership is the process of persuasion or example by which an individual (or leadership team) induces a group (followers) to pursue objectives held by the leader or shared with his or her followers. While this definition is more than a decade old, Gardner's work has been so influential in the field as to deserve retention.

Margaret Wheatley (1999): On effective leadership, the Leader's task is first to embody these principles—guiding visions, sincere values, organizational beliefs—and then to help the organization become the standard it has declared for itself. This work of leaders cannot be reversed, or either step ignored. In organizations where leaders do not practice what they preach, there are terrible disabling consequences (p. 130).

These writers adhere to leadership as something carried out by an individual, with or for others, toward a specific goal or outcome. Transformational leadership is consistently referred to as the most progressive of these descriptions in that it aims toward the deep transformation or emancipation of those led.

I am often asked the question, What is the difference between "constructivist leadership" and "transformational leadership"? The assumptions about the capacities of humans to grow and change are similar and complementary; indeed, constructivist leadership might be understood as arising from or growing out of many of the precepts of transformational leadership. Transformational leadership, studied more closely during the 1990s, has given rise to encouraging results. Transformational leaders help develop and maintain a collaborative, professional school culture, foster teacher development, and help teachers solve problems more effectively (Leithwood, 1992; Morgan, 1997; Avolio, 1999).

However, transformational leadership situates responsibility for the growth of others in the designated leader. It becomes paternal, although well-meaning, with such concepts as help, assist, and foster. Constructivist leadership separates leadership from leader and situates it in the patterns of relationships among participants. Reciprocity requires that the formal leader is growing and changing in concert with others. Relationships are dynamic rather than directional. Further, in constructivist leadership, the learning that is transformational is anchored in constructivism and community.

Early in the 1990s, Leithwood (1992) predicted that transformational leadership would subsume instructional leadership as the dominant image of school administration. In 1994, Poplin observed that instructional leadership encompasses hierarchies and top-down leadership, where the leader is supposed to know the best form of instruction and closely monitors teachers' and students' work. She argued that instructional leadership had outlived its usefulness. In truth, now in the early years of the new century, the accountability climate has floated instructional leadership to the top once again. Two encouraging observations can be made: Now there is more puzzlement over what is meant by instructional leadership, and people are realizing that there are a myriad of instructional leadership tasks, not all of which may need to be performed by the principal (Olson, 2000). These new insights reveal a convergence of more traditional leadership thinking as described above and transformational and constructivist leadership perspectives (U.S. Department of Education, January 17, 2001).

Third, some writers are puzzled about the meaning of leadership. I'm persuaded that puzzlement about the concept of leadership is a promising state of affairs. It is a sign of a concept in transition when thinkers in their own field are less sure, more speculative about the notion of leadership than they were in the early 1990s. In 1992, Roland Barth said that *leaders* make happen that in which they believe while working with all in a community of leaders. Today (2001), Barth notes that this sounds somewhat self-centered and misses the notion of "what is in the collective best interest." How about "assisting/engaging the group to bring to life what is in it's best interest? . . . or assisting the group to make happen what it believes in," I ask. "Oh well," he proclaims, "I'm not sure what leadership is." Unsureness, of course, may not be an apt description for thinking in transition. With each product of his prolific pen, Sergiovanni raises new issues and ideas about the concept. Unsureness can lead to abandoning the concept (or at least the word) altogether, or it can lead to a redefinition. New definitions are gathering strongly on the horizon.

Fourth, the movement to redefine the concept of leadership. Some writers are giving attention to redefining the concept of leadership and separating it from the interlocking sameness of leader. William Foster (1989) began this process when he described leadership as the reciprocal processes among leaders and followers working toward a common purpose. Constructivist leadership is situated in this fourth category. Since 1995, there have been multiple shifts in understanding:

Charlotte Roberts, in Peter Senge and colleagues' newest work, *Schools That Learn* (2000), describes constructivist leadership and proceeds to define leadership as problem-solving (with Heifetz), engaging, leading learning, and learner, rather than authority-based (pp. 404, 414–418).

Ann Conzemius and Jan O'Neill (2001) integrate constructivist leadership and the concept of "leadership capacity" to describe "Leadership as the capacity of the school for broad-based, skillful participation in the creation and fulfillment of a vision focused on student learning" (p. 5).

Richard Ackerman, Gordon Donaldson, Jr., and Rebecca Van der Bogert (1996) view leadership as a process, a quest that entails learning to think and act as a leader in response to the ever-changing challenges of learning and dealing with growing children and the adults who care about them. While the authors write primarily about the principal's learning quest, the definition does not demand that it be attached to a specific person in a specific role.

Fritjof Capra, who in 1995 (personal conversation) adhered to the "great man" theory of leadership, meaning that one person with extraordinary, charismatic qualities should lead, in 1997 suggested that "In self-organizing systems, leadership is distributed, and responsibility becomes a capacity of the whole. Leadership, then, consists in continually facilitating the emergence of new structures, and incorporating the best of them into the organization's design" (pp. 8–9).

Howard Gardner (1995) defines leadership as "a process that occurs within the minds of individuals who live in a culture—a process that entails the capacities to create stories, to understand and evaluate these stories, and to appreciate the struggle among stories. Ultimately, certain kinds of stories will typically become predominant—in particular, kinds of stories that provide an adequate and timely sense of identity for individuals who live within a community or institution" (p. 22; in Sergiovanni, 2000, p. 169).

James Spillane, Richard Halverson, and John B. Diamond (2001) hold that leadership, cognition, and activity are situated within an interactive web of actors (leaders and followers), artifacts, and situations that they refer to as "distributed leadership." The situation, or context, is not an external force but an integral part of the leadership dynamic. Leadership is "stretched over" leaders, followers, and activities within a reciprocal interdependency. School leadership, therefore, involves the identification, acquisition, allocation, coordination, and use of the social, material, and cultural resources necessary to establish the conditions for the possibility of teaching and learning.

Those who are redefining leadership situate it in the processes among us rather than in the skills or disposition of a leader. These processes include problem-solving; broad-based, skillful participation (leadership capacity); task enactment, conversations, and stories. William Grath (1998) uses the definition of constructivist leadership and concludes:

> The idea of leadership that seems to be emerging calls for rethinking the source of leadership. It will no longer be thought of as something initiated by the leaders (or by followers) but understood to begin in the reciprocal connections of people working together. This is a significant change from even the most current ideas of leadership, which are still rooted in the ideas that leadership is a product of individual initiative and action. Even in the modern idea, it is still usually presumed that the (formal) leader initiates the shared process. (p. 414)

TOWARD A NEW CONCEPTION OF LEADERSHIP

Above we examined perspectives and dimensions of the definition of *leader* and *leadership*. Constructivist leadership falls into the fourth perspective: redefining. It has been redefined by suggesting that leadership is beyond person and role and embedded in the patterns of relationships we will refer to as "reciprocal processes." These patterns enable participants in a community to construct meaning and knowledge together. We hold deep faith that, when individuals learn together in community, shared purpose and collective action emerges—shared purpose and action about what really matters. The balance of this chapter examines each dimension of this definition in turn:

> The reciprocal processes that enable . . .
> participants in an educational community to construct meanings . . .
> that lead toward a shared purpose of schooling.

Since leadership is viewed as essentially the enabling reciprocal processes among people, leadership becomes manifest within the relationships in a community, manifest in the spaces, the fields among participants, rather than in a set of behaviors performed by an individual leader. The school culture, the field in which we work, is permeated with opportunities for exercising leadership of this character. This culture, or field, among us is imbued with our histories, energies, emotions and thoughts, conflicts and affections. Greene (1988) finds in these spaces among us the possibilities for creating an authentic presence with each other . . . being real and vulnerable with each other in ways that engage us in genuine conversations. Hannah Arendt, Greene reminds us, called these spaces the "in-between" (quoted in Greene, 1988, p. 17). Vygotsky (1962) understood well the value of those fields, the in-between, as present in the "zone of proximal development" through which participants negotiate their own meanings, knowledge, and intelligence, influenced by social, cultural, and historical forces. He envisioned these spaces between and among people as being the central arena through which individuals in interaction make sense of what they think and believe and create new ideas and information. This is not unlike Kegan's (1982) "zone of mediation" for meaning-making, through which individuals labor toward new understandings. To this extent, leadership provides us with a "third dimension"—a set of untapped opportunities that exist within the culture of the school. There are the individual minds of educators in the school community, the minds of others in that community, and the richness of ideas and questions as yet unexplored or unasked that exist among us.

In this book we propose that leadership inhabits these spaces, fields, or zones among educators in an educational community. Leadership, like energy, is not finite, not restricted by formal authority and power; it permeates a healthy culture and is undertaken by whoever sees a need or an opportunity. Occupying these "zones," leadership is different from an act of leadership, for it can be omnipresent among and within all participants. Leadership possibilities permeate our interactions and inform our actions. A new teacher is having trouble? An experienced teacher might intervene, provide assistance, secure other resources and ideas, mentor. In a culture rich in leadership connections, this experienced teacher does not have to be recruited; he or she is a fully functioning professional leader. Barth (1988) seems to have had this notion in mind when he talked about a "community of leaders." Lieberman (1985, 1988, 1992, 1994, 2001), in her extensive and continual discussions of the relationships in collaborative work, understands the criticalness of human interaction and the emergence of professionalism.

THE RECIPROCAL PROCESSES THAT ENABLE . . .

Constructivist leadership involves *the reciprocal processes that enable* participants in an educational community to construct meanings that lead toward a shared purpose of schooling. It is important to understand that the capacity for reciprocity is the result of time spent in meaning-making with others (Kegan, 1982). To be able to move outside oneself, to differentiate one's perceptions from those of another, to practice empathy, to move out of the self and observe the responses and thoughts of another— all are prerequisites to reciprocity. Reciprocity, or the mutual and dynamic interaction and exchange of ideas and concerns, requires a maturity that emerges from opportunities for meaning-making in sustainable communities over time. As adults, we need to be able to engage in processes of making sense or meaning of our lives and work together in educational communities if capacities for reciprocity are to be developed. "Knowledge is not *extended* from those who consider that they know to those who consider that they do not know," pointed out Paulo Freire in 1973; "knowledge is *built up* in the relations between human beings" (p. 109, emphasis added).

The reciprocal processes that enable us to construct meaning occur within that context of relationships. The creation and expansion of our possibilities and capacities for reciprocity occur in communities rich in relationships. We need to stop thinking of roles or people as fixed entities and instead view them as relationships, as patterns of relationships that involve one another: "Patterns do not 'contain' one another, but rather 'involve' one another" (Wheatley, 1992, p. 71). "Patterns that involve" is reminiscent of Bateson's "patterns which connect" (1972), which encompasses both the relationship and the pattern of meaning. These consistent, repetitive forms reveal patterns of relationships that evolve and deepen over time.

Equity is deeply embedded in these patterns. Without equity—a profound respect for the worthiness of each other—we have dominance, not reciprocity. Further, caring is the relational aspect of such reciprocity (O'Neil, 2001). Our schools, as well as our communities, are still haunted by grievous racism, classism, and sexism, both personal and institutional. Symbols of institutional racism are pattern producing. These patterns— tracking, grouping, packaged curricula designed to imprison the mind in mediocrity, homogeneous teaching forces, nonrepresentative governance structures—evoke and allow relationships of inequity. Unless this condition is set right, reciprocity of relationships will not be possible. "Setting right" deep historical wrongs will require new conceptions of leadership.

Reciprocal relationships, the meanings of which must be discussed and commonly construed in schools, are the basis through which we make sense of our world, continually define ourselves, care about others, and "coevolve," or grow together. With relationships, we give up predictability for potentials. Potentials are those abilities within us that can develop or become actual, those personal passions and personal schemas that enable us to construct meaning and knowledge. They exist in possibilities; they are unpredictable, yet limitless; they are built on equitable relationships and connecting patterns; they are dynamic and paradoxical; and they are continuously renewing themselves. We must evoke or provoke potential (Wheatley, 1992)—it does not appear on command (or through "persuasion, recruitment, or enlistment").

While the chapters ahead provide a more detailed look at reciprocal processes along with practical examples, it is essential here to portray what is meant by these processes. These portrayals are examples and will undoubtedly give rise to thoughts of other processes as the reader ponders them. *Reciprocal processes* are mutual learning processes such as listening, questioning, reflecting, and facilitating—those relational endeavors that weave a fine fabric of meaning. When they are framed within a constructivist learning design, they are understood as those that

- Evoke potential in a trusting environment
- Inquire into practice, thereby reconstructing old assumptions and myths
- Focus on the construction of meaning
- Frame actions that embody new behaviors and purposeful intentions

Those processes that *evoke potential in a trusting environment* are those that enable individuals to call forth memories, perceptions, and assumptions that underlie and inform their work. These recollections may be elicited in the form of stories, conversations, brainstorming, writing, or even reenactment. These evoked ideas, drawn forth from their yearnings (Kessler, 2000, p. 118) and deep beliefs, create an essential foundation for constructing meaning and knowledge together, for making our schemas explicit and public, thereby enabling us to understand how we and others are making sense of the world.

Those processes that *inquire into practice, thereby reconstructing old assumptions and myths* necessitate a reexamination of accepted ideas and traditional interpretations. To "reconstruct old assumptions" is to loosen one's attachment, adherence, and dependency on the assumptions that formed current schemas in order to consider or entertain new assumptions. Confronting and processing new information or experiences that are different from those that formed the original schemas can cause an individual to disconnect from and reconstruct assumptions. This process can lead to the formation of new schemas and to changed perceptions and behaviors. This aspect of the conversation involves posing questions that will cause dissonance and disequilibrium between the held beliefs and new information, gathering evidence or data, and reconceptualizing or redesigning the ideas in question. This "redesign" function may involve speculation, reframing, visioning, or imagining possibilities. As assumptions are reexamined, we can begin to make sense of new information and ideas.

Those processes that include the *focus on the construction of meaning* involve many of the same evocation processes described above (conversations, stories, writing) and entail combining or recombining these ideas so that they make sense to those involved. "Making sense" (constructing meaning) also requires the creation of new symbols or images (examples, metaphors, patterns) that form the basis for construal and interpretation. As adults share common experiences and common inquiry, assigned meanings converge, becoming more common than uncommon. Teachers and principals begin to agree on—or at least to understand— the interpretations that they are making about teaching and learning.

Those activities that *frame actions that embody new behaviors and purposeful intentions* involve the most practical aspect of the reciprocal processes. Such activities may include establishing new criteria, planning approaches, identifying emerging goals and outcomes, implementing new actions, evaluating progress, and redesigning or reframing the actions in response to the information generated by the process. These are the specific actions that emerge from the conversations.

These are spiraling processes, involving and building on each other and circling back upon themselves. New actions become the means through which other potentials are evoked, new information is generated, and deeper meanings are constructed.

The following scenario from a school we will call Raintree Middle School describes how these processes may join together: As a staff that has deliberately planned to develop a collaborative working culture, they meet together for a professional development day to discuss their reading program. Two teachers are facilitating the work of the day, aimed at discovering where they need to go with the teaching of reading. The leadership team and the professional development committee have planned this day together.

> *First activity:* In small groups, staff are asked to recall how they now teach reading. When did they start doing it this way? Why is that so? They share experiences and stories. (*Evoking potential in a trusting environment*)

Second activity: They converse as a whole group. What patterns do we notice in how we teach reading? What questions do they raise? What do we want to know about how successful we've been? What evidence or data will tell us what we need to know? How will we organize ourselves to discover this information? (*Inquiring into practice thereby reconstructing old assumptions*)

Three weeks later. . . .

Third activity: They converse in groups with information and data posted around the room. What patterns do we see? Does this evidence support or challenge our current practice? In what ways? How do we make sense of this? (*Focus on the construction of meaning*)

Fourth activity: The last activity asks: Based on our conversations this morning, in what ways do we need to reshape our reading program? What different outcomes do we seek? Do we need more information—if so, what? (*Frame actions that embody new behaviors and purposeful intentions*)

The above example combines four phases of reciprocal processes involved in constructivism so that a staff can create together the parameters for their future work. These processes involve rethinking our structures as well. Structures provide the containers in which patterns of relationships occur. Structures are resources. The forms that support relationships are nodes of connections, channels of energy flow. Places or intersections where people and energy converge might include groups, such as leadership teams, study or action research teams; places, such as a professional library, faculty research and development center, even open supply closets or "user-friendly" faculty rooms; and events, such as workshops, district dialogue sessions, or parent conversations.

The essential criterion for enabling structures involves an element of high synergy, which Carlsen (1988) explains as the positive reaction and interaction that occur when people do things for themselves and at the same time do things for others (reciprocity). Carlsen recalls Buckminster Fuller's 1978 work, *Operating Manual for Spaceship Earth,* in which he explains, "Synergy is the only word in our language that means the behavior of whole systems unpredicted by the separately observed behaviors of any of the system's separate parts or any subassembly of the system's parts" (quoted in Carlsen, 1988, p. 71). Larger than the sum of the parts, synergy in schools is the interaction dynamic arising from opportunities for mutual conversation, work, and action. It is the by-product of true collegiality. We provide additional examples of school and district collegial structures in later chapters.

PARTICIPANTS IN AN EDUCATIONAL COMMUNITY TO CONSTRUCT MEANINGS . . .

In Chapter 1, we discussed the process of *meaning-making* as constructivism; above we discussed leadership as the "reciprocal processes that enable . . . participants in an educational community to construct meanings." By participants we mean *all* members of the educational community, not segregated as leaders and followers. Leaders are teachers, administrators, parents, and students, as well as others who make the schools their purposeful place. Crusty old paradigms might warn us that "too many cooks spoil the stew"; new paradigms are making a different stew. The patterns of relationships in this new "stew" contain rich possibilities and exist outside traditional lines of authority, roles, established norms, rules, and policies. At any given time, roles and behaviors will shift among participants based on interest, expertise, experience, and responsibility. In more advanced school cultures, as in good marriages, roles are integrated or transcended.

Together we create and engage in experiences that we imbue with meaning, meanings informed by common experiences and also by our own personal schemas. The above example of the Raintree staff working through a process for creating common work agreements is illustrative of this leadership work in schools. Kegan (1982) advanced the idea that "meaning is, in its origins, a physical activity (grasping and seeing), a social activity (it requires another), a survival activity (in doing so, we live). Meaning understood in this way is the primary human motion, irreducible" (pp. 18–19). This understanding is critical to the role of constructivism within the context of community. This notion, born of negotiating experiences together, gives force and purposeful direction to community. The Raintree staff will never be quite the same; making meanings together changes us and creates momentum (motion and direction) for our work together.

Bateson's (1972) concept of meaning as a synonym for *pattern* adds another rich dimension to our communal work: meaning-making for common patterns of understandings. When the Raintree staff members have practiced their new agreements for a few months, the pattern of their understandings will deepen. These practices will become the new "habits of mind." There has been set in motion a patterning process that gives rhythm and purpose, force and direction, to the educational community.

Experiences with educational communities that have evolved from sustained collaborative work have created an understanding of communities as the primary context for professional growth. "The constraints of constructed knowledge," point out Bransford, Goldman, and Pellegrino (1992, p. 116), "come largely from the community of which one is a member. In the absence of any community, we suppose that it would be possible for an individual to have an idiosyncratic view of the world—but then, because there is no community, the idiosyncrasy is irrelevant." In a community, views are brought into harmony or we agree to disagree—either way, we consider the other. Grath (1998) refers to such shared meaning-making as "joint or reciprocal interpretation of experience, especially experiences that are readily open to multiple interpretations. . . . the reciprocal social processes by which a group of people agree on how to understand some phenomenon and what values to place on it" (p. 415).

Since constructivist learning is a social endeavor, community is essential for substantive and sustainable learning to occur. In our definition of constructivist leadership, the educational community is considered the medium for meaning-making, for human growth and development. In this chapter, community is defined in terms of its natural ecological qualities and its relationship to constructivist leadership.

Why is it important to understand communities as ecosystems? To understand that leadership is embedded in the patterns of relationships and meaning-making in a social organization is to notice that everything is connected. The system is dynamic, interdependent in its learning processes. One leader doesn't direct the learning of others (although those participating as leaders frame, and invite others into, opportunities)—the learning of each is dependent upon the learning of the other and of the whole. This ecological portrait can change our schemas about social systems.

Fritjof Capra, author of *The Tao of Physics* (1975), *The Turning Point* (1982), and *The Web of Life* (1996) has given his attention for most of this decade to the application of the principles of ecology to work with whole-school cultural change and social transformation. This work is called "ecoliteracy," meaning literacy in environmental principles and practices; by "ecology" they mean the guiding principles informing the development of all organisms and systems. In translating the concepts of ecology into social systems, Capra joined in the tradition of Gregory Bateson in psychology and anthropology; Bruce Joyce, Elliott Eisner, John Goodlad, and C. A. Bowers in education; Robert Kegan in psychology; Robert Bellah in philosophy and political science; and Theodore Roszak in political and environmental philosophy. The principles of ecology are described by Capra (1993) as involving interdependence, sustainability, ecological cycles, energy flow, partnership, flexibility, diversity, and coevolution.

In order to create educational communities that function as ecological social systems, members of these communities work in *interdependence* with one another. They rely on and trust one another to provide the support and skills needed by the whole group. In order to evolve, educational communities must be *sustained* over time, since it takes time to deepen the spiral of meaning-making, seek shared purpose, and develop interdependent professional cultures. *Ecological cycles* require a fluid flow of information and feedback, spiraling processes that are essential to engagement with the disequilibrium that causes us to break set with old assumptions and construct meaning (often called a "cycle of inquiry"). The reciprocal processes described earlier in this chapter can be understood as an ecological cycle.

Biological systems are propelled by the *energy flow* of the sun. The energy driving social systems is meaning-making, which we have described as developmental, as motion. These energy sources keep communities in motion. To understand meaning-making as the primary energy source of a community is critical to the understanding of constructivist leadership, which relies on communities in motion.

> *Partnerships* with parents and the broader community are essential if information and learning opportunities are to enter and leave the culture of the school.
>
> *Flexibility* is basic to communities in motion if fluctuations, feedback, and surprises are to lead to change rather than disorientation in schools.
>
> *Diversity* brings a complexity to the network of relationships that contains multiple perspectives and multiple resources and talents. Static, homogeneous, and inequitable relationships cannot challenge the thinking of its members, since individual and group thinking will stem from experiences and biases that are too similar. Diversity introduces the opportunity for participants to think and act in more complex ways. Such cognitive complexity involves the ability to understand and work with multiple perspectives; the capacity to think systemically; the yearning for reciprocity; and the ability to access, generate, and process vast sources of information. Diversity in the learning environment improves our possibilities for developing such complexity and therefore the possibilities for variance and productive dissonance.

Coevolution refers to the idea that as we work together in collaborative professional cultures, we grow together. This book focuses on the multiple means of learning in a professional culture, including shared leadership, conversations, common language, and the use of narrative. Bransford and colleagues (1992) describe knowledge as "a dialectic process": "By continually negotiating the meaning of observations, data, hypotheses, and so forth, groups of individuals construct systems that are largely consistent with one another" (p. 116). This dialectic is an essential aspect of coevolution. Herein lies our confidence that a shared purpose will arrive from such dialogue.

A composite narrative of a social ecological community might be interpreted in this way: A community is an interconnected and complex web of reciprocal relationships sustained and informed by their purposeful actions. Complexity is manifest in the diversity of the system; and the more diverse, the more rich and complex. Such communities are flexible and open to information provided through feedback spirals, as well as unexpected fluctuations and surprises that contain possibilities. The coevolution, or shared growth, of the participants in this community is propelled by, and emerges from, the joint construction of meaning and knowledge and involves continual creation and adaptation.

To borrow generously from Carl Rogers's (1959) concept of the "actualizing tendency" in individuals, these ecosystems are "actualizing communities" in the process of becoming more coherent and more growth-producing for both individuals and social groupings. In the process, these communities are responding to the dual nature of human beings to be both independent and interdependent, self-directed and interconnected. However, Bellah, Madsen, Sullivan, Sidler, and Tipton (1985) would remind us that to focus too deeply on the nature and needs of individual human beings may lead us to narrowly therapeutic interpretations of community, designing communities that are aimed primarily at meeting the needs of the individual. Rather, we must seek communities that serve the needs of the broader society as well as the needs of the individual.

The work of the new communitarians focuses primary concern on "the balance between social forces and the person, between community and autonomy, between the common good and liberty, between individual rights and social responsibilities" (Etzioni, 1998, p. x). These communities, Etzioni contends, are webs of social relations that encompass shared meanings and shared values. Unlike biological systems, these social communities are deeply moral, driven by shared values that encompass reciprocity, equity, and democracy. Educational communities of this character concurrently attend to the professional development needs of the individual, to the professional culture of the group, to the engagement with the broader community, and to the outcomes of the students. Such educational communities have coherence, a wholeness and an integration that characterize sense-making.

Sergiovanni (2000) captured these understandings for schools as communities that enjoy discretion and choice:

1. Schools need to be defined as collections of people and ideas rather than as structures of brick and mortar.
2. Shared values that lead to the development of tightly knit communities of mind and heart need to be encouraged within schools, while at the same time respect for the defining differences that make a school unique need to be encouraged among schools.
3. Though some schools might function as schools within schools and others as free-standing schools connected to a larger complex of schools, all schools need to be tied together by common foundational values.
4. Layered loyalties to one's own school community and to the larger community of schools needs to be cultivated.
5. Nothing in the concepts of nested communities, neighborhoods within a city, or schools within schools should compromise the individual rights of students, parents, teachers, and other community members.
6. This emphasis on individual rights needs to be tempered by deliberately linking rights to responsibilities within a framework of commitment to civic virtue, defined as the willingness of all members of the community, individually and collectively, to sacrifice their self-interest on behalf of the common good.
7. Within practical limits, students and their families, as well as teachers, should be able to choose the particular school, school family, or schools within a school they wish to join. This "school" of choice should be part of a larger legal framework of school or schools and resourced in an equitable level.
8. Commitment to both individual rights and shared responsibilities that are connected to the common good should provide the basis for moral leadership. (pp. 72–73)

In spite of the promise of educational communities that are based on ecological principles, communities can become fragmented and incoherent without leadership. Leadership is the factor that enables meaning to be constructed together in that it engages people in the essential reciprocal processes. Without value-driven, purposeful leadership, communities can become balkanized, or focused on the self-serving purposes of an individual or a few individuals.

Studies of cult communities such as Synanon (Lambert, 1982) recognize that even though many of the aspects of community may exist (interdependencies, purpose, support, and security), individual and societal growth can be dramatically restricted, then reversed. If flexibility and diversity are disallowed by acts of leadership by an individual who focuses on control and conformity, the rewards of community can become counterproductive. Organization and community can be amoral concepts. Cult-type communities may articulate a purpose, usually the designated leader's purpose; however, this would not produce a moral community. What is it that creates a shared purpose of schooling to which people freely commit?

That Lead Toward a Shared Purpose of Schooling

Before the middle of the last millennium, the Gutenberg printing press found itself esconced in a warehouse in Victor Hugo's Paris. In one particularly powerful scene in *Notre-Dame de Paris* (1831/1978), a church archdeacon, on learning the purpose of the cumbersome machine, observed in outrage: "Alas and alack, small things overcome great ones! A tooth triumphs over a body. The Nile rat kills the crocodile, . . . the book will kill the building!" Hugo goes on to explain: "It was the terror and bewilderment felt by a man of the sanctuary before the luminous press of Gutenberg. . . . It was the cry of the prophet who already hears the restless surge of an emancipated mankind, who can see that future time when intelligence will undermine faith, opinion dethrone belief, and the world shake off Rome" (pp. 188–189). His prediction proved remarkably keen, for a fundamental shift in access to knowledge gave rise to the Protestant Reformation and the Enlightenment. For most of the last three centuries, the schools have been the center of knowledge for the "common man." Today, American schools have lost not only their monopoly on knowledge—even their corner on knowledge has shrunk.

Several educational figures had been paddling swiftly against the tide. In 1979, Goodlad published the small work *What Are Schools For?,* in which he set forth the knowledge and competencies that schools should teach. Hirsch (1988) claimed the centrality of a common knowledge base (albeit European), and Adler laid out his *Paideia Program* (1984) for "essential" knowledge. These statements and arguments for a common knowledge base gave additional credence to the role of schools as knowledge dispensers—purveyors of the canon—at a time when this ancient role is necessarily under scrutiny. Few have questioned the assumption that such content should serve as the foundation of schooling. Today, standards have set forth the current canon of knowledge to be learned.

Children can see the world and its people on television's National Geographic or Discovery series, experience news as it is made, observe re-creations of history, have access to the Library of Congress, and observe and fall victim to the conflict and violence on America's streets. Almost any question can be researched, any information can be found through the Internet. In schools, we can teach children how to pose the questions, to access, process, and challenge knowledge, but we are no longer the major knowledge provider. Yet we have returned with full force to the notion of a knowledge base, usually static, through the standards and testing movement. We have codified with the force of law those things that children need to know and be able to do. In the first chapter, we made the case that standards—properly used—had the potential for addressing the needs of all children. We need not let it lull us into believing that there is a static knowledge base and that learning it will create thoughtful citizens. It must occur within a supportive, vibrant community in which children and adults are continually making sense of their learning and their lives.

We agree with our colleagues from Dewey (1916) to Glickman (1998) that our major purpose in schools remains the preparation of children for democratic citizenship. However, our track record here is as wanting as our role in the knowledge business. It is not surprising that when we do not offer democratic learning opportunities for children and adults, as we generally do not, we cannot expect democratic actions. However, in those rare schools and institutions in which we seek to teach democracy through experience, we tend to seek our goals through individual involvement in decision making. Focusing on such summative actions as the polling booth and the moment of decision making does not engage the prerequisite lived experiences essential for democratic life. It is as true today as it was in 1985 when Bellah and colleagues reminded us that individuals remain individuals in this country; they have vague understandings of community but virtually no conception of interconnected, pluralistic communities or social vision.

An integrated concept of the good society or shared purpose can only be found in interconnected, ecological communities. We continue to propose that *the purpose of schooling is to engage children and adults within patterns of relationships in school communities that serve as centers for sustained growth.* Experiences in ecological communities can produce a shared purpose for schooling, encompassing aims that extend beyond self-interest to the growth and well-being of children, their families, and society. Moral educational communities come into existence as people learn to grow together. The purposes referenced in our definition of constructivist leadership involve a commitment to the growth of children and adults as well as a commitment to communities and societies that sustain such growth.

If participants are constructing their own meanings and knowledge, how can we be assured that the shared purpose of schooling will entail such a moral commitment? This confidence arises from a faith in ecological communities as communities enabling their participants to coevolve morally. As this coevolution takes place, caring, equity, and justice seem to surface as guiding values (Gilligan, 1982; Kohlberg, 1976). Poplin and Weeres (1993) claimed in the work *Voices from the Inside* that the process created shared meanings that led to a larger moral purpose—teachers reconnected with their reasons for going into teaching. There resides in each of us a deep yearning for community and purpose. When individuals and others share a common experience of growth in an educational community, they experience an increased responsibility for others. We become committed to "a cause beyond oneself" (Glickman, 1993, p. 15). Within the context of these lived experiences, diversity opens up possibilities, helping us see the multiple perspectives and worldviews of others, and transcend the "fault lines" of difference. This faith in the transformational capacities of communities continues to be echoed by others in Toronto schools, a Seattle high school, the National Writing Project network, and leadership preparation programs built around learning communities (Fullan, 1999; Grossman, Wineburg, and Woolworth, 2000; Lieberman and Wood, 2001; Norris, Barnett, Basom, & Yerkes, 2002).

This purpose of schooling demands a rethinking of all aspects of our educational institutions, a commitment to a new set of goals. Knowledge must serve as "grist for the mill" for both students and adults, a basis for framing big questions, for conversations, and for learning the thinking and collaborative skills essential to a democracy. Purpose, like vision, emerges from the conversations. This sense of renewed purpose can be made possible through the processes of constructivist leadership.

THE SPIRITUAL DIMENSIONS OF CONSTRUCTIVIST LEADERSHIP

Our discussion about purpose and community is in its essence a spiritual one. Constructivist leadership is a spiritual concept in that it embraces reciprocity and equity, meaning, learning, responsibility, community, and purpose. By "spiritual," says Palmer (1998), "I mean the diverse ways we answer the heart's longing to be connected with the largeness of life—a longing that animates love and work, especially the work called teaching"(p. 5). He continues, "The connections made by good teachers are held not in their methods but in their hearts—meaning heart in the ancient sense, as the place where intellect and emotion and spirit and will converge in the human self" (p. 11). Asa Hilliard (1991) asked us a decade ago if we had the will to educate all children. Such "will" can be found in the meaningful conversations in schools. Connectedness found in the conversations we have with each other includes essential questions framing the "largeness of life":

> How do we relate to each other?
> What contributions are we making to each other and to the larger society?
> How do we create community? How do we create caring communities?
> What is our shared purpose?
> What does it all mean?

Meaning-making requires "going to ground," coming to understand our inner terrain and therefore our most profound successes, puzzlements, mistakes, and avoidances. When we confront our failures to teach all children, a form of remorse and anguish is inevitable. Such anguish can only be survived and acted upon in supportive communities; otherwise denial is the expedient response. Many of our urban schools live in a state of denial created by the lack of an authentic community in which to translate the knowledge of failure with many children into what Etzioni (1999) refers to as "civic repentance." By civic repentance he means our capacity to acknowledge mistakes (privately and collectively), learn from them, get back in touch with our core values, and restructure our lives as professionals. This process, not to be mistaken for the lingering guilt that can result in illness, challenges us to create Palmer's "community of truth," a place where we can come face-to-face with the realities of our lives, embrace those truths, and learn from them. Such a community requires the "epistemological reality that knowledge is embedded in discursive community, and knowledge claims (any claim to truth) should therefore be evaluated and, where appropriate, modified in the context of cooperative enquiries with community members" (Etzioni, 1998, p. 64).

As adults in schools, we must model for and with children the value actions embedded in the large questions above. As we learn from and contribute to each other, so will students be encouraged and clear about their responsibilities and opportunities to commit to others beyond themselves. Programs that involve community service, peer teaching, service learning, problem-based learning with community agencies, involvement of whole families in the educational process, and Internet connections with developing countries, all hold great promise for enabling our youth to find their spiritual centers as they live their lives with us.

In our conversations with each other, Whyte contends (1994), we uncover our innocence, what it is to be "awestruck with wonder, ripe with the dumbest questions, and thirsting to learn" (p. 290). Such joy need not only reside with small children. Joy, wonder, and imagination bring perspective: We take ourselves less seriously, and we are more attentive to the greater world and to finding a sense of home in the exquisite patterns of relationships. Whyte continues:

> The new organization that honors the soul and the soul of the world will be what Peter Senge has called "the learning organization," an organization that is as much concerned with what it serves as what it is, as much attentive to the greater world as the small world it has become, as much trying to learn from the exquisite patterns that inform that greater world as trying to impose its own pattern on something already complete. (p. 296)

ACTS OF LEADERSHIP

An "act of leadership," as distinguished from role leadership, is the performance of actions (behaviors plus intention) that enable participants in a community to evoke potential within a trusting environment; to inquire into practice, thereby reconstructing old assumptions; to focus on the construction of meaning; or to frame actions based on new behaviors and purposeful intention. Everyone in the school community can perform an act of leadership. Leadership is an inclusive field of processes in which leaders do their work.

Those who perform acts of leadership need to have the following qualities:

- A sense of purpose and ethics, because honesty and trust are fundamental to relationships
- Facilitation skills, because framing, deepening, and moving the conversations about teaching and learning are fundamental to constructing meaning
- An understanding of constructivist learning for all humans
- A deep understanding of change and transitions, because change is not what we thought it was
- An understanding of context so that communities of memories can be continually drawn and enriched

- An intention to redistribute power and authority, for without such intention and action, none of us can lead
- A personal identity that allows for courage and risk, low ego needs, and a sense of possibilities.

Educators generally enter life's work with *a sense of purpose and ethics*. Perhaps it is primitive and sketchy, certainly it is vulnerable. A few years ago, I heard a young teacher, Susan, in her third year of teaching, say that she had entered the profession because she wanted to make a difference with kids. I have heard this statement of dedication hundreds of times. Midway through the second year, she had begun to question her options, her possibilities. Yet as she sat in an initial meeting to plan for a professional practice school, she reported that this feeling of purpose began to resurface. So easily lost; so easily regained. So vulnerable.

Perhaps all educators were Susans at one point. What has happened? Do educators still possess that sense of purpose with which they began their work? Can it be recaptured? We believe so. Those who initiate an act of leadership are usually those who have held on tight to their purposes or who have been reawakened, experiencing a pattern of relationships that has helped to resurface and perhaps redefine and extend those original compelling purposes into ethical behavior. For them, a sense of coherence and authenticity contributes to the establishment of trust in communal relationships. *Actions that reconnect us* with our values and purpose may include facilitating the development of a shared vision or difficult dialogues about the capacities of all children, and keeping the values agenda on the table.

Those performing acts of leadership find *facilitation skills* essential to creating engagement in reciprocal processes among leaders in a community. These skills are vital to everyone in "Leading the Conversations" (Chapter 3). When I entered my third year of teaching, I discovered in an interview that all teachers and administrators in my new school were expected to participate in 30 hours of training in open communication, shared decision making, problem solving, and accountability. This school, Bell Junior High in Golden, Colorado, was genuinely founded on these four principles, and everyone was a leader and expected to facilitate the processes. *Actions encompassing such facilitation* included convening and sustaining the conversation, asking questions that move the conversation deeper, and enabling other participants to learn from experiencing facilitation.

An understanding of constructivist learning for all humans enables leaders to pose questions and to frame actions that cause self-construction and collegial interaction as well as the design of constructivist curriculum, instruction, and assessment. Constructivism is not an evolutionary understanding that has naturally emerged from our training and experiences in behaviorism. Constructivism is a significantly different paradigm that enables us to frame new questions and create learning based on passion, unique learning gifts and perceptions, community, and authentic work and assessment. *Actions that address this act of leadership* include designing faculty meetings based on what we know about human learning, keeping teaching and learning at the center of our conversations, and studying professional literature that sets forth ideas and strategies based on constructivism.

A deep understanding of change and transitions is also essential to jointly designing the sequencing, timing, and duration of reciprocal processes. Change that is constructivist in nature emerges from the meaning-making process and is therefore unpredictable and evolving. Preset objectives, as well as predetermined strategies and techniques that are too tightly drawn, violate the very nature of constructivism. Constructivists have goals, outcomes, and a repertoire of change strategies that focus talent and resources toward a shared purpose. Attempting to harness real change that is being pulled by intention, not pushed by prediction, is so complex that its understandings can only be constructed in the conversations among co-leaders in a learning community. *Acts of leadership* in this area include using multiple forms of communication to enable people to work through change at many levels, keeping the vision and values in the conversation so everyone will keep in touch with why they are involved in the change, and coaching and mentoring people through the sense-making process.

An understanding of the context is essential to the unity of "communities of memories," which must be drawn forth and enriched and reinterpreted. Bellah and colleagues (1985) invite us to consider communities, in the sense in which we are using the term, as having history—in an important sense they are constituted by their past—and for this reason we can speak of a real community as a "community of memory," one that does not forget its past. In order not to forget that past, a community needs to be engaged in retelling its story, its constitutive narrative (p. 153). These composite and shared memories take on expanded meanings when retold together. They constitute a vital part of the meaning construction (and reconstruction) that goes on in schools. When a new principal enters a school, we advise him or her to talk with teachers, with families, with children, to find out about the memories. Embedded in these stories are the values and intentions that drive the work in the school, as well as the fears and lost hopes that form barriers to collective work. Further, schools are a part of an ever-changing context of culture, the context from which the students come. To develop viable curriculum and relationships we must know these cultures. *Acts of leadership* may include learning together about the culture of the families who are a part of the school, developing responsive teaching and learning, storytelling, and developing a histomap of the history of the school and community.

An intention to redistribute power and authority followed by action that both relinquishes power from formal positions and evokes power from others is essential to constructivist leadership. Such realignment of power is central to reciprocity and equity, to creating shared responsibility for our work. Uneven power arrangements have historically resulted in blame and abdicated responsibility. "A learning leader's work," claim Frydman, Wilson, and Wyer (2000) "is about skillfully giving away power, surrendering control, and rendering capacity for leadership in others. The word 'skillful' is key here. The devolution of power involves letting go of the reins in such a way as to free the potential for self-organizing networks to emerge" (p. 228). Block (1996) provides several profound reasons for replacing leadership with stewardship and thereby redistributing power: Stewardship is about service to others, not centralizing power to accomplish one's own ends; traditional governance is based on "sovereignty and a form of intimate colonialism" (p. 7). Leadership, he argues, has engendered dependency; our sense of purpose is disconnected from a sense of service. *Acts of leadership* that address these barriers may include truly involving others in reciprocal partnerships and governance, thereby gaining authority from the participants (Glickman, 1998); solving problems together instead of telling and directing; and holding continuing dialogue about the needs of children and their families.

The redistribution of power requires that formal leaders construe and interpret themselves as they construct meaning and knowledge with others. Their *sense of personal identity* allows for courage and risk, low ego needs, and a sense of possibilities. Personal identity forms in reflective interactions with others. They seek not so much to explain and describe, but to listen and to understand. These individuals have outgrown the need to "win" in the traditional sense, understanding that reciprocity and high personal regard reframe "winning" into concern for moving toward a shared purpose. With a growing clarity and confidence in the grounding values that guide their lives, these emerging leaders are able to cut through the cumbersome morass that sometimes envelopes our lives and ask the next essential question. Since personal efficacy is evolving in a trusting environment, these leaders work with others to create possibilities for all children and educators. *Acts of leadership* may include raising questions for which no clear answer exists, admitting mistakes, and creating multiple forums for conversations.

Full participation leads to acts of leadership; being fully engaged in meaning-making activates one's drive toward purpose and community. One cannot help but lead; one is compelled to do so by the self-directed drive toward self-renewal and interdependency. Responsibility toward self and others surfaces as an essential developmental process. Paulo Freire's (1973) ideas have long been persuasive: "Humankind emerge from their submersion and acquire the ability to intervene in reality as it is unveiled" (p. 44). We would add strongly, *"to intervene" and to construct and to reintervene* in their realities. We have seen this over and over as staff emerge into the leadership arena: The next essential question is asked, ideas and traditions are challenged, people volunteer to lead, groups form, curiosity is aroused, verbal and nonverbal interactions change. My experiences in tough-to-change schools and institutions is that these actions begin to emerge during the first year of active engagement and gain momentum about 18 months into the process. It is the participation processes that create the meaning and the understandings (the reality) to which people then commit themselves. Without these participatory opportunities, commitment is not possible, only compliance and disengagement.

This vision of the potential of educational leaders may not only seem ideal, it *is* ideal—and it is possible. Constructivist leadership enables human growth that was previously reserved for the few. Others were followers, relegated to second-class citizenship and second-class growth. In our traditional systems, growth was a limited resource; in ecological communities, interdependence and reciprocity require equal partners.

CONCLUSION

Since the mid-1990s, leadership has been bandied about in energetic and new ways—a ball in the air, it has been discarded, repainted, reshaped. It has evoked lively discussion and stimulated many to wander into uncharted territory. Leadership is in transition. Among the trailblazers of this new path has been constructivist leadership, boldly separating itself from the "one leader" and embedding itself within the patterns of learning relationships in schools and organizations.

In 1998, this path led to the concept of "leadership capacity" or the broad-based, skillful participation in the work of leadership. It emphasizes that leadership work is skillful and multidimensional, and that many need to be involved in such work. Further, it establishes the reciprocal learning processes of inquiry and reflection as cornerstones in the schoolhouse that ensure that all children are learning.

CHAPTER 3

LEADING THE CONVERSATIONS

LINDA LAMBERT

I'm saying that it is necessary to share meaning. A society is a link of relationships among people and institutions, so that we can live together. But it only works if we have a culture—which implies that we share meaning; i.e., significance, purpose, and value. . . . The different assumptions that people have are tacitly affecting the whole meaning of what we are doing.

David Bohm
On Dialogue, *1998, pp. 19–20*

"What is the use of a book," thought Alice, "without pictures or conversations?"

Lewis Carroll
Alice's Adventures in Wonderland, *Chapter 1*

It is in the conversation that we find shared meaning. Conversations give form to the reciprocal processes of leadership that make up the sum of the spaces or fields among us; they create the text of our lives. In Chapter 2, we discussed the concept of spaces, or zones, among us that constitute the texture of our relationships. The conversations serve as the medium for the reciprocal processes that enable participants in a school community to construct meanings toward a shared purpose about teaching and learning. Conversations are fractals of communities; that is, they re-create on a smaller scale the ecological processes of the larger community.

By constructing meaning, we evoke the imagination. It is imagination that makes empathy possible, observes Maxine Greene (1995). Imagination "allows us to break with the taken for granted, to set aside familiar distinctions and definitions" (p. 3). Through imagination we discover our questions and our capacity to entertain the possibility that things could be different.

Conversations are the visible manifestation of constructivist leadership, thereby encompassing the reciprocal relationships that make meaning and community possible.

The conversation is the major approach to constructivist change as conversations host meaning-making. This chapter explores the concept of conversations, provides examples of conversations in schools, and tells what it takes to lead them. Chapters 4 and 5 deepen the nature of the conversations through language, questioning and listening, narrative and story. *A primary role of the constructivist leader is to lead the conversations. In so doing, a leader opens, rather than occupies, space.*

THE CONVERSATIONS

Life in schools and in society at large has become too complex. As Kegan (1994) argues, we are "in over our heads." The demands of modern life and the mounting pressures of the high-stakes accountability press have pushed this complexity into untenable arenas. The artifacts of public knowledge—standards, examinations, core curriculum, policies—are continually changing. We must be able to construct new meanings around these artifacts. We would suggest that such clarity, focus, and internal congruence can best be found within the conversation. Within the conversation we find ourselves, our ideas, our priorities, and our capacities for relationships and understanding. We are referring to all forms of talk as "the conversations," even conversations with self. That does not mean, however, that all talk is conversation.

Conversations that are constructivist in aim and nature have some common qualities or characteristics distinguishing them from talk that has undeclared agendas or agendas that are directed by persuasion through power. By "undeclared agenda" we mean talk that appears to have a public purpose, but instead stems from a private purpose of manipulation. We speak of the qualities of dialogue, for "anti-dialogue does not communicate, but rather issues communiques" (Freire, 1973, p. 46). Talk that is directed by power involves those discussions through which individuals holding hierarchical authority over another are declaring a demand, or "request." This does not mean that there will never be a role for this latter type of discussion; it does mean that we would not consider this interchange to be a constructivist conversation.

In a constructivist conversation, each individual comes to understand the purpose of the talk, since the relationship is one of reciprocity. Each person is growing in understanding; each person is seeking some interpretation of truth as he or she perceives it. In our discussion of the spiritual dimensions of leadership we called upon Palmer's notion of a community of truth. What does this mean—"truth"? Truth, in the sense that we use it here, refers to the intention to bring to bear to the interpretation of the current experience our past experiences, beliefs, and perceptions so that we can come to understand. It is the genuine pursuit of understanding as it exists in the moment and within the context of the conversation, the relationship, and the community. This means, of course, that this understanding will be context influenced and developmental; therefore it will change with time.

Discovering an intention for truth in schools and organizations does not come easily. The development of our capacity for truth-finding emerges from trusting relationships over time. The more we are together, the more we talk about what matters; and the more we follow through in our commitments to each other, the more our capacity for truth is strengthened. The endless cycle of reforms, revolving-door principals, and unfulfilled promises have deeply wounded many who work in schools. Overcoming such tribulations and disappointments requires what we will reveal as "sustaining conversations," conversations that enable us to reconstruct meaning and purpose in our professional lives. Trust is especially important in constructivist learning, since, as Kegan (1982) points out, "there are few things as intimate as constructing meaning in the presence of another" (p. 16).

The conversations described in this chapter are characterized by *shared intention* of genuine "truth-seeking," *remembrances and reflections* of the past, a *search for meaning* in the present, a *mutual revelation of ideas and information,* and *respectful listening.* Participants share an intention to seek "truth" together. Remembrances and reflections are evoked by the genuine interactions in recalling the past with a critical eye. We recall our successes and failures, our purposes and intentions. As participants search for meaning, they try to make sense of what is being talked about together, revealing to one another their ideas, experiences, and insights. These rich processes are made possible by really listening to one another, listening for words, expression, emotion, and meaning.

A conversation may not include all of these elements during each interaction, for some conversations are short and informal. However, all of the elements are usually implied or understood, based on prior experiences with the relationships of the conversants. These conversations occur within the context of a trusting environment. We consider these elements to be central to constructivist conversations, although the content and goals of the conversations will vary, as will the entry points into the process.

A TYPOLOGY OF CONVERSATIONS

Whenever the word *typology,* or classification of types that have characteristics in common, is used, qualifications or caveats are required. The idea is being employed here to embody the common elements discussed above while revealing different initial purposes or entry points (see Figure 3.1). No category is self-contained; they are fluid, overlapping, and informing of each other. Sometimes they are one and the same; for instance, a one-on-one conversation can be both inquiring and sustaining.

A principal colleague, Rick Rubino, uses a trust-building activity in which a long piece of nylon rope, about 40 feet in length, is shaped into a square by four blindfolded people. The shape takes form as they talk together. While the rope may become a four-sided figure, it can also take on any other shape. This typology of conversations is the nylon rope.

PERSONAL CONVERSATIONS

All conversations are personal in that they involve our identity and meaning systems. Our evolving identity—who we are or how we perceive ourselves—is the basis for the construction of meaning. As teachers shift their identities, their beliefs about their work and purpose change. In a recent study of teacher-leaders in professional development schools, Gonzales and Lambert (2001) found that the basis for moving into leadership work was changing identity. One teacher declared: "I saw myself as a kindergarten teacher . . . now I see myself as an educator" (p. 10). The work of this teacher changed. She was still an outstanding kindergarten teacher, *but she also* shared responsibility for the improvement of the school community and teachers new to the profession.

One of the most persistent questions about this work has been, How do educators come to change their beliefs about students, about their work, about themselves? We explore our inner terrain within the context of communities of practice, within the conversation. As we discuss in the section below entitled "Sustaining Conversations," changing beliefs result in new theories of practice—theories that incorporate new perspectives. We change our identities in relationships, thereby continually changing

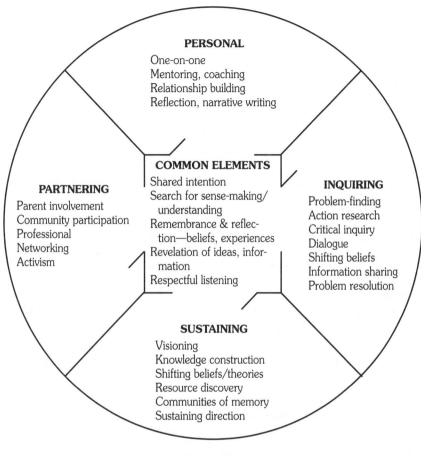

FIGURE 3.1
Typology of Conversations

our meaning-making system by exploring our theories about why we do what we do. Wheatley (1999) suggests

> Everything comes into form because of relationship. We are constantly called to be in relationship—to information, people, events, ideas, life. Even reality is created through our participation in relationships. We choose what to notice; we relate to certain things and ignore others. Through these chosen relationships, we cocreate our world. (p. 145)

As we have noted, convening and sustaining the conversation is the primary work of leaders, for it is the medium through which we become more fully ourselves and invent new ways of being together.

With ourselves, we often use the term *reflection* to denote the processes that can be most eloquently, although not exclusively, activated in the personal conversation. When calling forth our own experiences, beliefs, and perceptions about an idea, we are simply remembering or recollecting; when we also assess and reevaluate the assumptions underlying our remembrances (we stop and think), we are reflecting (Dewey, 1938; Schön, 1987). Reflection and self-construction are the central purposes of the personal conversation and this requires that we consider "conversations" with the self in this domain. Examples of personal reflection often include journal writing, moments of stillness, meditation, metacognition, self-assessment, and spontaneous thinking during rhythmic, repetitive activity.

Schön (1987) likened the conversation to musical improvisation. "Conversation is verbal improvisation. . . . the participants are making something . . . an artifact with its own meaning and coherence. Their reflection-in-action is a reflective conversation" (pp. 30–31). Conversation is discovery, constructed in interaction with self and one another.

Personal conversations take many forms; they can be the complete conversation of two colleagues talking through an idea, a preplanned conversation about teaching, an informal moment when we lift a cup from the stream of conversation that is ever-present in a relationship. Such conversations are part of mentoring and coaching, critical friendships, colleagueship.

Or, a personal conversation might be as formal as a postobservation conference within a cognitive coaching process. Cognitive coaching brings a strong constructivist approach to the "supervision" table (Costa & Garmston, 1994). The purpose of the postobservation of teaching conference, particularly, is the construction of meaning, of self-reflection and sense-making. Because the process is reciprocal, both individuals are seeking to understand the teaching episode and to learn from it. This purpose is not shared by all approaches to clinical supervision; many forms of supervision cast the supervisor in the role of teaching the teacher about "good teaching," using the conference as a forum. Under those circumstances, the supervisor is the expert, the teacher is the student.

The small portion of conversation below uses mediational questions to explore teaching practice in a cognitive coaching conference.

JASON: Sometimes it feels like we're just getting through the day. My students seemed bored by math.

LINDA: Can you recall a time or an instance when it wasn't that way? When students reacted differently?

JASON: Well . . . in geometry. In geometry they are more enthusiastic, involved.

LINDA: What is different in the two circumstances?

JASON: In geometry they can use tools, objects, and work with space. They create images in space based on the concepts.

LINDA: What can you infer from this observation? Can you imagine using some of these approaches in your other math classes?

JASON: Umm . . . I think so.

LINDA: Let's think about what that would look like. Can we construct a sample lesson in algebra using the geometrical strategies?

When self-reflection reaches this quality of construction, it is clear that there is a high degree of trust in the relationship and that both individuals understand the nature of their work together.

Another powerful relationship context for personal conversation can be that of mentoring and mutual or comentoring. While the mentoring relationship is initially uneven, it is nevertheless imbued with a caring investment in the growth of each other. As a teaching intern at James Logan High School in Union City, California, Stacy Kopshy entered into an unexpected set of mentoring relationships:

> As a beginning teacher I was excited to know that Ms. Sklavos would teach me to plan interesting lectures and show me ways to easily create multiple-choice tests. Instead of the lesson plans I envisioned, Ms. Sklavos [a recent California Literature Project graduate] challenged my own concept of the classroom. She encouraged me to think beyond the prepared lessons I could present to the students and, instead, to coach the students as they *discovered* literature.
>
> The following year I shared a common prep with Ms. Nelson. In the same manner as Ms. Sklavos, Ms. Nelson never just presented information to the students. Instead she modeled lessons that caught the attention of each student as he/she was forced to interpret the literature on an individual basis. (Letter to the California Literature Project, June 20, 1994).

These teachers taught Stacy to be a constructivist teacher and a constructivist learner; they altered her view of herself as a teacher and her worldview about teaching and learning. The relationship of a new teacher to an experienced teacher or a new administrator to an experienced administrator can provide for these fundamental processes in the construction process: a reexamination of the self and world view within the context of a supportive relationship. The process can also be similar in a cognitive coaching conference: Personal experiences and perceptions are elicited; feedback or information that causes dissonance can be introduced; the discussion and self-reflection centers on trying to make sense of any discrepancies that are encountered. Often the process is a coevolutionary one: Both mentor and mentee are redefining themselves and their worldviews. Eventually the relationship evolves into one of comentoring, or, if the mentor cannot make a shift to equity, the mentee tends to move out of the relationship.

Many of the qualities being described here as part of a mentoring relationship can also be found in the current term *critical friend*. A critical friend, writes Costa and Kallick (1993, p. 50), is a trusted person who asks provocative questions, provides data to be examined through another lens, and offers critique of a person's work as a friend. A critical friend takes the time to fully understand the context of the work presented and the outcomes that the person or group is working toward. The friend is an advocate for the success of that work. He or she observes, joins in the research process, provides feedback and data, and questions and probes. The critical friend, like the mentor, must be invited into life.

Personal conversation processes underlie the conversations that follow, for the reciprocal processes of dialogue evoke potential in a trusting environment, inquire of each other, focus on the construction of meaning, and help frame actions that embody new behaviors and purposeful intentions.

INQUIRING CONVERSATIONS

It is the inquiring conversation that distinguishes a self-renewing school from a stagnant or declining one. Just as personal inquiry is at the heart of the personal conversation, organizational inquiry is at the heart of this cluster of conversations. These are the conversations that occur around inquiry processes such as action research, critical inquiry, disaggregating school data, the protocol, and planned conversations around student work. It is inquiry that places "learning" into the learning community.

Inquiring processes are not new. Kurt Lewin originated the term *action research* in the 1940s. Robert Schaefer's *The School as a Center of Inquiry* was published in 1967.

These processes are being used in schools with increasing frequency. They are becoming central to administrative preparation programs, professional development schools, and national and regional reform networks.

Principal Anita Hayward routinely organizes the work of Hanna Ranch School (Hercules, California) around the uses of the reciprocal processes of constructivist leadership. Such processes involve surfacing current thought and beliefs, inquiring into practice, constructing meaning, and reframing action. Inquiry is characterized by the penetrating use of data and evidence to discover problems of practice and make sense of the work of teaching and learning.

Embedded within a framework of reciprocal processes is *dialogue*, perhaps the most elegant form of conversation. In dialogue we listen, seek to understand, and hold our assumptions in the air of critique. We do not seek decisions, actions, or justifications. The promise of dialogue is that we may invent visions of what could be in our schools and organizations. Greene (1995) suggests that

> reshaping imagination may be revealed through many forms of dialogue: dialogue among the young who come from different cultures and different modes of life, dialogue among people who have come together to solve problems that seem worth solving to all of them, dialogue among people undertaking shared tasks, protesting injustices. (p. 5)

Since the purpose of dialogue is to understand—to understand others and to understand ourselves—it calls upon us to find reflective stillness in our busy lives, to set aside time and space in which to mentally breathe. It is through understanding that we change who we are and what we do. Wheatley (1999) points out,

> We don't accept diversity because we've been told it's the right thing to do. Only as we're engaged together in work that is meaningful do we learn to work through the differences and value them. (p. 149)

Kegan (1994) describes the complementary thoughts of Burbules and Rice:

> There is no reason to assume that dialogue across differences (necessarily) involves either eliminating those differences or imposing one group's views on others; dialogue that leads to understanding, cooperation, and accommodation can sustain differences within a broader compact of toleration and respect. (p. 327)

A "compact of toleration and respect" is essential to a community of practice. Such safety allows alternative perspectives to emerge and to be examined; otherwise they haunt us.

While Greene, Wheatley, and Kegan may voice the value of dialogue, we find that it is rare in schools. Dialogue in its "pure" form (Bohm,

1998) suggests a boundless, emerging conversation that is unattached to action and highly time-consuming. In the center of the cyclone of schools, we tend to find just the opposite: An issue or problem arises, vaguely defined, and faculty move toward solution. Children aren't doing their homework or behaving well? Develop a new homework or discipline policy with incremental punishments. Understanding is a rare commodity in schools. While we have spoken of teaching for understanding for decades, we rarely lead for understanding.

We would suggest that dialogue can, and must, be nestled into the critical work of schooling by situating itself between the question (Why aren't children doing their homework?), the evidence (let's ask children and parents), dialogue (what does this mean?), and action (so, what shall we do about it?). Such dialogue might be placed anywhere in the agenda for 20–30 minutes during which people listen, probe, express, and seek to understand. Action is held at bay until later in the process. We find that action delayed is action infused with a deeper wisdom. Educators are smart people—we need to surface and appreciate that smartness through appropriate conversation designs.

Listen in to a slice of dialogue on standards and benchmarks in another high school:

JOAN (FACILITATOR): As you will note on our agenda, today we will continue with our dialogue on standards and benchmarks. Let me remind us where we left off last time. We had clarified the meaning and use of standards as "what students know and are able to do." We had agreed to set up a continuing process to examine our standards and curriculum in the light of assessment data.

JEFF: Further, I believe, we introduced the district's interest in collecting systematic data around the benchmarks.

MARIA: My concern at that point was the number of benchmarks—in California, nearly 9000—won't we be fragmenting learning and moving away from our commitment to the big ideas?

GARY: We need to clarify the implications of this approach to benchmarks in light of our further commitment to project-based learning and constructivism.

JOAN: So let us frame this dialogue with a question, how about the one that Gary just suggested by his comment? "What are the implications of using benchmarks in light of our commitment to project-based learning and constructivism?" (all nod in agreement)

TIA: My understanding is that benchmarks are indicators on the pathway to meeting the standard and that they can be anchor pieces of student work that meet the standard. In other words, they are ways in which students can demonstrate progress toward standards. They are not objectives.

JOSE: An interesting tension—we tend to treat them as objectives.

SAM: Yes, and as objectives, we have assumed that we need assessment data on each one. What are the implications of this tension?

THERESA: The implications are becoming more clear to me, I think. As indicators and expressions of progress, some benchmarks will be more appropriate to certain learning situations than others.

TIA: And, there will be indicators that emerge from the learning that had not been predicted on the state's benchmarks for a specific standard.

SAM: For instance, if the standards, or clusters of them, represented our "big ideas," the indicators would vary based on how the child is coming to know and on the instructional practice as well. Perhaps even the curriculum.

JOAN: . . . such as project-based learning. Can anyone think of an example?

GARY: That is challenging. Let me take a stab at it. Let's take a standard related to literary criticism. One pathway would be to understand the text as "text"—you know, language, writing style, narrative as appropriate to the subject at hand. In our integrated language arts–history project, we would also expect to find a heightened awareness of social values and civic virtues.

MARY: I think I understand what you're getting at—can anyone give me an example in math?

CYNTHIA: I'll try one for our math-science project. The concept of measurement is a big idea that students bring with them from elementary school. And, as we work with astronomy and physics, I would want them to also know the Heisenberg Principle. (quizzical looks) This principle tells us that in space that which is being measured alters itself during the act of measurement. Therefore, the concept of measurement becomes even bigger and less certain.

JOAN: Can we take these two examples and infer a few benchmarks and student performance indicators that would differ based on the interdisciplinary approaches in problem-based learning?

This piece of dialogue reveals many of the features of helpful dialogue in schools: (1) it was facilitated; (2) it started with a review and a question; (3) it involved respectful listening; (4) knowledge was built from each other's ideas; (5) assumptions were surfaced; and (6) openness to further understanding was pervasive.

As we have seen, dialogue begins with a question (or a quote or poem), a question that invites thoughtfulness and doesn't close perspectives. The power of questions fuels inquiring processes as well as informal interactions among community members. A question, once posed, stays in the mind, nudging and pushing, insisting on a response. The mind has a way of staying in the question until it is addressed. Further, as we have found in cognitive coaching, powerful questions, persistently asked, become internalized, and those who were asked, now ask themselves.

In inquiring conversations, questions can frame the reciprocal learning processes in many ways.

ON EVOKING POTENTIAL . . .
How do we teach reading in our school?
Why is that? When did we start doing it this way?
What beliefs can we infer from our practice about how students learn to read?
How do these beliefs connect to our school's vision?

ON INQUIRING . . .
What questions do we have?
Based on our questions, what do we need to know?
What evidence would be useful?
How can we find or discover this evidence?
When will we bring our evidence back to the group?

ON SENSE-MAKING . . .
Based on our evidence, what patterns do we see?
How do we make sense of this? Does the evidence confirm or challenge our working assumptions?
What conclusions can we draw?

ON REFRAMING ACTION . . .
Based on our findings, how do we need to change our practice? What will the changes look like in practice?
What will it take to accomplish this?
How shall we proceed?
How might we reflect on our process? What have we learned?

In Chapter 4, Zimmerman describes such questions as "cross-categorical" and describes further uses in schools. As we will see, such questions built into meeting designs can become second nature to staff. Ackerman, Donaldson, and Van de Bogert (1996) suggest that we *lead* with questions.

> Leaders who embrace open inquiry, the sharing of problems and solutions, and collective responsibility will foster creativity, resourcefulness, and collaboration in the work. . . . These characteristics are the earmarks of leaders who seek to learn and to invent through questioning. (p.3)

They suggest seven topic domains for questioning, each value-directed yet open-ended: justice, teaching, purpose, resources, change, ownership, and autonomy. For instance, "How can we be just to each child, as an individual and as a learner, and create a just and disciplined school as well" (p.7)?

The *protocol* has become another significant reflective inquiring tool in many schools. By "protocol" we mean a process by which teams of school community members converse in front of a team of reflectors and engage feedback to deepen understanding. In Box 3.1, Linda Starnes describes an example of a protocol.

Inquiring conversations involve action research, problem-finding and uses of evidence, and examples of reflective conversations such as dialogue and protocol. These strategies are central to inquiring conversations, as well as to the concept of sustaining conversations.

SUSTAINING CONVERSATIONS

The idea of sustaining conversations is drawn from the concept of "sustainable development." Sustaining conversations are those that continue, endure, over a period of time and are essential to sustaining the development of the community. Changes can be made, but we have to ask whether those changes represent true developmental changes in the staff and school. If the individuals are becoming different, that is, taking on new assumptions and acting out of new theories of action about teaching and learning, this is sustainable development, and it emerges primarily from sustaining conversations.

Clearly, personal and inquiring conversations can be sustaining as well. We are beginning to see an image of conversations more like this:)))—a pattern whereby each conversation is a part of another one because they share common elements. Sustaining conversations need to be tied to enabling structures and real work; it is almost impossible to contrive sustainability. Such structures might include the talk of leadership teams, team-teaching groups who share the same preparation period, regularly scheduled portions

Box 3.1

The Protocol Conversation

SCENARIO 1

Linda Starnes, a former vice principal at Granada High School in Livermore, California, describes a protocol that engaged staff. This suburban school, a participant in the California Center for School Restructuring reform effort, was making significant progress in restructuring and developing processes to support student learning. Teachers met on a regular basis to examine student work, to collect and use data to make decisions about student learning, and to explore various ways of assessing student learning.

THE PROTOCOL PROCESS

The structure of the protocol provides for an Analysis Team and a Reflector Team, each composed of four to six staff members. In the process used at Granada, the Analysis Team engages in a dialogue around its question for 20 minutes, during which time the Reflector Team takes notes, raises questions for further exploration, and prepares to reflect on the Analysis Team's dialogue. It is important to note that the conversation is within the Analysis Team and is not a "presentation." At the conclusion of the Analysis Team's conversation, the Reflector Team has a dialogue for 15 minutes about what they have just heard. The Analysis team then has a 10-minute dialogue about what they heard from the reflectors, followed by a 10-minute conversation between the two teams which includes a reflection on the process. Below is a brief segment of such a conversation.

THE SETTING: A high school faculty meeting, with each protocol team composed of five teachers representing several disciplines. The remaining faculty actively participates by taking notes, keeping track of their own questions, and providing feedback on the process at its conclusion.

THE QUESTION: How can we more effectively use performance-based assessment to measure student learning?

ANALYSIS TEAM DIALOGUE

TEACHER A: As a staff, we made a commitment to use performance-based assessment as one of our measures of student learning. But as you can see in listening to our conversation, we were having trouble with how to assess this performance-based work. The math example of giving students several choices as to how to demonstrate mastery of math concepts illustrates part of the dilemma, for we were unable to agree on how to "grade" them and be sure students are learning. It was certainly easier when we gave the paper and pencil tests!

BOX 3.1 (CONTINUED)

REFLECTION TEAM DIALOGUE

TEACHER D: They have given examples of how they have begun to incorporate performance-based assessment, but it's obvious they are still struggling with developing appropriate criteria. Maybe more data and examples from staff members who are regularly using rubrics would be helpful to them.

TEACHER E: I think that as staff continues to examine student work together, we may all get more clarity on criteria, too.

TEACHER F: I'm also wondering if the question is, "How do we implement performance-based assessment?," or is the real question, "Do we all agree on what we mean by performance-based assessment?"

ANALYSIS TEAM DIALOGUE

TEACHER B: The Reflection Team has given us some new insights on our initial question. We've made some assumptions about our own commitment to and knowledge about what performance-based assessment means. We may need as a staff to examine those assumptions.

TEACHER C: I appreciated being reminded that we do have resources within our own staff that we haven't really taken advantage of.

TEACHER A: Part of the problem may be that we're not sure of our own criteria, or that teachers all use different criteria. So students must be having trouble understanding the expectations as well.

ANALYSIS TEAM AND REFLECTION TEAM DIALOGUE

TEACHER D (RT): This conversation has made me think about how clear I really am with students. My lab classes are "performance based," but do all students understand the criteria?

TEACHER E (RT): I know some teachers involve students in developing the rubrics. That might be something we want to consider. I'm remembering a student telling me, "Giving me a rubric is like handing me the key that unlocks the mystery of grades." As we focus on student learning, that might be a way to involve students more in the process.

TEACHER C (AT): I am beginning to realize that we really didn't spend enough time as a staff determining just what we mean by "performance-based assessment," and how that relates to grades and student learning. We moved to implementing this concept without really thinking through the implications.

TEACHER A (AT): I don't think we answered our initial question, but we have raised some questions that are important to finding answers. When we have our next meeting, let's start by making sure we have a common understanding as a staff of what we mean by performance-based assessment.

of staff meetings, action research teams, study groups, school learning communities, and shortened-day staff meetings of various forms. The structure that allows for sustaining conversations includes a specific time set aside with predictable regularity, agreed-upon norms, a group understanding of the purposes of these times, an explicit focus on teaching and learning, and someone to facilitate the conversation.

"Sustaining" is the key element through which polite interactions work themselves into authentic talk about real work. "Authentic talk about real work" is tied to the processes of teaching and learning, although we observe that some programs seem to define these too narrowly. Teaching and learning are, and are affected by, all the experiences that children and adults have in and out of schools. In some programs, incoherence grows out of separating discipline, guidance, extracurricular activities, and parent involvement from the teaching and learning conversations. For instance, the protective factors for resiliency are significantly related to student performance. These include caring relationships, high expectations, and broad opportunities for participation and contribution. Conversations worth having need to connect the philosophy and actions of the school to all learning opportunities.

When educators are engaged in sustaining conversations over time, assumptions more safely float to the surface. People feel safe in self-questioning, in holding practices up to the light. It is within such environments that theories of practice are reconstructed. These changing theories occur as identity and beliefs evolve, as people grow and change together. For instance, an assumption that not all children may be able to learn will fall into question: "Perhaps they can learn. If so, how must I change the way I teach and relate to children in order to cause this to happen?" A theory of practice will emerge from this reflection: "If I use cooperative learning, personal support, and frequent feedback about performance, more students will learn than ever before."

Harri-Augstein and Thomas (1991) described "constructive modeling" as a vital part of theory development. By "constructive modeling" they mean modeling theory into practice and practice into theory or "intricately relating theory to explaining the results of actions and relating actions to the implicit expectations generating them"(p. 80). This is somewhat like talk-aloud problem solving. "I'm solving the problem in this way because more options will remain available . . . in using this action, it reaffirms what we thought we knew about how children learn."

As sustaining conversations occur a form of "sea change" begins to result. Imagine change as a process in which the sea moves in upon itself as the entire sea shifts forward. Feedback spirals, formed by personal conversations, inquiry, action research, and other forms of information, resemble the sea moving in upon itself. The shift forward of the entire sea results from the motion of meaning-making, of interpreting new information together. This is what is meant by a "self-organizing" system and this is what is meant by "systemic change." We have come to understand that systems spontaneously organize themselves when their inhabitants work together. In schools and districts, the most interesting examples lie in the moments in change when people begin to re-form themselves into collegial clusters, usually around approaches that respond to new understandings of the nature of professional work. These might include peer coaching pairs, study groups, action research teams, leadership teams, ad hoc planning groups, and on and on. *As professionals find new meaning in their work together, the patterns of relationships and the structures change.*

Yet, effective schools have not often been able to sustain themselves. Why is this? We would suggest that the leadership of the schools has been defined as the principal and that person-dependent schools do not last. By investing leadership in the reciprocal, purposeful learning within a school community, the school's sustainability becomes much more possible. This thesis insists that everyone has the right, responsibility, and ability to serve as a leader. Like constructivist learning, this work is collective, reflective, and based on continually constructing a purposeful community of learners and leaders. In Chapter 6, Principal Del Bouck describes how such assumptions have significantly changed Winterburn School.

In such communities of learners and leaders, sustaining conversations take many forms. Dialogue can become nearly addictive in its power to engage, clarify, and bring understanding. Chris Weaver (1999) describes the use of the Talking Circle at Pathfinder School, a Native American focus school in Seattle. "The Talking Circle is so simple that one is tempted to expect that its results might also be simple. But in practice, the talking circle is so important in building trust and giving voice to diversity, regardless of any notions of authority, that I truly cannot imagine the school working without it on matters of any importance" (p. 9). By passing a talking stick around the circle to all present, everyone has his or her say.

The Found Poem has a similar and mesmerizing effect when attached to an inspiring piece of text. The chosen text relates to an area of group development (e.g., emergence, purpose, diversity, imagination, or empathy). Each participant highlights meaningful passages. Participants enter the dialogue as their passages relate to the one that has gone before. One must listen intently and make connections (two essential elements of dialogue). The group creates a new text, or Found Poem, that constructs new and enhanced meanings around the idea and is now the possession of the group.

Such forms of dialogue create space for people to get in touch with ideas and each other. They enable people to break set with currency, old assumptions and old practices, an essential struggle in the evolving transitions that signify growth.

All groups and all cultures that engage in sustaining work and change together go through phases of transition. William Bridges's work in *Managing Transitions* (1991) has been very helpful to educators in numerous schools and districts as a way of understanding the processes that people encounter as they undertake substantive change. The phases of *letting go* of old ways of thinking and acting, *experiencing the neutral zone* of transition, and engaging with *new beginnings* has much relevance to sustaining conversations.

During the "letting go" phase of change, participants need to listen to the losses that each is experiencing. Letting go of old ways of thinking and acting is painful and may not occur unless we go through a "grieving" process. Fortunately, when we work through a constructive mode, people do take a piece of the past with them; their selves are carried forward as they redesign their work. However, when new data challenge old ways of thinking, we need to help each other be explicit about what we are leaving behind.

As we let go, we enter what Bridges refers to as the "neutral zone," a time of disconnectedness before we take hold of something new, for instance, when schools consolidate and lose their culture, site, and some of their staff, or when grade-level teams are disbanded in favor of vertical teams. It may be a short time, or it may last several months, depending on the magnitude of the change. Grieving continues during this period, but, intriguingly, creativity is also high. We need an abundance of accurate information, because rumors run rampant. It is a time to envision new ways of working and to ask ourselves, How does all of this fit together? By using the "reciprocal processes" of leading we deliberately escort each other through the phases of transition.

"New beginnings" can coalesce around purpose and vision. At this time, we need concrete images of what this new work can look like. What does this purpose look like in practice? How will my teaching be different? What student work can we expect? For example? Feedback is even more important now as we formulate new images of a practical vision.

Roles that have been emerging and changing now become more explicit. Specific knowledge and skills are brought to bear, and it becomes more clear what additional knowledge and skills are needed. We can develop policies, procedures, and new parameters to fit the new changes. And we are able to reflect on the processes that we have experienced. This awareness of the effects of change on each of us can become an enlightening journey.

This knowledge of transitions is vital to all participants in a school and needs to inform our conversations together. It is particularly important to our sustaining conversations; otherwise we get stuck in transition and are handicapped in our own development. Making sense of what is occurring to ourselves allows us to make sense of what is occurring to others.

The constructivist process of meaning-making is motion, it is developmental. Unless experiences are created and negotiated together, this development usually does not take place. Conversations in school often cease when conversants encounter discrepancies, opposition, or rough spots; people back away, become silent, divert their interests elsewhere. Encountering and negotiating such struggles can be assisted through well-designed conversations and skillfulness.

PARTNERSHIP CONVERSATIONS

Partnership conversations engage individuals and groups who are physically outside of the school into reciprocal relationships—parents, community groups, universities, governmental agencies, businesses, professional organizations, networks, cultural organizations, other schools and school districts. *Reciprocity*, or the mutual and dynamic interaction and exchange of ideas and concerns, requires a maturity that usually emerges from opportunities for meaning-making in sustainable communities over time. We need to enlarge the circle of community to be more inclusive than we have been in the past if we are to develop reciprocal partnerships with parents and members of the broader community so that together we can improve learning for children and adults. Such conversations require a confidence on the part of educators that emerges from regular and thoughtful personal, inquiring, and sustaining conversations. Lack of such confidence can result in holding parents at arm's length or mechanizing interactions with those outside the school.

School relationships with parents and community are notoriously non-reciprocal, with the lack of equity moving in both directions, as the following examples show.

1. Parents are recruited to serve the school—sponsor fundraisers, work in classrooms, donate time to a school beautification effort, set up for the science fair.
2. Social agencies are called on in emergencies to handle problems that schools are unequipped to deal with.
3. Student outcomes may include community-related goals, but usually as a means of meeting an individualistic student outcome.
4. Businesses contribute to schools as a function of their charitable work.
5. Other schools, regional education agencies, and professional networks are sought out to provide training or when they host a program or possess expertise thought to be superior to that in the initiating school.
6. Universities seek out schools in which they can conduct research on human subjects.

In the first three examples, the school's stance is often one of usage; it seeks to "use" parents, agencies, and communities for the perceived welfare of the school. In the second three examples, the one-way relationship points the other way, and the school is the object of charity, expertise, and research. Some key questions arise:

What does each entity have to give as well as receive?
What do they have to learn from each other?
What knowledge can these partners construct together, thereby creating something that did not exist before—something that each had to learn?

If the conversations with these agencies involved a shared intention, a search for sense-making and understanding, remembrances and reflections on their own experiences and beliefs, an openness to ideas and information, and respectful listening, how different would the relationships be? Below are examples in each of the six areas that hold potential for building reciprocity in school communities.

The *relationship of schools to parents* has probably been the most problematic area because of the centrality of the parent-child-school relationship to learning. Many educators eagerly accept the research findings telling us that student achievement is directly linked to parent involvement; however, in many schools we have not changed our paradigm about the notion of "involvement." Hollins (personal communication, 1994) challenges us to understand that parents have much to teach us about how their own children learn. And if we ask the questions and listen for the answers, we might be able to create a new joint pedagogy (not necessarily a joint curriculum).

Fullan and Hargreaves (1998) argue for the importance of learning relationships with parents. Such relationships suggest that "When schools involve communities with them in the uncertainties of change at the outset, support and understanding are more likely to be forthcoming" (p. 71). Further, taking the journey together through data gathering and analysis, problem solving, and resolution will insure support when things go awry, as well as when things go well.

Perhaps the most hopeful conversations I have experienced have been in schools in which parent-teacher conferences were thoughtfully organized and planned through advisement programs. Such conversations have become more common in the past five years. This small portion of such a conversation was conducted by the student, Emil:

EMIL: I want to thank you both for coming to this conference today. Let me show you some of my work and tell you how I think I'm doing.

PARENT: I'm very eager to see it. Do you have any examples of your writing?

EMIL: Yes, here are two samples that I think are a "4" on the rubric.

PARENT: What is a "rubric?"

EMIL: A rubric tells me what good work looks like.

TEACHER: Our writing rubric has four columns for four levels of work. Here is an example. Emil, why don't you read your mother the fourth column on creativity?

(Emil reads.)

PARENT: I like that! May I have a copy at home? I can see several ways that we might use it.

TEACHER: Certainly, this will be your copy.

Emil's mother felt increasingly competent in using multiple measures in understanding her son's work. Deborah Meier, former principal of Central Park East, once commented that parents ought to feel better about themselves as parents when they leave the school. In a reciprocal relationship, each partner becomes *more* clear about his successes and his common courses of action.

Peggy Bryan, principal of Sherman Oaks Community Charter School, a highly diverse school in one of the poorest areas in San Jose, California, established the school's emphasis by meeting with every parent to discover what they wanted for their child. Parents wanted technology, art, and excellent communication. These are now the cornerstones of the school.

Public exhibitions have become outstanding examples of respectful work with parents. Parents and community members come to school events, usually in the spring, to witness performances and products of children and adult conversations around data arising from actions to improve student performance. Sherman Oaks Community Charter School holds events in which parents and children together examine and discuss student work. Mary Jo Pettigrew, principal of Indian Valley School in Walnut Creek, California, organizes a major community event in the spring in which parents and community members observe a protocol conversation around student work and other evidence of student achievement.

The new work of schools and regions in *interagency collaboration* has great potential for redefining partnerships. In California, the Healthy Start Program is designed to enable elementary schools to develop partnerships with social service agencies (e.g., child protective services, probation departments, housing authorities, community health groups, and welfare agencies) so that planning, thinking, and serving can be coordinated and focused around agencies and organizations. At Wyandotte High School in Kansas City, Kansas (see Chapter 6), a section of the school is devoted to offices for social services, the probation department, and other community agencies that work closely with the school teams. Principal Walt Thompson reports that these agency representatives are a part of the school, coming to know the students and staff.

Heretofore, *student outcomes that are community related* have been generally one-way and individualistic. In other words, we figure out how to use the community to accomplish student outcomes that are not reciprocal in nature. If we arrange for students to work in senior centers, the outcome may say: Students will perform community service and experience the rewards of contributing to the lives of individuals from different age groups. *A reciprocal outcome might read:* Students and senior citizens will contribute to the lives and learning of each other through the sharing of their stories, ideas, interests, and time.

In order to develop outcomes such as this, we need to involve the community members in writing the outcomes and to let go of a felt need to control all of the named participants in the outcome. We have designed outcomes narrowly and thus missed the vital interconnectedness of children's lives with those of all others in the community.

Businesses have generally been seen as the senior partner in their connections with schools. We have not talked with many businesspersons who have thought about what they can learn from schools. Those business leaders who have been involved in "shadowing" principals come away with a new understanding and respect for the work of schools. Perhaps this bridge of observing and understanding each other's work needs to be crossed before full reciprocity can be undertaken. Many businesses do articulate their understandings of the connection of their involvements to societal goals: preparing students for successful performance in the workforce and in the democratic process. The fertile field of partnership might include common questions to be explored as well, the answers to which will improve both businesses and schools. Some examples of such questions include the following:

> What are some of the many ways in which students and adults learn together in their work?
> What democratic practices do individuals and groups need to experience in the workplace?
> How can education's work in authentic assessment inform business?
> What does it mean to have "clients"? How does it change your relationships toward those who become identified as clients?
> How can education's understandings about diversity and equity inform business policies and practices?
> Can we design a shared vision that is oriented toward the betterment of society and to which we could all commit? What would that mean for our work together?

The changing nature of partnerships is altering the course of our conversations together. As the ripple enlarges and unfolds we continue the image of))))—personal, inquiring, sustaining, and partnership conversations moving out from a shared set of understandings and interpretations about our interconnectedness. These newer conceptions of partnerships are essential to educational communities since reciprocity and interdependence create equitable relationships that form the patterns that give rise to learning for children and adults alike. The search for reciprocal partnerships can be hindered by naiveté, however, if educators do not understand the need to attend to issues of authority and seek to shift power relationships.

Schools and school districts are among the more hierarchical of organizations. Such structures of domination and control have been considered the backbone of "efficient" modern organizations for several centuries. The larger and more complex the organization, the more complex and tightly drawn is the organizational chart. We see this form of organization particularly in our large urban school districts. Hierarchy and roles establish and maintain authoritative power, that is, power and control over the decisions and behaviors of others. While there is a legitimate role for authority (for instance, in convening and sustaining the conversation), professional cultures created exclusively or primarily by such arrangements have resulted in uneven power relationships, unilateral flow and control of information, fear of reprisal, codependencies, and censure for overtures made across hierarchical levels. The invisible bonds that hold hierarchies in place imprison the inhabitants of each level, fragmenting their lives and their work and making it difficult to construct a shared purpose for teaching and learning.

Working with, rather than through or on, people means that the conversation becomes the medium for realigning relationships. Communities based on the more democratic facilitation of power (Goldman, Dunlap, & Conley, 1993) and the principles of ecology are marked by networks (webs of relationships) rather than hierarchies (Capra, 1994). These networks are characterized by feedback spirals bringing information and knowledge to everyone in the community, thereby breaking the "cult of expertise." Such communities require leadership that engages participants in the reciprocal processes described in this book. We have found that these conversations bring with them the familiarity and regard that can shift the meaning and definition of roles and authority. However, as powerful as these respectful and sustained conversations can be in building equitable partnerships within professional cultures, they must be accompanied by district and school structures that replace hierarchy with networks and redefine roles, practices, and policies that have historically created and protected uneven power relationships (see Chapter 7).

LEADING THE CONVERSATIONS

In order to hold conversations that can lead to professional cultures, educators need to construct understandings about the nature of constructivist conversations and acquire facilitation skills in order to convene, move, and deepen our talk together.

Leading the conversations is not a neutral role; it is a role of active involvement through which leaders insist on the conventions of conversations, facilitate the reciprocal processes, and connect participants to the vision, values, and established norms of the group. Conversations such as we envision here do not occur naturally, at least at first. Yet they do not have to be scheduled in usual ways. Conversations can hold "strange attractors" (the design created by the magnetic pull of random data in chaotic systems), that is, inherent incentives that pull people into shared talk. For instance, such attractors might include constructivist approaches that engage individuals in learning, conversations that do not insist on closure but encourage continuance to deeper levels ("let's continue this talk at lunch tomorrow"), and decision timetables by which one can anticipate closure and some resolution. These processes and forms result in complex networks of relationships. Professionals who are participating as constructivist leaders need to pose the questions and convene the conversations that invite others to become involved.

Leading the conversations is the work of everyone in the educational community.

In order for leaders and potential leaders to actively convene, frame, and move the conversations, these predispositions, understandings, and skills are highly important. These can be learned in a number of settings, including preservice education; professional development within a district; working in a culture in which these processes are regularly experienced; regional workshops or site-based workshops; and observing, modeling, and coaching. Figure 3.2 describes some of these behaviors as they relate to the four forms of conversations described in this chapter.

We are persuaded that plans, approaches, and strategies for leading the conversations need to originate initially from some group such as a leadership team. Otherwise, the principal is apt to attempt to go it alone, and this greatly limits the early construction of knowledge around school change that needs to occur in a group as well as the potential for teacher leadership. Further, it eliminates the "multiplier effect" of the patterns of relationships through which team members create feedback spirals by consistently interacting with a particular group of participants. Spirals gather others into the leadership arena.

CONCLUSION

Leading the conversations is at the heart of constructivist leadership. It is the facilitation of the reciprocal processes that enable participants in an educational community to construct meanings toward a shared purpose for teaching and learning. It is a skilled undertaking for which each participant needs to be prepared; it is a shared responsibility.

In this chapter, we described a typology of conversations that include personal, inquiring, sustaining, and partnership conversations that are informed by common elements. These common elements involve shared intention, a search for sense-making and understanding, remembrance

PERSONAL	INQUIRING
• one-to-one conversations • mentoring • cognitive coaching • on-line coaching • reflection • journaling • questioning • distribute articles to encourage new knowledge/reflection • create time • peer planning • graduate work	• reciprocal processes • action research • data collection and analysis • the protocol conversation • dialogue • action planning • meeting designs based on inquiry • questioning • study groups • technological data software support
SUSTAINING	**PARTNERING**

• dialogue
• theory construction
• constructive modeling
• feedback
• on-going communication
• convening and sustaining the
  conversations
• talking circle
• found poem
• professional learning of
  conversational skills
• histomap
• networking
• chat rooms, e-mails
	• interviews, focus groups
	• exploratory conversations
	• parent–school conferences
	• exhibitions of student work
	• participatory governance structures
	• forums
	• co-learning structures
	• shared classroom teaching
	• shared curriculum development
	• open school as a learning lab
	• new parent orientations
	• partnerships
	• video conferencing

FIGURE 3.2
Acts of Leadership in Support of the Conversation

and reflection, revelation of ideas, and respectful listening. In the next chapter, Diane Zimmerman makes explicit and examines linguistic moves embedded in conversations. This dimension of the reciprocal processes plumbs the depths of interaction and reciprocity.

CHAPTER 4

THE LINGUISTICS OF LEADERSHIP

DIANE P. ZIMMERMAN

I have always felt that the action most worth watching is not at the center of things but where edges meet. I like shorelines, weather fronts, international borders. There are interesting frictions and incongruities in these places, and often, if you stand at the point of tangency, you can see both sides better than if you were in the middle of either one.

Anne Fadiman
The Spirit Catches You and You Fall Down
(1997, p. viii)

As constructivist leaders, we listen differently. Consequently, we learn to silence our own inner chatter to achieve momentary stillness. With a quiet mind, we can focus deeply on other voices, searching for themes and ideas, finding boundaries and intersections, and seeking out frictions and incongruities. In response to others, we employ our linguistic abilities to restate, inquire, or add to what we hear; we encourage others to listen and converse, building the group understandings as we go.

In Chapter 3, we emphasized that leading the conversation is not neutral and that how the leader chooses to respond shapes the conversation. Accordingly, the leader actively engages in framing the conversation, facilitating the reciprocal processes, and connecting participants to the vision, values, and norms of the group. This chapter further describes the different ways that the constructivist leader employs simple linguistic tools to facilitate the reciprocal processes and support the thinking of the group. The constructivist leader's goal is to explore meaning with others as a way of deepening understanding, producing clarity, or reframing thinking. By using linguistic moves and being conscious of language choices, a leader creates spirals of meaning that are continuously formed and re-formed.

Common knowledge about linguistic moves allows any participant to perform an act of leadership. In this chapter, we propose some new ways of thinking about these moves and choices that enhance a constructivist leader's capacity to facilitate conversations. When a group member applies the skills outlined in this chapter, he or she assumes a leadership stance, becoming the linguistic leader for the group. We begin this chapter by viewing linguistics through the lens of the new sciences that have evolved from quantum physics and chaos theory.

LINGUISTICS—THROUGH THE LENS OF THE NEW SCIENCES

Like all complex systems, conversations are unstable. As with the weather, only general patterns are predictable. For example, one might expect a particular friend to add humor to a serious discussion or to bring up a topic of common interest; however, one can never predict exactly what will be said, how it will be said, or what effects it will have on the listener. Patterns of conversation, like clouds, continuously self-organize, moving in and out of a larger pattern formed by the interactions between speakers. Most importantly, leaders cannot expect to control conversations, but rather only to influence or shape the conversation. By employing linguistic moves and making careful language choices, leaders bring continuity and fluid form to the meaning-making process. For example, when one person's words escalate into a massive issue for a group, leaving others' words unnoticed, leaders can employ a simple paraphrase to communicate to the louder voice that the message has been received, opening the space for other voices to enter the conversation. In another example, an important but ignored comment, when paraphrased for the group, gets amplified and gains prominence in the conversation. Paradoxically, a paraphrase serves dual functions. The paraphrase communicates "I understand" to the assertive voice and reduces the need for repetition; it also amplifies the quiet voice and helps the group attend to all ideas.

Just as systems have forms that create a set of boundaries, so do conversations (see Chapter 3). The field or holding environment created by the conversation serves as the medium for the reciprocal processes. A few reciprocal linguistic moves, such as reflecting, summarizing, or inquiring, can frame, deepen, and move the conversation. The purposeful application of these linguistic moves is a leadership act that creates a basis for meaningful shared conversations. We propose that these linguistic moves widen the space for conversation, allowing groups to explore and eventually self-organize around important ideas. In conversations, self-organization becomes evident when a conversation moves from "my idea" to a shared "center." Isaacs (1999) describes this center in dialogue as "taking the energy of our differences and channeling it towards something that has never been created before" (p. 19). David Bohm (1989) describes dialogue as a "*stream of meaning* flowing among and through us and between us" (p. 1). Although not all groups are structured as forums for dialogue, we have found that the application of the linguistic tools, as described in this chapter, create small holding environments that share the quality of coherence described in dialogue forums.

The way groups act within the linguistic fields distinguishes a meaning-making community from communities of advocacy. Senge (1990) states that in most organizations, group meetings tend to be places where individuals articulate their own views but learn little from one another. From our perspective, these are not meaning-making communities. Senge suggests that a learning community must actively pursue a balance between advocacy and inquiry. He states that the goal in balancing inquiry and advocacy is to "find the best argument" (p. 199). From a constructivist perspective we would say that the goal is to find the best understandings through a balance of paraphrasing, inquiring, and articulating ideas.

When members become excited about the emerging relevance of the conversation, the group self-organizes around the interesting concepts. Just as the joining of simple sentences compounds ideas, so does the juxtaposition of ideas in conversation. When ideas are combined, the group's drive to understand sorts out confusions and seeks cohesion in the ideas. Together groups negotiate meaning and labor toward new understanding. Instead of trying to control through telling, leaders can create spirals of meaning by expanding and clarifying the common conceptual fields. Asking questions and rephrasing ideas helps others create common maps from which to act. Stacey (1992) states that managing ambiguity and the unknowable are necessary skills for the postmodern world. We maintain that reciprocal linguistic moves are a powerful way to manage the unknowable; by applying them, the leader creates a holding environment for the emerging conceptual thinking that deepens and sometimes shifts to new understandings.

The linguistic moves of questioning and paraphrasing, which are designed to fold back the meaning, serve as simple rules to change the jumble of sentences into meaning-making contexts. Significantly, these linguistic moves create a reciprocal relationship in which the language of the group iterates, or repeats itself, to form feedback spirals that continuously define the field. The simplest analogy comes from fractal geometry, in which simple iterating equations create wild and complex visual patterns that self-replicate, not unlike the way a compelling question generates a wide variety of possibilities, all relevant to the conversational field yet each nuance a little different than the others. In addition, these moves demand a specific type of listening—that of attending to the other. Thus, silence and the suspension of one's inner critique are essential linguistic moves as well.

SELF-ORGANIZING PATTERNS OF THINKING

Any discussion of linguistic processes must also take into account the self-organizing patterns that guide human thinking. The traditional notions of cause-and-effect relationships no longer provide adequate explanations of psychosocial systems. To further our own thinking as constructivist leaders, we have embraced the work from generative linguistics. These models describe how thinking self-organizes into patterns.

In 1980, George Lakoff and Mark Johnson published a seminal work on the metaphors of language. In this book, they proposed that the human conceptual system is metaphoric—that metaphors are the bedrock of human thought processes and that these create meaning. (See Chapter 5 for more information on metaphors.) Lakoff and Johnson identified a paradoxical quality of metaphoric systems in that they both structure and invent reality. To describe this phenomenon, they coined an oxymoron— *imaginative rationality*. This paradoxical quality describes one of the qualities of an emergent system, a system that cannot be defined by the properties of its parts. Because our work with groups is complex and sometimes difficult to quantify, we have turned to the study of patterns in thinking to assist us in navigating this complex territory. In Chapter 2, we wrote of patterns of relationships. This chapter focuses on how we enhance the conceptual worlds of educators; the next chapter extends this work into the narrative domain. The emerging brain research suggests that these patterns bring a predictable form to our work and foster our ability to help the meaning-making process self-organize around the patterns.

Lakoff (1987) theorizes that concepts are categories composed of radial networks. His analysis of category structure finds that categories do not form hierarchical structures with a limited number of essential attributes, as in classical studies, but rather a radial structure learned through social conventions. Category structure is a complicated network of resemblances rather than defined similarities. As educators, for example, we teach for *reading comprehension*. However, when queried about reading comprehension, we each have a unique conceptual map or definition with attributes that are important for us: One response might be about "creating mental pictures," another about "making inferences," and yet another might be "recalling the facts." Rather than clearly defined similarities, each conceptual map resembles the other.

Lakoff's (1987) work suggests that creating radial bubble maps in visual form to capture complex ideas is one way to help groups make semantic patterns visual and available for ongoing consideration by the group. We suggest that taking the time to develop radial concept maps assists the leader in holding the conversation still so that the group can reflect back on their own thinking. Novak and Gowin (1984) claim that concept maps help the learner recognize what they are coming to know, compare with what they already know, and record what is worth remembering—all worthy purposes for the construction of meaning. David Hyerle (1996) extends the work of semantic mapping and identifies different visual mapping tools that parallel fundamental thinking processes and provide practical schemas for groups to demonstrate shared understanding by producing explicit graphic representations about the group thinking. For example, after talking about how a new text supported reading instruction, the first-grade team graphed their thinking using a branching diagram (Hyerle, 1996) that showed three different foci—phonemic awareness, fluency, and comprehension; under each branch they listed the instructional strategies discussed. This branching map made the group thinking explicit and available to them as a reference when thinking about their teaching. When the group came together several weeks later, the graphic organizer helped them retrieve the focus so that the conversation could start about where they last left off.

By encouraging groups to explore different ways of graphically organizing and representing their thinking, leaders allow the group to choose between free-flowing generative maps or the more traditional hierarchical maps. Sometimes groups will decide to organize the ideas in both ways, and we speculate that this may have more to do with the thinking styles of different group members. When groups create their own graphic organizers, they create a memory tool that can be used by the group over time to reflect on their own thinking. In the next chapter, we will describe how narrative also serves the group memory and helps groups retrieve the conversation over time. Even the simple narrative device of paying attention to the beginning and the ending are useful structuring devices. In this next section, we explore how these simple structures, such as initiating, constructing, and closing, help open and close the space for the conversation.

ENABLING STRUCTURES FOR DISCOURSE

The purposeful application of the linguistics of leadership requires a commitment to public discourse, which produces a reciprocal relationship that enables adults to construct meaning and knowledge together. As we have noted in our earlier discussions of breaking set with old assumptions, instead of ignoring the uncomfortable topic or assuming no news is good news, leaders and group participants must be tenacious in both seeking out compelling themes and uncovering the unspeakable. Kegan (1994) describes conversations as having tremendous potential if only groups would take the time to talk. He states, "Potentially they amount to a fascinating lived conversation between equally respectable parties who care deeply about the outcome of philosophical conflict because it has real implications for their own lives and the lives of their students" (p. 48). In the remainder of this chapter, we outline some ways of defining structure, moves, and choices that foster the "lived conversation." These approaches enable us to facilitate the four relationships—personal, inquiring, sustaining, and partnering—within the holding environment of the conversation.

Structures serve as guides for leaders but often remain invisible to the group. We argue that these structures must become explicit so that group members learn to apply them both within the group and across contexts. For instance, taxonomies of question types serve as guides for asking questions, just as the levels of paraphrasing described later in this chapter guide leaders in the revoicing of ideas. Structures must not intrude on the meaning-making process; instead they must enable it. Furthermore, for structures to be enabling, they must capture the interests of the group. The structures can be as simple as paying attention to the *initiating*, *constructing*, and *closing* activities.

Initiating activities bring focus to the group by assisting members in bridging from personal to group experience. When designed well, initiating activities help each person transition from outside the group to become fully present in the gradually enlarging space for conversation. An essential quality of initiating activities in the constructivist environment is that these activities must foster engagement and be meaningful within the context. To illustrate, a group might start by analyzing an interesting metaphor or story related to the topic at hand. In another example, a facilitator might play with the tension between individuals and the group by framing questions that invite participants to compare personal views to those of the group. The facilitator might ask, "What do you value most about this topic? What do you think others value?" Asked in this way, the questions serve as a focusing device, triggering a search for answers.

As they evolve, initiating activities set the tone and purpose for the work of the group. At this stage, group members build patterns of relationships that are respectful of one another and of the group. When groups develop respect, they can persist through conversations that accentuate differences, emerging with a heightened sense of professional efficacy. Group members report that well-planned opening activities reenergize individuals, making them productive and ready for group work. The facilitator knows to move to the next phase of constructing by paying attention and moving on once the group is grounded in the public space. Skilled facilitators learn to observe the ebbs and flows of group focus, changing the structures and activities to sustain momentum and focus.

Constructing shared knowledge and understanding is the essential work of a leader. In this phase of the work, the leader invites the group to engage in meaningful conversations by identifying themes of mutual interest. The most important leadership act is framing compelling issues and constructing opportunities for focused conversation about these issues. For example, in one school a group of teachers joined together to debrief an unusually rough school year. One teacher served as the leader by framing two simple questions: "What made this year so difficult? What could we have done differently?" By focusing the conversation, group members find greater clarity and also more space for open, honest conversation about these themes.

When working with larger groups, the facilitator shifts between small-group discussion to help keep the focus and larger-group discussion to broaden the conceptual space. Small-group conversations increase engagement and assure that more voices enter the conversation and engage with the topic. When working with larger groups, the questions are posed for consideration by the smaller group, and then the leader needs to simply ask the larger group: "What are we learning from each other?"

To do this work well, leaders must learn to live with a certain amount of ambiguity and uncertainty. Experience has taught us that groups go where they need to go, not necessarily where the leaders want them to go. Therefore, leaders must be flexible and trust that out of chaotic and sometimes confusing conversations can come complex understandings. Initially, these types of conversations can frustrate some group members, so leaders need to encourage persistence; once the benefits of the subsequent deep understanding and insight are experienced, group members learn to help each other persist. The conversation processes enable groups to learn to respect differences and to listen and paraphrase to seek understanding. As the ideas gain momentum, differences will occur and conflicts may arise. If groups take time to listen and inquire of each other, the tension raised by differing assumptions, values, and beliefs often generates deeper levels of understanding. Diverse viewpoints and multiple responses help members break set with unexamined ideas and entertain new ways of thinking and acting. When group members notice the discrepancies between thought and action, new questions emerge and compel the group to think differently.

When conversations become complex, some group members will lose focus. Graphic organizers and thinking maps assist leaders to create tangible products for group members to think about and respond to. Initially the appointed leader may suggest an organizer for capturing the ideas, but as the group grows in the knowledge about constructivist processes, they should take responsibility for choosing appropriate organizers.

Finally, *closing* activities create communities of memory and commitment. Lively discussions during the constructing process can produce information overload and forgetting. Taking time to summarize, finding patterns that connect, creating metaphors, generating new questions, and committing to action bring closure. Equally important is the recognition of the lack of closure. By summarizing a lack of consensus and agreeing to continue the process, the leader helps groups accept differences. In leave taking, participants need to be able to shift from group to personal meaning. When group members take time to personalize the meaning, they are able to use the new knowledge to inform practice. Two simple questions will generate this closure: "What have I learned?" and "How will I use what I have learned?"

Closing rituals should also reflect on the work of the group. Valuing activities provide structures for evaluating and improving. The facilitator should take time to ask questions such as, Did the group produce new insights together? Did the participants discover some new ideas? Will this discussion make a difference? How were the members renewed by the synergy of the group? These are but a few of the many questions that might be asked to help a group become more aware or metacognitive about themselves as a group. The following is an example of the use of this enabling structure:

Initiating: A group of educators have come together to think about ways for the local university and school district to collaborate. Traditional introductory activities for these types of collaboration often begin with the leaders welcoming the group and then describing the purpose of the meeting. After these introductions, the facilitators decide to forgo the round-robin introductions with each member giving his or her name and job title in favor of a simultaneous introduction. To actively engage the group and honor the need for the group to become acquainted, the group members are instructed to get up, find someone not known by them, and introduce him or herself by stating name, role, and his or her thinking or feelings about the proposed collaboration. This simultaneous introduction gives voice to each person in the room and provides time for personal reflection about the opening comments. By structuring listening and talking activities, the facilitators foreshadow the communicative expectations for the meeting and time is managed in an efficient way.

Constructing: When the group sits down, they are focused on the facilitators and appear eager to go to the next step. To honor the past and to entice the group about possibilities, the group is asked to talk in small groups about opportunities gained and lost regarding a K–16 collaboration. Once again, the small-group discussion is designed to bring individual focus to the task. After about 15 minutes, the groups are given strips of paper and asked to write out a few key ideas that emerged from their discussion.

To help the group learn about the thinking in other groups, the strips of paper are then brought to the front and posted on the wall. The facilitators help the group organize by categories under the headings "opportunities gained" and "opportunities lost." When group members find similar themes, the strips are clustered together. By the end of the allotted time, the wall is full of ideas and the group is energized by their own thinking. A note taker simultaneously enters these into a computer so that the thinking can be captured and distributed soon after the meeting. Capturing the thinking of the group in visual form enhances the group's ability to reflect on their own thinking and provides a reference for later.

Closing: In closing, the group members are asked to address the entire group. They introduce themselves by name and role and then describe what most intrigued them about the meeting. It may seem odd that introductions are saved for later. The constructivist leader knows that introductions linked to meaningful interactions are richer and therefore memorable; he or she also understands the need for summarization or statements about commitment. As before, the comments from the group are captured on charts to be referred to at a later time. Like all fractal patterns, each small section of initiating, sustaining, and closing contains a subset of the same three structures. The facilitator must learn to nest these structures so that the primary purposes—group engagement and learning—are maintained at all times.

THREE LINGUISTICS MOVES

THE SIMILARITIES BETWEEN THE QUESTION AND THE PARAPHRASE

When used as meaning-making moves, questioning and paraphrasing share common characteristics. First, both the paraphrase and the question are reciprocal, as they are dependent on the conversation for their focus. When applied in a constructivist context, they draw their potency from the field of meaning, not from autobiographical thoughts or ideas emerging from one's own thinking. To further the meaning-making process, the leader designs linguistic moves in order to understand or help deepen the conceptual field. In contrast, when discussions are driven by each individual's individual perspective, the conceptual field is often fragmented into positions or points of advocacy. To inquire, we must listen deeply to the other person's message and for a moment silence our own inner talk. When each person takes the time to inquire or paraphrase about points of difference, insights can lead to new understandings.

Second, the paraphrase and the question are selective tools because they establish focus. Consider the situation in which a friend complains that the district office was not supporting the schools and is hindering the implementation of the shared decision-making process. The listener-responder, whether consciously or unconsciously, selects the focus. One paraphrase suggests emotion, "the lack of support is frustrating"; another focuses on the central office, "the district office does seem to be the hindrance"; or another, on process, "shared decision making is not so easy." In another example, it poses a question for clarity: "How is shared decision making being hindered?" Each response establishes a different focus for the conversation. Later in this chapter we describe how conceptual frameworks for paraphrasing or questioning aid in this selective process and enable groups to break set with old assumptions.

LINGUISTIC MOVES — THE QUESTION

As language develops, the ability to pose questions is acquired naturally. However, the art of asking open-ended questions that mediate meaning must be learned, practiced, and refined. How leaders learn to frame questions either limits or enhances the group's ability to construct meaning and act in concert with others. For example, a broad question such as "How can we use student writing samples to inform our teaching?" requires teachers to spend time talking and finding commonalities in student work, whereas narrow questions run the risk of fragmenting the group into positions. Consider this narrow question, "Should we teach quotation marks in third or fourth grade?" Asked from an either/or frame, the question limits the responses and detracts from the larger idea of teaching grammar in the context of writing. In the constructivist context, failing to frame meaningful questions confuses the process and keeps educators from the real work of improving learning. By framing a question that cannot be immediately answered, leaders ensure that group members will ponder a topic long after the discussion is finished. Group members often report that they continue to think about unanswered questions beyond the normal confines of a conversation. In this next section, we review the art of asking questions beginning with the narrow frame: the rhetorical question.

The Rhetorical Question. In English, a rhetorical question is formed with a desired response in mind. When a speaker does not expect an answer, has a predetermined answer, or forces choice, the question becomes rhetorical. Rhetorical questions have great value for clarifying truths in a court room; however, in a learning context, this type of question closes down thinking. Furthermore, when leaders ask questions with embedded commands, such as "Don't you think we should . . . ?," they cause groups to adopt either compliant or defensive postures.

To generate a little humor, the rhetorical question does have a place. Often the extended probing required for meaning-making can be taxing, and thus poking fun at the process of question-asking can lighten the tone. Recently a friend teased the group, "Who would ever do that?" We all laughed because we knew we were guilty of the implied offense, and we moved on without ever answering the question.

The Categorical Question. A second type of question is one that limits the range of responses to specific categories. We call this type of question the categorical question because a "what" question asks for a label, a "where" question asks for a place, and a "why" question asks for a justification. Often these questions can be answered with one word or a short phrase. In English some "wh-" questions and the yes/no question would be of this type.

If a member wants some specific data, desires clarity, or wants to know more about someone's knowledge, this type of question is useful within a meaning-making context. However, because the categories are self-contained and have a limited range of interpretation, they are only a small part of the processes of conversation. Furthermore, this type of question can limit the breadth of the thinking or insult by asking for a justification.

The Cross-Categorical Question. A third form of question searches for meaning by inviting the generation of new contexts or reframing the group focus (Costa & Garmston, 1994; Laborde, 1988). Questions that open up possibilities and do not restrict answers to narrow categories focus thinking in a much broader way; they elicit a broad range of possible answers within cross-categorical boundaries. For our purposes here, we have labeled this type of question the cross-categorical question. Notice how these types of questions invite a wider search for an answer: "What kinds of vacations do you enjoy most?" (places, activities, types of travel); "How did you come to that conclusion?" (data, hunches, decisions, plans). Open-ended questions create feedback systems in which they *amplify the meaning* created by the group, allowing it to ebb and flow in many directions. Questions that amplify feedback are essential tools for building constructivist conversations. In Chapter 3, we proposed additional cross-categorical questions that can draw out constructivist reciprocal processes.

A new teacher recently returned from a workshop on thinking. When asked what she had enjoyed the most, she told her principal, "I learned how to ask thoughtful questions like those that you ask us. The essential idea was that powerful questions are ones in which no one knows the answer, and I realized you ask those types of questions all the time." When the answer is not known, the members in the group must negotiate to find answers that satisfy the group. This becomes a meaning-making activity at its finest, as the elements of surprise and discovery are fostered and further deepen understanding.

A fundamental task of shared leadership becomes one of asking questions that do not have answers embedded in them or that do not privilege one group member's preconceived views over another's. In early stages of group work, it is not uncommon to have members ask questions with embedded opinions, such as "Don't you think that we should be using authentic assessment tasks?" The underlying assumption is "we should use authentic assessments." In contrast, a more open-ended question might ask for values, such as "In what ways would authentic assessment enhance learning?" The assumption here is that a decision will be made based on how assessment enhances learning; this is a larger frame from which to consider action. The linguistic leader helps groups learn to self-regulate the conversations around powerful unanswered questions. A gifted teacher helps others generate new questions, keeping the conversation spiraling through multiple cycles of meaning, always deepening the understanding.

We believe that it is essential for communities of learners to spend time learning how to ask questions that further the meaning-making process. Exploring the contexts and boundaries of a concept through questioning is one aspect; an equally important aspect is how to summarize and amplify messages to create meaning.

LINGUISTIC MOVES — THE PARAPHRASE

The word *paraphrase* is derived from the Greek *para* (through or beyond) and *phrazein* (to point out or to speak). Most dictionaries define it as a restatement in another form. From a constructivist viewpoint we would define paraphrase as the way we communicate understanding through speaking or writing. We also assert that the paraphrase points the way in conversation and that it can shift a group's focus beyond their current thinking. Used in this way it becomes a powerful tool enabling groups to break set with old assumptions.

In its simplest form the paraphrase is a restatement in the listener's own words of what was heard. When the paraphrase captures the essence of the message, it acknowledges; when it misses the mark, it clarifies. The act of acknowledging reinforces, encouraging the speaker to go deeper or extend his or her thinking. The act of clarifying paired with a tentative intonation communicates "I am listening; tell me if I understand correctly."

Because the paraphrase places emphasis on part of the message, it guides the conversation by creating a selective focus. For example, in a conversation about cooperative learning, the linguistic leader can emphasize key points about cooperative learning by paraphrasing aspects important to group understanding and encouraging a closer look at a particular aspect. The leader might say, "It appears that many of us believe it is essential to require either a self- or group evaluation." This encourages others to expand on or clarify opinions about evaluation. To create a different focus, the linguistic leader can shift the emphasis by paraphrasing what has not been said by saying, "We have been talking about how to use the strategy, but we have not discussed the impact of this strategy on learning." Alternatively, if the group is hung up on a certain point, such as individual versus group evaluation, the linguistic leader can paraphrase in a way that expands the options. He or she might say, "We have been focusing on only two types of evaluation; an hour ago we were asking about all the ways that accountability shapes the cooperative learning lesson." This paraphrase shifts the focus away from a debate on method and toward a conversation about assumptions and beliefs related to accountability. For each of the above examples, the paraphrase directs the conversation in different ways, and for this reason we maintain that the paraphrase is not a neutral linguistic tool; like questioning, it requires a mind-set of respectful listening or it can become manipulative.

When teaching groups about the paraphrase, we have found that many adults have a false clarity about the simplicity of the paraphrase, causing it to be underutilized in conversation. Like question-asking, paraphrasing is a linguistic skill that requires practice. By practicing the use of paraphrasing and building in process steps that require the paraphrase, group members learn to acknowledge or clarify the meaning. From time to time, group focus can be regained by requesting a summarizing paraphrase. One enlightened leader stopped a group after about an hour of lively conversation and requested, "There are so many ideas on the table, I am getting confused. Can we take a moment and summarize the ideas that are important for us?" This simple intervention shifted the group focus and produced elegant paraphrases about what had been said. When members learn the habit of summarizing what the group has been saying, the group learns to appreciate the power of the paraphrase in building on the group's ability to think together. When groups routinely paraphrase messages, members report higher trust levels and a climate of respect that encourages honest, open communication. Once the group demonstrates mastery of the basic paraphrase, they are ready to learn how to use an advanced paraphrase to shift focus, which is a highly refined skill.

The Advanced Paraphrase: A useful framework for interpreting and understanding messages is the advanced paraphrase developed by Costa and Garmston (1992). They describe a framework that extends thinking in the coaching relationship. We have adapted this model and propose that it be used as a framework for deepening thinking in constructivist conversations. In keeping with the original model, we propose four logical levels organized from global to specific (see Figure 4.1 for examples of each of these types). At the core is the simple form of restatement about *content* or *emotion*. The content paraphrase summarizes; the emotion paraphrase empathizes. The next higher logical level uses listener inference to shift to a broader conceptual level. When the listener paraphrases using a *broad concept label,* or a statement of an *inferred goal,* or a statement of an *inferred value, the conversation necessarily widens by requiring new information to build clarity and understanding.* At the highest logical level of paraphrase, the focus is shifted to a contextual level, enabling groups to think in contexts that extend beyond the current field of meaning. Leaders suggest new meaning by *juxtaposing context,* or inferring *long-range intention,* or creating a *metaphor.* These two logical levels help groups break set and consider meaning-making fields that are wider and more inclusive than those generated by the simple paraphrase. Moving below the simple paraphrase, the logical level drops, moving toward specificity or clarification. Leaders build clarity through *counter-examples*, through *examples*, or by *clarifying emotions*.

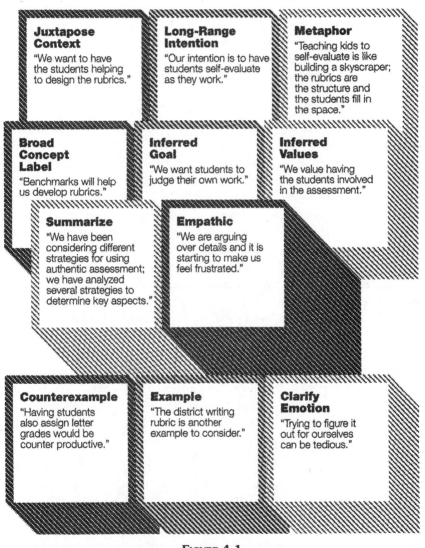

FIGURE 4.1
Advanced Paraphrasing. (Adapted from a figure designed for the Institute for Intelligent Behavior)

Although this model is complicated, our experience with conversations in which group members regularly paraphrase demonstrates that these types of paraphrases occur spontaneously. As linguistic leaders gain confidence and come to appreciate the power of the paraphrase, we encourage them to explore aspects of the advanced paraphrase, because it provides a sophisticated map for navigating the meaning-making field and helps groups explore ways to refine and extend meaning. Groups need not learn the entire model at one time. Instead, a leader can ask the group to focus on one or two of the advanced paraphrases, eventually helping the group explore the entire repertoire.

LINGUISTIC MOVES — THE REFLECTIVE PAUSE

For the purists, the reflective pause may not be considered a linguistic convention at all. We suggest otherwise, for pauses give speech its cadence and shape. The pause in conversation is literally a breath-taking moment—a time for both listeners and speaker to take a deep breath. Pauses give both the speaker and the listener fractions of seconds to think. We suggest that groups consciously pay attention to the cadence of a group and impose quiet time for reflection when appropriate. Metacognition, the ability to think about thinking, increases with focused quiet reflection time. Again, this is a reciprocal process in that reflection time is governed by the group's need for time to think.

These pauses need not feel artificial; however, groups do need to explore comfortable ways of working with silence. When individuals or groups do not respect the need for silence, pauses longer than 15 seconds are usually filled with more words. Palmer (1998) reflects on his own panic when encountering silence in the classroom: "As the seconds tick by and the silence deepens, my belief in the value of silence goes on trial. Like most people, I am conditioned to interpret silences as a symptom of something gone wrong" (p. 82). However, he goes on to question his assumptions:

> But suppose that my panic has misled me and my quick conclusion is mistaken. Suppose that my students are neither dumbfounded nor dismissive but digging deep; suppose that they are not ignorant or cynical but wise enough to know that this moment calls for thought; suppose that they are not wasting time but doing a more reflective form of learning. (p. 82)

Group members not sensitive to the poignant pause described above unconsciously violate norms about silence and the need for time to think. To be congruent and to value this tool, each of us must learn how to read the posture of "give me time to think" in our colleagues. The first and most noticeable clue is an extended break in eye contact paired with a shift in posture and breathing. An astute group member, noticing a colleague in deep thought, can voice this want for the group and suggest that they take a moment to think about what has just been said. To maintain congruence in the message, the initiator must have enough comfort with public reflection to then break eye contact and follow his or her own suggestion to take time for personal reflection. When leaders sanction by modeling, silence and contemplation are accepted and can become expected norms.

Leaders not yet comfortable with public silence or who need a chance to practice pausing can help groups learn to respect silence in a natural way by stopping the flow of a complex discussion by asking for summarizing paraphrases. At this juncture the group will naturally pause to reflect on what has been said. Another strategy is to direct the group to take time to think about what is not being said; this request often sends groups into deep, contemplative thinking. Asking groups to write about what has been discussed is another way to invoke quiet time. In Chapter 5, Cooper describes the use of narrative writing in schools as a process of reflection and meaning construction.

Palmer (1998) emphasizes that solitude within community invites time for reflecting on and absorbing information in a way that maintains the integrity of each person's inner self. He states: "in authentic education, silence is treated as a trustworthy matrix for the inner work students must do, a medium for learning of the deepest sort" (p. 77).

Questioning, paraphrasing, and pausing are but a few of the linguistic conventions used in conversations. They are highlighted for their value in creating reciprocal processes and patterns of relationships within a school community. In Box 4.1 below these linguistic tools are brought together in one example to demonstrate the power of their use. Next, we look at the way frameworks or mental maps can guide leaders in extending the meaning-making process. Each framework described below can be used as a template for forming a paraphrase, for asking a question, or for deep reflection about the shape of a conversation.

LINGUISTIC FRAMEWORKS

B. Bloom, Engelhart, Furst, Hill, and Krathwohl (1956), Taba (1957), and Costa (1989) have suggested hierarchies for framing questions that extend student thinking. We refer readers to these frameworks as alternative ways of framing questions. Here we explore how cross-categorical questions

Box 4.1
A Story about Applying Linguistic Moves

Setting

Several years ago, the staff at Patwin Elementary in Davis conducted five different action research projects designed to encourage students to become avid readers. One research project had generated underlying tensions between the librarian and the 6th grade teachers about allowing students to choose novels. In an attempt to get more students engaged in print, the 6th grade teachers had involved the students in choosing what they wanted to read. A group of avid readers had quickly moved beyond the library or school collections and was bringing in books from home. The dilemma rose when the adults working with the students were reading the story along with the students and material came up that was questionable for that age or for a public school (e.g., religious issues or racial slurs). At the symposium in which the research groups were sharing their findings, a verbal argument was started between the educators.

The Linguistic Moves

It was obvious to the principal that unless this unresolved conflict was framed for the teachers in a way that helped them discuss the issues, rather than argue points, this conflict would continue to escalate. By *paraphrasing* or labeling the conflict, she assisted the teachers to frame the problem by stating, "A conflict has just surfaced and we have disagreements in the room about allowing 6th grade students to choose books. Take a moment and think. *(reflective pause)* What are the various positions in this controversy?" The principal then followed her own directions and sat down, moving into her own personal thinking posture; the teachers also assumed reflective postures. After about two minutes of *silence,* the principal then elicited from the group several *paraphrases* of the various positions. Each time the principal also *paraphrased* what was said. As the positions were moved from specific people to the open space for discussion, the teachers in conflict visibly relaxed; their opinion was now elegantly stated and was before the entire group for discussion. Once the group was satisfied that all the issues had been identified, the principal challenged the teachers to work in groups of three to generate all the *questions* that these issues brought up. Ten minutes later the staff listed on a chart 15 *questions* about censorship in classrooms and libraries; one set of questions moved beyond censorship to ways teachers could work with students and parents when students were exposed to unsettling experiences either in reading or in the school in general. The principal then set aside the questions for discussion and exploration later and asked the research team to give their research conclusions. They were able to do this without debate as the tension in the room had dissipated.

BOX 4.1 (CONTINUED)

IN REFLECTION

When group members are in conflict, defending positions occupies the thinking space; this position of advocacy closes down the space for listening. By employing the *paraphrase* and a *reflective pause,* the space for listening by all involved was opened. Once the conflict had been framed, rather than resolve the issue the leader moved the group to *inquiry.* The act of asking questions sent the teachers in many different directions and further opened the space for thinking about a complex issue. The principal did not realize it at the time, but this 20-minute diversion also ended up settling the issue. When asked later, the teachers did not feel further need to discuss the topic; in their mind, it was resolved. The irony was that censorship ended up not being the issue. Through the *questioning,* the teachers in the project came to understand that keeping parents informed and being ready to deal with tough issues when they came up seemed to resolve the immediate dilemmas they had faced. This example demonstrates how linguistic moves, not just knowledge or ready-made answers, can help a group learn productive ways to work through conflicts and powerfully demonstrates the efficacy of these moves.

---

expand and extend the field of meaning. At the simplest level, these frameworks provide a scaffold for question-asking that enables members to ask questions that expand perceptions and create rich fields for meaning-making. We do not recommend the continual application of a frame; it is offered as one possible example of how to purposefully broaden perspectives.

THE STATES-OF-MIND FRAMEWORK

Costa and Garmston, together with a group of colleagues including L. Lambert and Zimmerman, identified five states of mind that are useful for mediating teacher thinking. In *Cognitive Coaching* (1994), Costa and Garmston describe ways in which these concepts can be used to frame questions during coaching. We have found this framework useful in our conversations.

The states of mind were identified through the categorization of specific linguistic moves that are useful for shifting thinking. We identified five states of mind: (1) searching for inner resources and determining who has the locus of control determines the level of *efficacy;* (2) what one is aware of and not aware of establishes the level of *consciousness;* (3) how to consider options determines *flexibility;* (4) how to think about perfecting a craft develops an ethic of *craftsmanship;* (5) how to think about building relationships establishes the level of *interdependence.*

In coaching, we envisioned these five as desired states of mind and use them to design questions that shift thought. For example, to cause a person to think in terms of efficacy, we might ask "What resources can you bring to bear on this problem?," or "What elements of the problem are within your control?" Figure 4.2 provides a framework, developed by colleagues Bill Baker and Stan Shalit (1992), that enables groups to ask questions in order to develop these states of mind in their conversations. We have found that asking questions from one state of mind often generates responses from other states of mind. These states are not discrete categories; they are overlapping fields of meaning.

A conversation in which the members use these states of mind as an inquiry map might be as follows: A staff had been working on the issue of building respect in the student body. They were working together in a staff meeting trying to define what they mean by respect. The first question that was raised by the group was, "To whom or to what should students show respect?" (interdependence). In exploring this question, the teachers started to question their own assumptions regarding respect. Some were more concerned with the teacher-student relationship; others were more concerned about student-student relationship. Another person brought up the issue of respect toward property. The group consensus was that all levels of respect are important. When one member suggested that respect really needs to start at the teacher-teacher level, a shift occurred in the conversation. Later, several staff members began to inquire, "What are we learning? What are we becoming more aware of?" (consciousness). Someone else asked, "Where does the responsibility lie?" (efficacy). Again a shift occurred; this time the group had different opinions. Initially one teacher felt that it was the parents who should be responsible; another teacher challenged this assumption since parent responsibility was not within her control. The conversation was lively, with many different viewpoints finding voice. Finally, the focus shifted to conversations about how to build respect (craftsmanship). By this time, there was a high degree of consensus within the group.

Metacognitive capabilities can be enhanced through the application of states of mind to a conversation. A person proficient in linguistic skills can switch between listening for understanding and contributing to content, or analyzing and inquiring from the states-of-mind framework. A metacognitive conversation might go as follows:

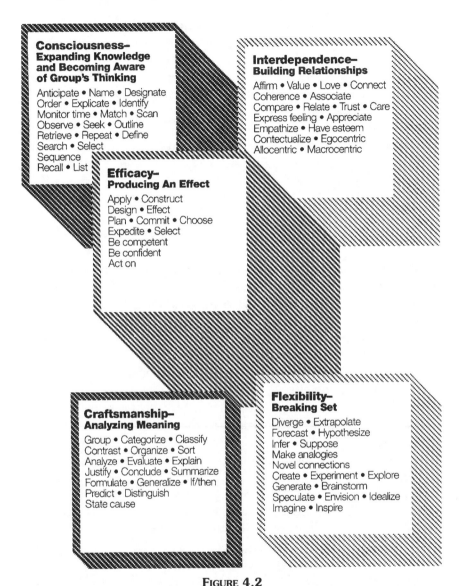

FIGURE 4.2

A Framework for Meaning-Making. (Adapted from a figure designed for the Institute for Intelligent Behavior by Baker and Shalit, 1992)

"It does seem like we are coming to consensus about appropriate strategies. Is there a state of mind that has not been represented? I notice that we have left few options for the students." I ask, "I wonder what options we want students to have in this process." Another person comments, "This is pretty tight on the kids." Again the conversation is off and running in a new direction. We are now exploring ways to expand the options for students.

The advanced-paraphrase, logical-levels, and states-of-mind frameworks are complex communication approaches. Since they are advanced ways of examining our linguistics dynamics, their uses may evolve as conversations become practiced and constructivist in nature. These frames provide some additional perspectives for a group of professionals who are intrigued by the meaning of their own engagements in the conversational processes.

LANGUAGE CHOICES FOR A POSTMODERN WORLD

Undoubtedly, the planks of a paradigm are constructed with language; beliefs, assumptions, and therefore actions emerge from that language. In our daily work in schools and in our personal lives, we make language choices that carry with them multiple assumptions. This chapter suggests that the constructivist leader is aware of the power of word choices and understands how different group learning experiences can be when at least one enlightened leader knows how to apply the linguistics of leadership. Lambert and Gardner (1993), in their inquiries into transformative leadership, developed a lens for considering language that is primarily reductionist and is contrasted with language that is transformative or constructivist in nature.

By "reductionist" they mean language that carries assumptions that are mechanistic, static, exclusive, hierarchical, manipulative, directional, and/or predictable. "Transformative" or constructivist language tends to imply assumptions that are dynamic, engaging, inclusive, participatory, open, reciprocal, and/or unpredictable. For instance, reductionist language might include such common words or phrases as *impact, mechanisms, objectives, buy-in, input, alignment, deal with,* and *getting results through people.* When replaced by *influence, approaches, outcomes, integration, work with,* and *working with people,* the same ideas become transformative in nature.

As staff develop their professional language (which all communities do), it can be interesting to discuss words and the meanings they carry for others, especially students and parents. Groups working on developing constructivist understandings will ultimately move to discussions about meaning on their own; however, an enlightened leader can raise these issues earlier when appropriate.

CONCLUSION

The ideas in this chapter are complex and raise the need for a few caveats, primary among them being: How can teachers find the time to learn such complex language patterns? And, if they cannot, don't such practices tend to keep power and leadership in the hands of the "expert?" Notice the stories of schools in Chapter 6 and how they handle time.

It is essential that the language moves described in this chapter be undertaken with a "talk-aloud metacognitive" approach; that is, that uses of such moves be made explicitly part of the dialogue. If we were to choose a professional development focus from the ideas in this chapter, it would be that of teaching groups about the various linguistic frameworks through direct instruction paired with guided practice. Carry-over of these approaches requires that these frameworks be applied to the conversations that take place about professional practices. Asking groups to set goals and choose which part of a framework to focus on simplifies the task and reminds them to share responsibility for generating the linguistic moves. We have found that conversations that are focused in this way produce quality work in shorter periods of time. We present these ideas as a rich repertoire of linguistic moves that will have different meanings for different people.

CHAPTER 5

CONSTRUCTIVIST LEADERSHIP: ITS EVOLVING NARRATIVE

JOANNE E. COOPER

Without a narrative, life has no meaning. Without meaning, learning has no purpose. Without a purpose, schools are houses of detention not attention.

Neil Postman
The End of Education *(1995)*

Postman (1995) underscores the importance of narrative to the meaning-making processes of educators. Without a narrative, Postman asserts, school life has no meaning. It is a central tool in the process of making meaning. Narratives, or stories of experience, not only help us make meaning of our lives and work, they facilitate emerging relationships, an element of school life that we have cited as the most important factor in our past, present, and future possibilities. Narratives or stories also connect us across differences of race, gender, and class. They remind us that we are all human. They begin the important work of creating relationships with the self and others. Both of these elements of relationship are essential to leadership, especially leadership that reaches across difference. According to Ramirez (1996), two essential ingredients are needed in leadership for diversity: (1) the journey of leadership and self-invention, and (2) the leader's role in shaping organizational culture in the face of diversity and inequality. Ramirez underscores that the journey to self-knowledge in the context of diversity requires the space and time for reflection again and again. Reflection often includes the creation of narratives about one's experience, narratives which facilitate meaning-making conversations with the self. Here, then, is where constructivist leadership begins, in conversations with the self. These conversations, or narratives, become the foundation for a school leader's articulation of values and vision.

The study of narrative and the use of stories in the work of educators has been a growing phenomenon over the last decade (Brunner, 1994; K. Carter, 1993; H. Gardner, 1995; Hallinger, Leithwood, & Murphy, 1993; Jalongo, 1992; McEwan & Egan, 1995; Mezirow et al., 2000; Osterman & Kottkamp, 1993; Witherell & Noddings, 1991). Narratives or stories are central to our lives in that "the stories we hear and the stories we tell shape the meaning and texture of our lives at every stage and juncture" (Witherell & Noddings, 1991, p. 1). Think back on your own life: Do you have stories of experience that embody much of what you have come to understand about your life and its meaning? I know I do. Stories about the time I paddled 75 miles down the Salmon River in Idaho in an inflatable kayak embody what I learned about facing my own fears and learning to "paddle like hell" straight into my problems. Stories about my daughter saving a man who had been stabbed in the park embody all the love and pride I feel in the process of parenting. Stories about my mother beating cancer speak of my heritage, the strength and courage that have been passed on to me. Stories I tell myself in my journal help me sort out who I am and what I believe and care about in this world. All these stories speak of the power of narrative in human lives, its capacity to help define us, to help us grow, and to help us form visions of our future.

The fluid character of narrative or story encompasses a capacity for reinterpretation and change. Stories can be retold, reframed, reinterpreted. Because they are fluid, open for retelling, and ultimately reliving, they are the repositories of hope. They are also a balm to the multiple and fractured images of self we encounter as we enter the postmodern world of the twenty-first century. A sense of leading rushed and fractured lives is a central ingredient to the postmodern life. Kegan (1994) describes it as feeling "in over our heads," overwhelmed and unable to cope. Women and minority leaders feel this most acutely, because they are frequently not viewed as traditional leaders. By their very existence they defy the "great white male" image of a leader. Yet women and minority leaders are most needed as role models for our increasingly diverse society (Bloom & Munro, 1995).

Reflection through narrative conversations with the self can begin to heal our fractured lives, helping us pull the disparate pieces of ourselves into some kind of cohesive and meaningful whole. Rachel, for example, a Japanese-American elementary school vice principal, talked of having a *life sense* rather than a *career sense,* an "inside sense of who I am and how tiny I am in the universe" (Benham & Cooper, 1998, pp. 112–113). She likes the idea of being insignificant in the natural world because it gives her a sense of humility, a sense that she really is like everyone else, the same fears and joys as the school custodian or a parent. She says it also adds to her sense of wonder at the vast world we live in. This sense of self places Rachel clearly on the path of leadership and self-invention. For Rachel, it is a way of knowing what kind of a leader she wants to be, as she attempts to shape the organizational culture of her school in the face of diversity and inequality. Through this narrative, Rachel is able to create a sense of herself as an individual and subsequently of herself as a leader within the world of education (Benham & Cooper, 1998).

Stories are a powerful tool for understanding our own lives, for organizing that understanding just as one would draw a map to organize information about a place, and for using that map to begin to move in a desired direction. This is true for individuals and organizations. Stories provide a vision and a desired direction for adults working in schools, both administrators and teachers. Stories embody the hopes of these adults on both an individual and organizational basis. Narratives or stories are easier to remember than lists or disconnected facts:

> If you doubt this is true, attend an all-day workshop and consider what you recall in any great detail by the end of the day or much later. Chances are, it is a personal anecdote shared by a workshop leader or participant. (Jalongo, 1992, p. 68)

Anecdotes are easier to remember because they carry more information in them than the average set of facts or research findings. They carry with them powerful emotions, an understanding of what it is to be human, a sense of connection. They also carry within them tacit knowledge, knowledge gained through experience that is difficult to explain but communicated and understood through the narrative mode. Narratives or stories are little packages of understanding, which not only support the process of constructivism, but also are essential to it.

How is narrative essential to constructivism? First, recall the major assertions of constructivism: (1) human being is meaning-making—in other words, people all construct their own reality or make meaning, often with little awareness as to the exact shape of their own reality; (2) these meaning systems shape and give rise to behavior (Kegan & Lahey, 1984); and (3) we often make meaning in relationship—that is, we are social beings and our worlds are socially constructed. Thus it is not the events and particulars of someone's life that matter most, but how they privately compose or make meaning of what happens to them. In this way, people do not act irrationally but in a coherent manner that is consistent with their construction of reality. However, the construction of that reality must be shared through narrative and dialogue if leaders are to create communities in which they can construct meanings that lead toward a shared purpose for teaching and learning. And, as we have noted in previous chapters, narrative and dialogue help create school cultures rich in leadership connections so that all organizational members can become fully functioning professional leaders.

When applied to the understanding and leading of organizations, constructivism stands in sharp contrast to the objectivist philosophy that has been the basis for past organizational theory. Educational administration in the past has relied on the understanding of organizational theory as a set of truths that can be utilized to properly lead organizational members. Recent theorists have begun to recognize that organizations, such as schools, are merely constructed realities, created through the collected understandings of organizational members. Given the theoretical move to constructivism, questions arise about how leaders, both principals and teachers, can begin to understand their own behavior and that of other teachers and staff. How might leaders begin to change the constructed realities of schools to form new and more powerful understandings of organizational events?

Narrative and dialogue are powerful tools in the construction of meaning by educators. Sarbin (1986) states that "Human beings think, perceive, imagine, and make moral choices according to narrative structures" (p. 8). Thus narrative structures are essential to the work of leaders, a way for school leaders to capture understandings that others might not be able to articulate. By listening to and fostering dialogue and narrative construction, school leaders are better able to understand and manage meaning systems with others. In addition, narrative and dialogue provide the reciprocal processes essential to constructivist leadership. K. Carter (1993) claims that narrative or story is a way of capturing the complexity, specificity, and interconnectedness of life. Often a sense of trust and reciprocity is evoked as each organizational member tells his or her own story.

Stories not only support meaning-making of present events, they help form visions of the future. Witherell and Noddings (1991) underscored the power of narrative truth as a means of envisioning possibility in one's life. In the case of professional educators working together within a single school, it is a means of envisioning possibility at the individual and the organizational level. Clandinin and Connelly (1991) described this complex process as "growth toward an imagined future," which involves "restorying and attempts at reliving" (p. 265). For the members of a particular school, it means not only retelling and reliving at the individual level but also collaborative retelling and reliving at the organizational level. One elementary school experienced enormous change and growth when teachers and administrators began meeting regularly to retell and then relive the story of their math curriculum. Teachers told stories about what worked, what didn't, how children were learning, and how it felt to teach math in the way it was being taught. The stories gave rise to insights about all aspects of teaching and learning and initiated a journey toward whole-school change. As their math curriculum changed, teachers and administrators grew, forming more open and collaborative multiage classrooms and a more collegial school culture.

Narratives or stories serve at least three functions in the constructivist process. First, they create connections across difference, an element of school life that will become increasingly important as our society becomes more diverse. Second, narratives provide structure for the ways in which human beings think, perceive, imagine, and make moral choices (Brody & Witherell, 1991). Third, narratives elicit and clarify tacit knowledge (Jalongo, 1992).

CREATING CONNECTIONS ACROSS DIFFERENCE

Our need for story and connection becomes greater as educational communities become more diverse. Narrative is at the heart of individual and organizational sense-making. We need

- stories of the self in action
- stories of the self in community
- stories of the school as community

All three of these powerful meaning-making systems are vital to the constructivist process and to the work of school leaders. Educators must first understand their own role in leading the school. Second, they must articulate their understanding of that role and the role of others in the community we call "school." Third, leaders must be able to articulate stories of the school as a community of learners, a task that has become increasingly challenging.

The challenges educational leaders face become greater as the society in general becomes more diverse. Ramirez (1996) states, "Diversity calls up the most deeply felt passions about who we are, as individuals and as members of multiple groups, and about the kind of society we aspire to shape" (p. 440). Leadership for diversity demands courage and creativity, both traits that "can only be earned through a process of self-knowledge and self-invention" (p. 450). An elementary teacher writes about her struggle with finding the courage to speak up and how reflective conversations in a trusting environment have helped her. As a Japanese American, she often struggles with a cultural sanction to remain silent rather than to speak up and perhaps make waves:

> At times I've had difficulty expressing myself, communicating, and then I find I've almost withdrawn and let the "squeaky wheels" take charge. Perhaps the way I was brought up and instances along the journey made me resistant to conflict, attack. Then, I was left with the emotional war of *needing* to speak up but not doing so for fear of being verbally attacked. My writing and thinking and talks (with other teachers in her school) have helped me find some courage, some listeners and others who share many of the same feelings. (Cooper, 1995, p. 130)

Story or narrative is essential to the process of self-knowledge and self-invention for both formal and informal leaders in schools. As Benham and Cooper (1998) have stated, "to talk meaningfully about *how* life experiences shape one's work as a school leader requires a storied approach that is descriptive, personal, and concrete" (p. 6).

STORIES OF THE SELF IN ACTION

As leaders create narratives of the self in action, they communicate and model self-respect for other professionals in the schools, as well as for the students. "If our children are to approve of themselves, they must see that we approve of ourselves. If we persist in self-disrespect and then ask our children to respect themselves, it is as if we break all their bones and then insist that they win Olympic gold medals for the hundred-yard dash. Outrageous" (Angelou, 1993, p. 103).

Jolie, an African-American teacher, struggles with the crippling stereotypes of both gender and color in her work in schools. She frequently needs to be clear with people about "who I am and am not. They have these conceptions that I must be married, have children, be loud and aggressive. . . . It's both a gender and color issue, I believe. . . . I am not married and my three dogs are my children. I am pretty no-nonsense and I tell people this" (Benham & Cooper, 1998, p. 84). Several layers of stereotypes impact the work of this woman in schools, those of gender, color, and concepts about what it is to be a leader. Teacher leadership has become a well-established concept during this past decade, but has taken hold in some regions more strongly than others, just as both gender and racial stereotypes have varying influences on the moral imagination. These stereotypes frequently have served to exclude women of color from participating in educational leadership. Jolie has been confronted by comments such as "Oh, you're here because you're filling a quota." She states, "Because of this, we have had to learn to speak with certainty, especially if you're going to be a leader. We have to confront head on those who doubt our intellectual capabilities because we're Black or Brown and women." Jolie went on to say, "I have had teachers and administrators in my building who have said to me, 'Good girl.' I have had to stop and say, 'No, you can call me a woman, you can say good job, but don't do the *girl* thing.' It's taken me years to get that out of their minds" (pp. 91–92). This kind of dialogue can only happen after the individual has had a dialogue with the self, reflecting on who she is and what she is about.

STORIES OF THE SELF IN COMMUNITY

In addition to understanding the self through narrative and dialogue, educational leaders need to clarify how that self plays out in the larger context of the school community. Here narratives across school members help leaders to understand difference and similarity across ethnic and cultural lines and to create a sense of the self in community rather than in isolation. Here is where the sense of the school as an interdependent learning community, discussed throughout the text, comes into play. Leaders clarify their own identity both in isolation and as part of the larger community. Stories of the self in community not only help facilitate a sense of identity and community, but they help ward off detachment. In this way they guard against one of today's great dangers, professional detachment (Brody & Witherell, 1991):

> one of the greatest challenges for professionals today is to guard against their own detachment—from themselves, from their community, and from those with whom they form particular relationships. (p. 258)

Western cultures tend to overvalue individualism, autonomy, and competition, values that have structured our social relations, guided our professional lives, and deeply defined the character of our educational institutions.

Sometimes it takes a major event to awaken us to the debilitating power of detachment, and what often awakens us is a story. Here is one such story. It is a reminder of the power and importance of narrative in the construction of meaning.

> I experienced the death of one of our teachers this year. He went on leave before Christmas, letting only the SASA (school secretary) know. A month later his family wrote saying he had passed away. . . . We never had a chance to say goodbye. Slowly over the past few years he had withdrawn from his peers. . . . New teachers never knew him beyond the hello in the hallway, and so he evolved into an odd character on campus.
>
> After his death many stories emerged that shed light on him as a person as well as a teacher. Particularly insightful were the students' stories and perceptions. He touched the lives of more students than he was given credit for. I realize the loss of never having shared his stories with him. Moral: Don't wait to share stories. Also, teachers share (either purposely or inadvertently) their lives and stories with their students: ask them.

This principal realized the power of stories to create community only after it was too late. Through sharing stories, we create healing communities and guard against the kind of detachment that allows people to slip away unnoticed.

Stories among school professionals, as well as with students, can be a powerful catalyst for the construction of self in community. Frank, an administrative intern, shared the ways in which his sense of self was facilitated by his discussions with his principal at the end of the school day:

> The most significant moments were opportunities we had to dialogue at the end of the work day. It was nondirective and intellectually invigorating dialogue, and thus the collaborative reflection truly helped me process and make sense of my emerging development as a school leader.

These conversations and stories made an impact on Frank at the time, but they also had a more lasting effect on him. In essence, the conversations stayed with him, echoing in his mind, as he moved into further responsibilities as a leader. He states,

> Even now, I tend to recall many of these conversations as I make decisions and effect action. In addition, wherever I am, I usually think in terms of the philosophy of education that I began to embrace during that short semester.

Because Frank is Japanese American, his reflections on his place in the school community often include considerations of culture and gender. He writes about his conflicting professional identities—"the self as school administrator, the self as doctoral student, and the self as resource teacher"—and how each of these selves fits into the larger community. In reflecting on his role as a school leader, he says, "As comfortable as I am in the organization, I am plagued by the possible realization that somehow I am not fitting into the larger organizational structure of the Department of Education." In addition, he wonders about his place in the community he has encountered as a doctoral student—academe:

> While advancing to candidacy and the dissertation seem to be so far off in the future, I sometimes wonder if I will continue to have the motivation and energy to work toward attaining this goal. And even when I reach this goal, will the sociopolitical structure in the academy be willing to accept a middle-aged, local Asian male?

Exploring the self in community is a complex matter. It involves a defining of the multiple selves leaders may inhabit and then reflection on the accompanying communities surrounding these selves. Each of these constructions of self and the accompanying reflections on the place of that self in community can be supported by shared narratives with others to create connection, enhance and clarify one's educational philosophy, and simply support the daily struggles all leaders face. These shared narratives, such as the one between Frank and his principal, are not only important at the time, but stay with participants long after the last echo of the conversation has died in the hallways of the school, underscoring their importance in the construction of a professional self.

STORIES OF THE SCHOOL AS COMMUNITY

Finally, we need stories of the school as community in order to understand where we are headed collectively and to clarify the identity of this community as a whole. Without the value of narrative and dialogue to help form community, connection, and collective vision, leaders may feel isolated and lost. One principal reflected on his own need for connection to the larger community: "So often the stresses of being a principal tend to be destructive and demoralizing. At the end of a day you are left in little pieces that someone sweeps up and empties into the trash. You don't get the feeling that your efforts were valued and appreciated." In essence, without a chance to share thoughts and stories, we remain disconnected from ourselves as well as others. As a school leader, this man has a large share of the responsibility for creating that sense of community for himself and those around him. When we remember and share stories of educational practice, we are literally "re-membering" the pieces of our professional life.

As teachers and administrators "re-member" together, they are able to build trusting relationships, which are the backbone of community building in schools. By making meaning together, both individual and organizational growth is fostered. Here, a teacher reflects on the impact of this process in her school:

> How nice it is to see how our "coming together" is evolving. The trust is building, and it becomes easier to share, the longer the time we're together. It's nice to see this—everyone wanting to hear each other's thoughts and appreciating ideas, uniqueness. I think I'm feeling more positive about our school now than I had been feeling. I can see how we are really able to work together.

For school leaders, this sense of trust and the appreciation of individual ideas and uniqueness is fertile soil to begin the important work of organizational development. Through reflection on individual lives and shared dialogue, teachers and administrators can begin to construct new organizational realities that allow all members to grow and work more productively together. In such an atmosphere of support for individual growth and a sense of community, the earlier stories of pain and hurt might not occur. The construction of new organizational realities might be accomplished in a variety of ways, such as through specific programs of professional development, grade level meetings aimed at improving the curriculum, or the work of a leadership team searching for alternative forms of assessment.

As we noted in the previous chapter, one way to build a sense of community and identity is through the use of metaphor. Metaphors are really condensed narratives or ministories that carry a lot of information. They provide us with a "felt sense" of ourselves and our schools, while pushing us to think more creatively. One elementary school created metaphors for their school, first individually and then in collaborative groups. These are some of the descriptions of the school:

> A prison in which each teacher stays confined to a cell and the prisoners are dying to communicate with each other.
> A huge ship adrift on a calm sea. We're on it and just floating around

with no sense of direction. Even the captain doesn't know where
we're headed.

A cushion being squeezed from all directions. There is the administration pushing down from the top and the teachers trying to push up
from the bottom. The students and parents are pushing in from one
side and the DOE (Department of Education), Board of Education,
and District Office are pushing in from the other side.

An untamed animal preserve with cages and gates where zookeepers
and animal tamers work daily to herd animals to their sprawling
assigned stalls for daily animal behavior response training sessions.

These metaphors communicate the sense of frustration, isolation, and
lack of direction some teachers felt about the school. This in itself is tacit
knowledge that school personnel often prefer to leave these feelings unarticulated. Yet only through facing the truth of our feelings can we move
on to make needed changes. In a meeting of teachers and administrators,
one teacher, after hearing each teacher's metaphor for the school, had a
sudden realization that much of the school's frustration was blamed on
the students:

Each metaphor talked about the low morale and the divisions
within the faculty and the lack of direction/leadership that really
seem to be the trouble. I guess when morale is low, and there seems
to be little support coming our way, we find outlets for our frustration. The kids seem to get the brunt of it—yet when you come
down to it—kids are kids.

Here the articulation of a sense of community through metaphor allowed
the teachers to first acknowledge their frustration and then to reach the
insight that students were taking the brunt of their frustrations. By
acknowledging this fact, the teachers and administrators were able to
take the needed steps to change it. This teacher's final statement was to
question how this knowledge could help, unless administrators were
involved in the work of reflection and dialogue. This seems to be an essential component. Formal school leaders may not like what they hear when
teachers and staff begin to reflect upon their organizational life, but by
acknowledging what is and beginning to work together to construct a
new organizational reality, schools can change.

When they are not allowed to articulate what they know, educators
are left "voiceless," unable to confirm their own worth, knowledge, and
ability and thus unable to connect what they already know to new infor-

mation. By eliciting stories of community through reflective writing, narrative, and dialogue, school leaders can support the constructivist work of all adults in schools. If this work is done collectively, teachers reach insights about their own work as they listen to others struggle to articulate what they know through story and dialogue.

Thus, constructivist work in schools can provide teachers with the supportive audience they need and the courage to speak up rather than to remain mute, leaving valuable stories of experience unarticulated. Constructivist leaders need to be alert to all voices in schools, not just those heard on a regular basis. They must provide opportunities for school personnel to form and share stories of the self in action, stories of the self in community, and stories of the school as community.

PROVIDING A STRUCTURE FOR THINKING, IMAGINING, AND MAKING MORAL CHOICES

Narratives or stories, both read or experienced and told, can become powerful guides in helping us make moral choices. These stories reach across time and cultural boundaries to remind us who we are and how we want to live. They can be stories read in adolescence, such as J. D. Salinger's *The Catcher in the Rye* (1951), and remembered for the critical understanding they carry or stories of experience, which gain power when they are shared with others.

The following story of an elementary principal in Hawaii illustrates how he found narrative useful in the construction of his meaning-making system. Here he is struggling with one of life's central questions: how to be human from a male perspective.

Our principal recalls the story of Holden Caulfield in *The Catcher in the Rye,* which he read as an adolescent and which became a powerful guiding force in his life, both when he first read it and now, in his work in education:

> I approached the reading of the book with a typical high school know-it-all disdain, thinking this was about baseball or something equally dumb. . . . What a revelation the book turned out to be. . . . (one) incident that stood out was Holden's encounter with a psychologist friend who he confided in. After listening to Holden's troubles, the psychologist gave him a piece of advice. He said, "The mark of an immature man is that he die nobly for a cause; the mark of a mature man is that he live humbly for one." I never forgot that

piece of advice. It took some of the wind out of my sails. I felt as if the psychologist was speaking to me. . . . Here I was full of idealism and fervor only to be told I was being immature. Of course I quickly rejected the implication at that time and believed what I wanted to (youth is quick to recover). In retrospect I knew I secretly took that advice to heart. Today, as a principal, when I have a choice of dying nobly or living humbly in a tense political situation, I remind myself of my responsibility to children and my ultimate effectiveness . . . in the long run.

This story embodies much of what it is to be a mature man. It helped this principal confront and make difficult decisions in uncertain times. The story serves as a reminder to live humbly even when there is pressure to do otherwise. This wise advice for leaders was first heard at a young age, and yet it has remained an important guiding force in the making of moral choices for this principal. That the story has remained with this principal for so long reminds us of the power of stories to teach and guide us long after they have been heard and sometimes thought forgotten. Thus, stories like this provide a structure for thinking, imagining, and making moral choices. This is true for organizations as well as for individuals. Stories of the struggles of one elementary school to mainstream and care for their special education students help remind them that all students can learn. Their motto for the year was "I care. You matter." And their efforts made them a national blue ribbon award-winning school. This story carries with it powerful institutional memories of the school's core values.

ELICITING AND CLARIFYING TACIT KNOWLEDGE

Both writing and sharing our stories helps clarify what we know and believe. Often our understanding of complex tasks such as teaching or leading are so deeply buried in our everyday experience and grounded in our intuitive sense of how best to perform our jobs that we are unable to readily articulate what we know. Schön (1987) calls this kind of intuitive knowledge "artistry" and asserts that it is elicited through reflection both in and on our actions. Here, an elementary principal writes about his own misconceptions of reflection and the power of reflective writing to reveal tacit knowledge, thoughts that lie buried and unexamined:

I always envisioned reflection to be a Buddhist monk sitting lotus fashion in hushed silence, a pebble rippling a still forest pond, or a wizened holy man sitting atop a Himalayan peak. I never envisioned that reflection could occur through a simple act of writing, especially amidst the hustle and bustle of daily living. But it can, it has, and hopefully will continue to be. . . . To think it was possible only for a holy man to reflect was a falsehood. Luckily it is available to ordinary persons caught up in the throes of daily living through the process of reflective writing. Therein lies the hope for us all.

It is only through reflection on our actions that we are able to clarify and articulate what we know. If, as constructivism suggests, we are continually reframing and reinterpreting our experience in the face of new information, school personnel must first be able to articulate what they already know. Much of that information is buried in stories of practice. The elementary school staff mentioned earlier who transformed their school through stories of their math curriculum and teachers' individual efforts to improve their own teaching and learning is an excellent example.

CONCLUSION

The words of these school leaders are powerful testimonies to the transformational possibilities of sharing our stories. Through reflective writing, dialogue, and the creation of shared histories, organizational members are able to reflect on the meaning and direction of both their individual professional lives and the life of the school within which they live and work. Writing and conversation, as forms of critical reflection, are powerful components of this meaning-making process.

Throughout their lives adults engage continually in the construction of meaning from the events of their lives. Narrative or story is a central tool in that process. Stories have the power to help define who we are, foster growth and development, and help us envision our possible futures. School leaders need to provide opportunities for educators to continually engage in the process of retelling and reliving the stories of their lives, both individually and organizationally.

Narratives or stories provide a structure for thinking, imagining, and making moral choices. Whether these stories are read and carried with us through the years or are shared in a staff meeting or at the end of the school day, stories can act as guides to our daily living. In addition, narratives elicit and clarify tacit knowledge. Through devices such as metaphor, a kind of condensed narrative, we are able to elicit both thought and feeling, to tap our own intuitive knowledge, to find our own voices, and to gain helpful insights about ourselves and our organizations. Reflection in writing and dialogue can help us pick up the pieces of our lives and deposit them, not in the trash, but in a community of understanding colleagues. In a study of community organizations that have long histories of bringing people from the margins into voice, Belenky & Stanton (2000) found that "a leisurely, highly reflective conversation" was probably "the most salient of commonalities" (p. 97). It is through dialogue that we begin to form trusting professional bonds that can sustain us individually while they move us organizationally to new insights and visions. In the most powerful sense, narratives help all of us begin to "re-member" who we are as educators and who we are as communities of professionals engaged in the construction of meaning about our lives and our work.

In the next chapter we present the stories—stories of six schools told by principals and their colleagues. These stories of successful elementary, K–8, and high schools exemplify the power of constructivist processes. Their stories took form through reflection, inquiry, dialogue, and narrative. The result was vibrant learning communities for all children and adults.

CHAPTER 6

CONSTRUCTING SCHOOL CHANGE— SCHOOL STORIES

LINDA LAMBERT AND DEBORAH WALKER

Leadership is a process that occurs within the minds of individuals who live in a culture—a process that entails the capacities to create stories, to understand and evaluate these stories, and to appreciate the struggle among stories. Ultimately, certain kinds of stories will typically become predominant—in particular, kinds of stories that provide an adequate and timely sense of identity for individuals who live within a community or institution.

> *Howard Gardner*
> Leading Minds: An Anatomy of
> Leadership *(1995, p. 22)*

In the first five chapters we explored the history, theory, and processes of constructivist leadership. Now we bring forth stories: vignettes that describe critical moments, turning points in the history of six schools. These are schools engaged in reciprocal, purposeful learning in a community. These are schools that are making a difference for all children. These schools were chosen because they represent constructivist leadership in action: commitment to purposes of community and equity, commitment to both student and adult learning and leadership, and commitment to constructing school change together. All are urban, and all are diverse in population. Geographically, they include Kentucky to California, to Canada. Three are elementary schools, one is a K–8 school, and two are high schools. Two are schools of choice: a charter school in Campbell, California, and a basic school in Edmonton, Alberta. Two elementary schools have some form of year-round scheduling. While separated by geography, they are drawn together by a shared philosophy, a shared approach among educators and children.

The schools have journeyed this road for differing lengths of time. The Manitoba high school has been engaged in this work for more than 10 years, while the elementary school in San Leandro, California, has just started. The schools that we have chosen for this storytelling are the following:

Engelhard Elementary School, Louisville, Kentucky
    Theresa Jensen, principal and author

Glenlawn High School, Winnipeg, Manitoba, Canada
    Donna Burlow, principal
    Rosemary Foster, University of Manitoba, author

Sherman Oaks Community Charter School (Elementary), San Jose (Campbell), California
    Peggy Bryan, principal and author

Garfield Elementary School, San Leandro, California
    Jan Huls, principal and author

Winterburn School (K–8), Edmonton, Alberta, Canada
    Del Bouck, principal and author

Wyandotte High School, Kansas City, Kansas
    Walt Thompson, principal
    Arthur "Gus" Jacobs, director of University of Missouri at Kansas City's Kauffman Principal's Institute and author

ANTICIPATING STORY THEMES

This chapter will present the stories of these six schools. From these stories we will infer lessons learned about constructivist leadership and the processes of change. We invite the reader to do the same by attending to certain themes and examples. While all share similar themes, some exemplify certain principles more strongly than others. For instance,

- *Creating a school culture that provides opportunities to create shared meaning in the work of teachers, principals, students, and parents.*
  Trust and relationships are prominent themes at Wyandotte, Winterburn, and Glenlawn. Collegial norms at Winterburn gave form to these relationships. Democratic participation patterns at Sherman Oaks and Engelhard frame both relationships and governance.

- *Having the principal serve as a powerful initiator of change.*
  These principals are "strong" but not in the take charge, direct, and control style. By "strength," we suggest someone who is forthcoming with his or her own values and passions and taps these sources in others as a way of creating a shared vision—someone who convenes and sustains the conversation, someone who asks provocative questions and clears the way for the voices of others.

  These are principals for a new age. Notice the styles of Walt at Wyandotte, Jan at Garfield, Peggy at Sherman Oaks, and Del at Winterburn as we reconstruct the public notion of the job of principal. Notice also that the two high schools had change facilitators/coaches in addition to the principal.

- *Investing leadership in teachers as well as in the principal.*
  Like Del at Winterburn, these principals recognize that not only could they not go it alone, but they should not go it alone. Peggy at Sherman Oaks, Jan at Garfield, Donna at Glenlawn, and Walt at Wyandotte invested authority and responsibility in teachers as a fundamental step in the process of establishing reciprocity. As leaders emerged from each school they changed their perceptions of what it is to teach, as well as what it is to lead. Relationships with each other changed, as well as relationships with students.

- *Ensuring that all students are well served, including poor and minority students.*
  While these assurances and commitments were part of each story, look to the dominant themes around equity and diversity at Engelhard, Sherman Oaks, Garfield, and Wyandotte. Notice how shared values made it possible to confront evidence about student learning, shift beliefs, and eventually shift action.

- *Engaging and codifying constructivist practices that build the leadership of the school.*
  Each school confronted evidence about student learning as a central feature of their commitment to inquiry, reflection, and dialogue. The courage to encounter and make sense of what was happening—or not happening—for children created purposeful learning communities and collective responsibility. Particularly notice such shifts in thinking at Glenlawn, Garfield, and Wyandotte.

- *Designing change in social organizations.*
  The fluidity of change and its emergent qualities can be observed in each story. While the direction is influenced by values and commitments,

no preset objectives could have signaled the outcomes. Each school exceeded its own expectations. The new communities and schedules at Wyandotte, Sherman Oaks, Engelhard, and Glenlawn altered the basic relationships among students, teachers, and parents.

Each story that follows is of a school weaving whole cloth from multiple strands.

THE STORIES OF SIX SCHOOLS

ENGELHARD ELEMENTARY SCHOOL
by Theresa Jensen

AUTHOR'S NOTE. By every measure, Engelhard Elementary is a high performing school, one that promotes continuous learning for students and the adults who work in the school. On Kentucky's battery of state-mandated tests and in comparison with schools having similar demographics, Engelhard is a star performer. It did not achieve this status easily and in fact has overcome many barriers to do so. Shared leadership and a belief in the ability of students and teachers to excel paved the way for a series of innovations that have helped students perform at high levels. Following the adoption of the 1990 Kentucky Education Reform Act and its high-stakes accountability, Engelhard began a journey to empower learners to achieve.

Back Stage
Engelhard, a prekindergarten through fifth grade school in Louisville, Kentucky, serves an urban population of 475 students, including children from five area shelters for families in crisis, three separate housing projects, and recently emigrated families from 10 countries speaking 12 different languages. Seventy-five percent of the students qualify for free or reduced lunch, 49 percent are African American, 71 percent live in single-parent families, many with a female head of household, and 56 percent of families live in one of the lowest per capita income census tracts in Jefferson County.

In the early days of my first year as principal, I came to learn much of the culture of this, my first public school. I remember one day vividly. I was walking down the hall. It was spotless, empty. Only the clicking of my pumps disturbed the silence. When I turned the corner into the primary-grades hall, I spotted two teachers talking. As I approached, they looked toward me, registered terrified expressions, and quickly, without speaking, ran to their rooms and closed the doors. This behavior so alarmed me that I spun around to confront the weapons-wielding vagrant I was convinced must be there. I was alone. My mind reeled as I understood the implications of their fear.

During all the times I had envisioned myself as principal, I never thought of myself as someone to fear. Instead, I pictured myself as a colleague who would work collaboratively to move our school forward. My hope was to help create a sense of shared leadership and responsibility for improving learning for our students. This scene in the hallway was my introduction to the incongruity in the way I desired to lead and the way the faculty viewed leadership.

Act I: Making Sense of Our Situation

If my encounter with teachers in the hallway was my introduction to the role of the principal as school leader, my first test as a leader came at the time our state assessment results were released. Given the many risk factors faced by our students and our low achievement, sharing these data with the faculty in a way that elicited constructive analysis and solution seeking would not be easy. To complicate things, I still had not established the kind of trust and reciprocity with the faculty needed for us to function as a team of leaders.

Before sharing the data collectively, I tried to lay the groundwork by meeting with a volunteer leadership team comprised of parent officers of the PTA and a cross-grade group of teachers. This team learned to disaggregate the data and came to understand what the numbers meant. During most of the week, we worked with partners looking deeply at one content area. On the last day, we shared our data with the other teams and planned to develop next steps.

As each team stepped forward with charts and handouts, the image of what we had achieved cleared. The results painted a picture of our learning community indicating students were not successful. Most students were ranked in the lowest testing category, demonstrating below grade-level achievement in every content area, and African American males were the least successful of all. I glanced across the table and saw tears roll down the face of Oliver, our PTA president and the father of an African American male in our first grade. I knew in that moment that we must develop a learning environment responsive to the needs of all learners.

Act II: Constructing Shared Meaning

Although our team represented many roles, the group was not ready to face the staff and share our findings. Instead, they insisted that I present the data and preliminary findings. At the next staff meeting, armed with charts, handouts, and transparencies, I stepped forward to share our work. As chart after chart was displayed and explained, I studied the faces around me. Expressions ranged from "What can you expect?" on the faces of the primary teachers to horror, tears, and "We can only do so much" on the faces of fourth- and fifth-grade teachers. I believe this was a defining moment, not only in confronting the learning challenges that faced us but also in deciding whether we would be able to share leadership and thus responsibility for our school, now and in the future.

I put the charts aside and began to talk. I shared my beliefs: that we all worked very hard and were good teachers; that the students could learn the content; that a culture built on trust of each other and ownership of the work needed to be established. I believed that if we were to develop a climate to support learning for children, we needed to support adults as active learning partners, to allow them to take risks and even fail without repercussions, to reflect, to discuss, to learn, and to implement change. I believed that I could not do this alone, but that working *together* we could develop the skills needed within the context of our work to fundamentally change the roles, responsibilities, and behaviors of the entire learning community. I promised that to do this, I would give my total support as we embarked on new ways of engaging learners. I asked for their help.

We then began to talk together. Our first conversations focused on the question, "If we believe that we have good, capable teachers, smart students, and caring parents, what are the barriers to student success at Engelhard?" This process of sharing our thoughts, accepting all input, and working to address all issues collaboratively energized our work and helped us construct new meaning of how to lead change efforts in our school.

Act III: The Language of Leadership

Two things became apparent in our conversations. First, we needed to develop a common vocabulary that would lead us to dialogue rather than debate. Second, we needed to learn to frame questions that would guide our improvement efforts on behalf of students.

Developing a shared language took patience and persistence. At first there were misunderstandings. Role differentials sometimes contributed to the misunderstanding. Even though I worked hard to be a colleague and to shift responsibility to teachers for important functions like professional development, it was easy to slip back into old ways, to give authority to the principal rather than assuming responsibility for school-wide outcomes. For teachers, being responsible for the success of the school beyond the individual classroom required new ways of talking about roles and opportunities to engage in dialogue, to describe this kind of leadership.

We used weekly study groups and frequent professional learning sessions to develop common ways of talking about, and ultimately thinking about, our work. Involvement in a whole-school reform model, *Different Ways of Knowing*, enabled us to describe the kind of child-centered, experiential, integrated learning we wanted for our students. It also gave us the vocabulary and common understanding to change our classroom practice.

Learning to frame questions in ways that promote inquiry was a challenge. Because of the urgency of our work, it was easy to look for quick solutions without really understanding the scope of the problem. Yet all of us agreed, as we came to know in greater depth what it means to lead school change, that it is in framing the questions that we have an opportunity to seek lasting and significant solutions to school dilemmas. We asked ourselves these questions:

- How do we encourage all learners to extend their learning?
- How do we continue to find the time and resources to engage in necessary learning?
- How do we maintain energy on projects when results are not immediately forthcoming, or when baby steps, though representing a ton of effort, yield very little progress at first?

We face the most serious of problems at Engelhard: deep poverty, homelessness, underperformance of minority students, and lack of hope and confidence. These problems take our best thinking and a commitment to long-term action. But because we were able to frame questions well and engage each other in inquiry about our practice, we implemented significant changes in teaching and learning, including a year-round calendar and a 4-day instructional week, with the 5th day optional and devoted to enrichment. We are not aware that any other school in Kentucky—or in the nation—has adopted this calendar. It enabled us to extend the time students were engaged in learning by adding one-fifth to the school year, since most of the students attend the 5th day. More time for our students enables them to make progress and catch up with their more affluent peers. This unique arrangement was possible because we learned to question and reflect as a means for achieving creative solutions.

Act IV: Leaders as Learners

We quickly learned that the fundamental changes we were envisioning required us to work in very different ways. We developed over time the trust, communication, and reciprocity needed to share leadership. In addition to constructing new patterns of leadership, we also committed ourselves to

- accept that we had much to learn
- not fall back into comfortable patterns when risk-taking failed
- realize that we could not change overnight
- accept our failures as readily as we accepted our successes
- codify the work we do as we moved toward sustainability

Our journey continues. We are developing a different kind of learning environment, one in which the roles of all the learners—teachers, students, principal, university professors, parents, community partners, and cultural and educational resource personnel—are often exchanged and renegotiated as our unique perspectives are honored and valued. Our change process has been active and healthy. We have remained focused on children and their needs while recognizing and supporting the learning needs of the adults who support them.

Each year we begin again in earnest to take the lessons we have learned and apply them to the work that children and adults do in all the classrooms in our school. Only then can we attain the vision that we all strive to achieve—success for all learners, children, and adults.

THE GLENLAWN JOURNEY OF SCHOOL IMPROVEMENT
by Rosemary Foster

"THE GLENLAWN ADVANTAGE." This bold statement appears on the cover of the student handbook and on promotional materials at Glenlawn Collegiate. Some long-time staff and graduates of Glenlawn would say that the "advantage" refers to the school's history and achievements in its academic, athletic, and fine arts programs. Several staff, students, and parents would say that the "advantage" also refers to recent innovations including the popular student advocacy program and the graduation portfolios. Being a student or teacher at Glenlawn, however, has not always been seen as an advantage. In the late 1980s, changing demographics combined with government reform initiatives including school choice gave rise to issues associated with increased student absenteeism and dwindling enrollments. In particular, the staff at Glenlawn were concerned about a sizeable group of students who seemed disconnected from the school. So began the Glenlawn journey of renewal and school improvement.

Glenlawn Today

Glenlawn Collegiate is located in an older area of Winnipeg, Manitoba, a Canadian city with a population of 650,000. The original school was built in 1923 and has undergone several renovations and additions over the years. This Grades 10–12 high school houses approximately 1,000 adolescent students from diverse racial and socioeconomic backgrounds. One principal, 2 assistant principals, 60 teachers, and 20 educational assistants are involved in delivering a broad-based program designed to accommodate the students' wide-ranging academic and athletic interests and abilities. The program comprehensively provides for the needs of all students, including those identified as gifted or having other special needs and those wanting to return to school after having dropped out in either elementary or junior high school. Today, Glenlawn Collegiate enjoys a positive reputation and is recognized for its capacity to adapt to changing times and the demands of a changing urban population.

Stage 1: Acknowledging the Need for Renewal

In 1990, the issues caused by changing demographics, the introduction of school choice, and increased student absenteeism gave rise to a sense of urgency among the Glenlawn staff. But dealing with the issues was not easy. Over the years, the stable and highly departmentalized teaching staff at Glenlawn had developed great pride in its unwavering belief that the school's chief task was to prepare students for university study. With dropping staff morale, dropping enrollments, and decreasing student and parent satisfaction, then-principal Brian Thorarinson formed a committee of volunteer teachers, students, and parents. Their task was to ask the "tough questions" and generate ideas for school renewal.

Stage 2: Asking the Questions and Gathering the Evidence

Through its connection with a school improvement network, the committee was successful in procuring enough funding to engage an educational consultant who had expertise in action research. The consultant and committee created and administered a survey to find out what students, parents, faculty, and community members thought of the school programs and expectations for graduates. The evidence was surprising. It showed that most Glenlawn students did not go to university, but instead chose other postsecondary programs or entered directly into the workforce. The data also showed that the reason students were dissatisfied and not attending was because they felt they were being forced to learn material that was not relevant to their lives. Worse still, students in general did not feel that their teachers viewed and respected them as individuals as well as students.

Stage 3: Lessons Learned and Development of a Vision
"Relationships and relevant learning" are words that have come to embody the major findings from that 1991 investigation. This phrase has become part of the school language and culture and captures the renewed belief in the "Glenlawn Advantage." That initial inquiry also revealed that parents, community members, most staff, and many students believed that getting a postsecondary education may be important to some, but that every graduate of Glenlawn should have the opportunity, and be accountable for, acquiring such fundamental life skills, such as working with others, problem solving, and lifelong learning.

These "lessons learned" in 1991 served as a critical turning point and a "wake-up" call for the staff of Glenlawn. The evidence produced from this initial research undertaking provided the impetus that the principal and committee needed to initiate conversations and debate around changes for Glenlawn. In the wake of these findings, staff, student, parent, and community focus groups were formed. With the help of the consultant, these groups worked through a process that culminated in the construction of the vision statement that can be found posted in classrooms and appears in student handbooks:

> Glenlawn students are required to complete 28 instructional credits and demonstrate mastery in three outcomes in order to graduate. These outcomes are: Working with Others, Lifelong Learning, and Problem Solving. These outcomes are a general set of skills integrating more traditional disciplines such as language and mathematics with a long "shelf life" that will provide an advantage to all graduates in their postsecondary endeavors—work, university, vocational school, or college.

Stage 4: Developing Action Plans
At the end of the 1990–91 school year, the school secured funding from the network for released time for staff development and committee work. In Brian's words, "I have learned that more heads generate more ideas and lead to better decisions." Two new ad hoc committees were charged to find ways to implement the shared vision. One committee, which later became known as the Advocacy Committee, put together a comprehensive plan for staff development activities that would help teachers become more proficient at building relationships with students and making learn-

ing relevant to all. The staff development activities for the following year were to include workshops in cognitive coaching, peer coaching, cooperative learning, differentiated instruction, and portfolio assessment. The other committee, which became known as the Outcomes Committee, developed a curriculum to achieve the three identified life skills. The consultant now worked as a "critical friend." This friendship involved reminding faculty of the "lessons learned" and coaching them to stay focused on the shared vision and the evidence. By June 1992, a student advocacy program and a compulsory portfolio assessment were in place. Within 3 years, these initiatives would lead to the attainment of the overarching graduation outcomes: Working with Others, Lifelong Learning, and Problem Solving.

Stage 5: More Lessons Learned and the "Big Questions"

Significant changes have occurred at Glenlawn over the past 10 years. Brian Thorarinson, who moved to central office administration in 1995, describes the changes that have occurred in the following way:

> Many staff would say that involvement with the school improvement network was the catalyst that helped people shift in their thinking to a schoolwide focus on learning and to the importance of becoming involved in problem solving and decision making. Not all staff felt comfortable. Some retired or moved to other schools, claiming it was all "too much work." Staff meetings and conversations got very heated at times that first year.

One long-time staff member describes the changes this way:

> It took us a long time to learn that *people will not hear the answers if they are not asking the questions.* I guess over time we have all become better at asking one another the questions about our kids and their education. We have learned the importance of action research and decision making that is based on evidence. We spend more time asking the "big questions," namely, *How do we know what we think we know? How are we doing? Can we do better?*

Stage 6: Sustaining and Extending the Conversation

Donna Burlow, who was vice principal and on the original committee, became the principal of Glenlawn in 1995. In outlining the accomplishments and strengths of the school improvement initiatives, she highlights the relationships and increased involvement:

We use the word "leadership" a great deal more today than we did in 1991. If you listen, you will hear that staff, students, teachers, and parents use the word to refer to "groups of people" being responsible and involved in problem solving and making decisions. This is particularly true of our committees where teachers, students, parents, and community members sit together as equals. People take turns chairing meetings. Decisions are made by consensus. There is a lot of trust and respect that has developed. It is safe for people to disagree and debate. The same is true of the student advocacy classes. During these classes, it would be difficult to tell who is the "teacher" and who are the "students."

A Grade-12 student who had sat on the advocacy committee for 3 years echoes these comments:

Students get to pick their teacher and have the same teacher for all 3 years of high school. You really get to know that teacher as a person and they you. My class, for example, has Grades 10, 11, and 12 students from all different programs in the school. We get to meet and talk to people we wouldn't otherwise. We help one another with problems and talk about outcomes and our portfolios. You could ask any student or teacher around here, and they would tell you that advocacy classes are the best.

In describing the challenges, present and future, Donna Bulow emphasizes that the journey is ongoing.

We are constantly looking for ways to help people feel like they are important and have a voice. The advocacy program and portfolios are just the beginning. I really believe that people are starting to see that becoming involved in the committees is important if we are going to continue to move forward at Glenlawn. Our newest committee is working on a process for reexamining our vision statement. After 10 years and all the changes, it is time.

Principal as Constructivist Leader
Donna Burlow believes that Glenlawn Collegiate "grows leaders." She also believes that leadership capacity increases when more people become involved and skillful at leadership. Donna sees the development of teachers as critical to the leadership capacity at Glenlawn but acknowledges

that the organization of high schools and the teaching culture can be obstacles.

Since becoming principal, Donna helps teachers see themselves as lifelong learners and part of the Glenlawn advantage. One initiative about which teachers and principals speak with tremendous enthusiasm is the "Career Planning Meetings." For the past 5 years, Donna, along with the two assistant principals, meet with teachers and ask, "If no jobs were assigned and it was wide open, what would you like to do? What would the perfect job at Glenlawn look like?" At these meetings Donna learns about the individual teacher's interests, talents, and goals. Donna knows that to build capacity she must first understand and support the goals of all staff. She must take the time and have the conversations with individuals and together learn the ways in which personal aspirations become congruent with the goals for teaching and learning at Glenlawn.

Reflections on the Glenlawn Journey

How do the Glenlawn school members perceive and understand their participation in school leadership? The evidence suggests that many at Glenlawn regularly experience and participate in constructivist leadership. Many of the teachers and principals will refer to their participation in the reciprocal learning processes as "shared leadership." Those who participate in committee activities would also describe their participation as "shared leadership." Inquiry, reflection, conversation, and change focused on improved student learning are the processes by which beliefs and assumptions are challenged and decisions are made.

Some teachers, students, and most parents, however, are less apt to see their involvement as "leadership," yet they describe relationships and interactions that are constructivist in nature. In classes and meetings, people come together as equals to participate in conversations that lead to shared purposes around schooling and learning. How are the patterns of relationships in the "Career Planning Meetings" and advocacy classes different from, and the same as, the pattern of relationships in staff meetings or in the regular classes? How is the learning that occurs the same as, and different from, the learning that occurs elsewhere? How can these promising relationships at Glenlawn be sustained and extended so that all teachers, students, and parents can become full participants in constructivist leadership at Glenlawn? These are some of the questions that are shaping the next stage of the Glenlawn journey of school improvement.

SHERMAN OAKS COMMUNITY CHARTER SCHOOL
by Peggy Bryan

Our Community

Located in an older, first-ring suburb (Campbell) of one of California's largest cities, San Jose, Sherman Oaks Community Charter School serves 450 kindergarten through fourth-grade students. The original school, serving a predominately middle-class community, was closed over 2 decades ago and the "new" Sherman Oaks opened in the fall of 1997. During the 20-plus years between closing and reopening, the local neighborhood changed from largely middle-class to low-income, immigrant families from Mexico, Central and South America, Vietnam, Eritrea, southern Asia, and the Middle East. The area is now dedicated to high-density, low-cost housing—many overseen by negligent, absentee landlords. Eighty-two percent of the students come from ethnic minority heritages, 55 percent speak a primary language other than English (mostly Spanish), and 75 percent live in poverty. The problems associated with at-risk families were clearly evident in our students. High mobility rates, absenteeism, low achievement, and disciplinary problems plagued the children. *We intended to change all that.*

Our School and Staff

Starting in the spring of 1994, with the passage of a school bond measure, funds were set aside to not just reopen but rebuild Sherman Oaks as a brand new facility. A broad-based committee of educators, parents, and community members from the public and private sector met and planned over the course of 3 years. Our goal was to create a true twenty-first-century learning community by adapting the best established models, but we also reserved the right to create our own unique systems. Schools around the country with innovative architectural or programmatic features were visited, corporate and civic officials interviewed, and multidisciplinary research analyzed. The end result was a program and building design that promoted staff and student collaboration and interdependence. Clusters of six classrooms called "Houses" ring a "Great Room" commons area full of networked technology and library resources. Each House has a garden and kitchen. Children and adults jointly share restrooms. The cafeteria was traded in for increased square footage for instruction—children benefit from learning environments one-third larger than traditional classrooms. Weather permitting, children eat at picnic tables under colorful sun umbrellas. Eliminating the institutional nature of our buildings guided the architectural design, so that when children or adults walk through our doors the message is "Welcome Home." The instructional program was built around constructivist pedagogy, project-based learning, exhibition cycles, and a strong commitment to dual language (Spanish/English) acquisition. We wanted the adults on campus to serve as true cultural role models for our students and families, so our hiring practices reflected that goal. Latinos, Vietnamese, Filipinos, African Americans, and Native Americans comprise over half of the staff and two-thirds of them speak Spanish.

Student Achievement: Improving and Proving

As a brand new school, we opened in 1997 with vast plans and many new programs on our plate. When we completed reading and writing assessments, the bleak academic achievement projections we expected were confirmed. Only a handful of students schoolwide were reading at grade level and less than 20 percent of our students could write a paragraph without multiple structural errors that rendered the content of the composition indecipherable. Math was in no better shape. But with a handpicked, highly trained staff, which was, to a person, completely dedicated to the mission of Sherman Oaks, we took the plunge. At the end of our first year, based on performance assessments, we saw academic achievement jump in all core academic areas. Concurrent to our start-up, the state of California initiated a high-stakes testing program requiring all 2nd- through 11th-grade students be tested on the SAT-9, a standardized, norm-referenced test given only in English. Our student results in the first year landed us on the state's "low-performing" school list. We low-performing designees, of course, were given great visibility in the local press. Rewards and sanctions were next: the state would pay cash bonuses for increased test scores or would ultimately shut down schools consistently posting low test scores. By year 2 our results improved significantly, especially in math, and we escaped "the list."

However, by the end of our third year, 2000, we noted that Spanish-speaking students were not gaining the English fluency and literacy necessary to demonstrate academic mastery on the SAT-9. We knew our kids understood the material because these same students would score above average to high in reading, writing, and math on a standardized test in Spanish, the SABE-2. But that test did not count in the eyes of the California Department of Education. Only the English-based SAT-9 mattered, and it mattered in a *big* way: Student retention and promotion policies, summer school assignment, faculty and administrative job security, and the actual viability of a school were all measured by this single, norm-referenced test.

Beyond the state tests, we as a staff were also concerned that as our students moved into third and fourth grades, they were not as fluent or literate in English as we would expect. In addition, our Dual Immersion Program was becoming so popular in the community that two-thirds of the student body were participating. We began to wonder and worry that parent choice was actually creating two student groups: students from families who took the time to examine and value bilingual or multilingual education versus those from families who didn't. Students not participating in the Dual Immersion Program were more likely to have behavior problems and suffer low academic achievement. In essence, we were dividing our school into two tracks: Dual Immersion (parent choice) and English-only (in reality, parent indifference).

Decision Making: The "Sherman Oaks Way"
With all of these variables on our minds, we determined to find a better way. At one staff meeting, the question prompt was posed: "Why should we change the Dual Immersion Program?" A pro and con list was developed, and the rules of brainstorming prevailed: no right or wrong answers, no value judgements—every reason was recorded. Our next step was to cross-check all ideas with validity; reasons for changing or not changing had to be supported with a data source. It should be noted that "teacher instinct" was acceptable as long as it was supported with anecdotal evidence. From this mountain of evidence and ideas, we determined it was in the best interests of our students to modify the program. As our first investigative move, we visited other schools that had established reputations of excellent language immersion programs.

Staff teams visited schools in Florida, Arizona, and California. Parents from our Curriculum and Instruction Council were invited to join a visitation team. When all the visits were completed, we set aside a series of days to discuss our findings. Our school has a unique master schedule that builds staff collaboration time into the contractual day. The Mid-Day Block is from 11:30 a.m. to 1:00 p.m., Monday through Friday. The faculty is released for lunch and staff development while students go through a daily cycle of Running Club (a lap program), Study Hall, and lunch recess, all supervised by paraprofessionals. When we developed our instructional program, we knew that teachers needed time to talk and work together on a daily basis, not once a week at a staff meeting usually held after school. Our typical weekly Mid-Day Block schedule covers content training, grade-level meetings, guest speakers, staff meetings, and so forth. This routine schedule was suspended to focus upon Dual Immersion.

Over a 2-week period we went from large to small, big idea to details. Several communication protocols were used to facilitate the process, starting with visitation teams providing feedback to the entire staff on their specific site visit. Recorders copied notes, insights, and "ah-ha's" on chart paper that hung up around the faculty room. After the staff heard exhaustive details of the visits, we turned to a "fishbowl" strategy to take our conversations deeper into inquiry. The prompt was changed from "Why should we change" to "How shall we change?" Visitation teams formed a conversation circle, and the remaining staff sat on the outside of the circle listening intently to the dialogue taking place between team members. After the inner circle dialogue ended the staff could ask clarifying questions and then offer feedback to the fishbowl team. The next step of the process was another fishbowl, but this time comprised of some people in favor of and some reticent toward making a program change. This self-selected group formed an inner circle and waged another debate. The new fishbowl prompt—"Is the new Dual Immersion model better for students?"—kept "adult convenience" out of the dialogue. Any reason that didn't support a student-centered decision was challenged. The final step cycled back to the beginning with a staffwide discussion summarizing the complexity of our prior conversations. After some compromise we decided to change the model for incoming kindergarten students, but keep the older model for matriculating students. Starting in the fall of 2001, all kindergarten students would participate in Dual Immersion, with half of the day taught in English and half in Spanish. The classes will be mixed equally with Spanish speakers and English speakers. Our goal is to transition to a schoolwide program over the next 5 years, thus ending linguistic tracking. And, by increasing instructional time in the second language, all students should demonstrate increased academic achievement as measured by both Spanish and English assessments. The staff decision-making process took 2 weeks. We never rushed to end any debate; if we ran out of time, we took it up the next day. The final round of checking for consensus included a public check-in with every faculty member, one by one. Full consensus was required to move forward. We call this the "Sherman Oaks Way."

Making a Difference

This type of process requires a high level of trust among staff and between staff and administration. At Sherman Oaks, we've worked hard to cultivate an environment where all opinions are valued and all voices heard. As a principal, I define my job as the "keeper of the vision." I have learned the hard way that rushing to a decision—even a decision which I advocate—is never worth the victory. I am persuaded that good people combined with a solid vision will keep moving confidently toward a horizon of hope and high expectations. Sometimes the march slows as people catch their breath and check their internal compasses. Sometimes the path includes dead ends and tricky forks in the road. But passion and commitment, if cultivated and nurtured, will ultimately override exhaustion, confusion, and inertia. A journey that energizes and empowers *every single staff member* and maintains *every single student* in our line of sight will endure— far longer than slick, quick, top-down maneuvering. The democratic process is messy at best but better than any alternative. Try the "Sherman Oaks Way." You won't be disappointed. Trust me.

GARFIELD ELEMENTARY SCHOOL: WEAVING EQUITY INTO ACTION
by Jan Huls

The Setting
Located between Oakland and Hayward in the urban corridor of the East Bay of San Francisco, Garfield Elementary, a year-round school, opens its doors each year to 450 students from the neighborhoods. Students arrive from the apartments and small homes of San Leandro and join the only school in the district that is on a year-round schedule and has a uniform dress policy. Garfield and nearby schools lie in a sometimes turbulent area of the city of San Leandro where 40 percent of the city's crime takes place. Nearly half of Garfield's families are eligible for free and reduced meals and two-thirds of the families have all parents in the labor force. Yet there is a quiet and close sense in the immediate neighborhood that spills into the hallways of the school. Threads of neighborhood culture have been strong for many years and remain to support the school. A branch of the library, a small Baptist church, the recycling and waste management facilities, and many businesses surround the school. The local spring Cherry City Festival parade finds its route through the Garfield neighborhood streets to the San Francisco Bay. Fresh paint, new portables, well-maintained lawns and classroom gardens all tell the story of this thriving community of learning in a typical California school setting.

In like manner to the whole community of San Leandro, Garfield has experienced a transition of its people. San Leandro, called the "Cherry City," began the twentieth century with a population consisting mostly of Portuguese fruit and flower farmers and fishermen and has quickly transformed into a diverse collection of people from many races and cultures. In the past decade, San Leandro schools have shifted from a majority of white students to a majority of students of color. Garfield now has just over 20 white students, with the majority of the children being Latino (30%), Asian (18%), and African American (17%). The mosaic of races found at Garfield provides both opportunities and challenges. Our way of conducting business and creating instructional programs leads us to consider matters of race and culture, poverty and language, traditions and institutionalized practices, and learning styles and behavior expectations. Consequently, we continually strive to weave the best programs, policies, and practices together for our students and their families.

The Garfield Journey Begins

I came to Garfield a year ago, having served as an administrator in two other local schools for 8 years. I had taught English Language Development and/or Special Education at most of the other 11 schools in the district and had lived in San Leandro for nearly 20 years. My desire to bring all of the skill and spirit that I had developed as a constructivist leader was in great harmony with the need of the school to build successful systems of learning and community. The strength of the school community was mostly felt in an outstanding teaching staff that had already addressed many of the instructional needs of students. Although not all students had reached grade-level performance, Garfield was 19th in the state for improvement according to the test scores from the recent state assessment administration. However, the data that we examined by race showed us that a large majority of our Latino and African American students did not reach the 50th percentile in reading and language assessments, while most of our Asian and white students did.

Parent groups included a core of passionately committed women who served the school in meaningful ways, like providing recess supervision and printing the school's parent bulletin. Yet there were significant pieces missing in the tapestry of the school, such as an absence of parents of color on governance boards, a school plan, a parent handbook, a discipline policy, and a mission and vision that was collaboratively established. Many teachers, office staff, and one-fourth of the students changed each year. What was needed was a sense of community and belonging for all students, parents, and staff.

During the first month of my tenure as principal, I sat down with each staff member, student representative, and parent-leader and asked them to give me ideas about the programs, policies, and procedures at Garfield. I asked them to list three things that they would like to continue and maintain at Garfield and three things that they would like to change or add. By the second year, we would have accomplished most of our list.

Every step of the way involved focused and engaged learning by everyone. Whenever we began planning for professional development and research, we brought together a team to think collaboratively. We involved the whole group (usually teachers first, then follow-up training at PTA and summarization with the School Site Council) to conduct training, research, or a "Cycle of Inquiry." Our team review and planning also used a Cycle of Inquiry. The cycle always followed a system of collecting data, creating a plan, moving the plan to action, and then assessing the success of the action. Much trust was built with this process, as leadership was developed in each member of the group and shared with the staff very openly.

Three teams led our work, weaving the major threads of our vision together regarding equity, the best instructional practices, and school-wide planning. The staff had held the district vision of "All students can learn" for several years, yet had not made it their own. The teamwork led teachers and parents to agree that our purpose and hope was to find all available services and programs for each student to achieve their best at Garfield. The vision phrase became "All means *all*" in the last part of our first year together. This vision stimulated a close look at individual student progress as well as the programs and policies that provided achievement for all students, regardless of race, gender, socioeconomic status, or learning ability.

The first team, called "Dreamkeepers" (named after Gloria Ladson-Billings' 1996 book), served as a race relations focus group for Garfield, paying close attention to our changing consciousness about equity. This mixed-race team of teachers and parents conducted collaborative action research for equitable practices and examined institutionalized racism in schools. They began their research by reading Takaki's book *A Different Mirror* (1993); its focus on history from a multicultural perspective led to a plan to revise the History/Social Studies text so that those lessons reflected a truthful historical experience for the Latino, Asian, and African American students in our school. At two retreats, Dreamkeepers shared their personal stories of race relations and created pilot lessons to teach at each grade level in History/Social Studies. These lesson samples would be shared with the whole group in late summer. Our goal was to strengthen our school plan by weaving in a strategic plan for equity at Garfield that could be shared with all staff, parents, and students.

The second team, the Program Quality Review Team, connected work of other groups and led the charge to write the School Improvement Plan. The staff and parents learned to write measurable objectives for students, based on student data. They created plans of action for individual students, grade-level groups, whole-school groups, and target students. Academic growth, behavior expectations, participation in programs, and opportunities to learn in a culturally conscious atmosphere were all regarded in our processes of inquiry and planning.

A third group of staff and I, the Systems Leadership Team, participated in a district-level planning and training collaborative. We systematically brought information about assessments, data, and instruction back to the full staff. I found additional support in a regional group, Creating Equitable Bay Area Schools, that focused entirely on leadership for equity.

All groups began by looking at student work and disaggregated data. In every area that we examined, our essential questions centered around the following:

> What are the performance levels of all of our students?
> What more do our students need to know and be able to do?
> What instructional practices do we use to teach them?
> What will we do if they are not able to achieve?
> What resources are available to meet the needs of all of our
>   students?

The Second Year

As this story is written, we are beginning our second year together. All classroom teachers have returned to their positions. We began the year with 3 days of professional development and reviewed the hopes and dreams from the previous year. We observed that in just one year we had accomplished most of our wish list: We had come far in a relatively short period of time.

Our 3 days were planned around our need to work more deeply with our relationships with students, our work in equity, and our work with student data. On the first day of our professional development, we reflected on our successes of the first year and participated in training for Conflict Resolution instruction. We wanted to match our new rules of respect and responsibility with support for the skills needed to create a learning environment that is safe and personal for everyone. All teachers and parent representatives engaged in this full-day workshop, which prepared the staff to help students become more skilled in conflict management.

On day two of professional development, the Dreamkeepers shared the leadership of this session. Participants were asked to chose one square of fabric that best represented their ancestry and themselves and hang it on the wall. The staff took great pride in the quilt they had created. We then completed a survey (from *Unpacking the Knapsack of Privilege* [1999] by Peggy McIntosh and adapted by Glenn Singleton and Pam Noli) that demonstrated access by different racial and ethnic groups to various places and positions in our community. The participants scored themselves according to the access that they had to things such as shopping, group membership, leadership roles, or representation in the media. Staff members then stood in a line in the order of their scores on the survey: One end, the most privileged in the group, was white, and the other end was darker and darker brown to black. We noted that people of color are frequently left out of the picture in our history as well as in our institutions of power. Participants in the lower half of the line removed their quilt squares to represent the absence of their stories in history.

Dreamkeepers reviewed the pilot lessons that they had created while on retreat. Teachers met in teams to examine the History/Social Studies texts to find lessons that needed revision or expansion to secure the representation of people of color. As each grade-level group came up with an idea for broader inclusion, they replaced a square on the quilt. Teachers celebrated as they created truthful, accurate lessons that reflected all Americans for what they had contributed to our country's history. They joyfully placed the quilt pieces back, reweaving history for their peers, their students, and themselves. One of the Dreamkeepers, teacher Jane Steele, read her vision from the retreat:

> We are all here now—everyone has a history that is part of
> what made this country what it is today.
> We are all pieces of thread and woven together.
> If we leave out pieces, the textile gets bigger and bigger holes,
> but with all the threads we get a rich, intricate tapestry.
> We know that our history books don't include all those threads
> and, therefore, what we look at is very different.
> Every one of our students has a historical thread.
> Let it be seen, heard, felt, celebrated!

On the third day we began with an enhanced consciousness about equity. We looked at schoolwide data, using our essential questions listed above. All specialists presented their programs with focus on students with special needs. One by one, leaders of special services reviewed their services and gave examples of how they intended to serve all students. Special Day Class teachers, a Speech and Language therapist, the English Language Development director, Healthy Start and Twenty-first Century grant coordinators, the Literacy coach, and Reading Recovery teacher all reviewed their assistance and intervention programs for students needing services beyond regular classroom instruction. With an eye on equity and a heart for inclusion, the staff then reviewed individual and grade-level SAT-9 scores. In grade-level groups, they investigated content clusters for areas of weakness and strength and returned to the School Improvement Plan, created the previous May, to ensure that areas of instructional focus were still aligned with student needs. The staff had come light-years in knowing what a "measurable objective" might be for their students. They were able to quickly form target groups from the disaggregated data they were given and discuss the instructional strategies that would be most effective with their students. The feeling that we had come full circle in 3 days to extend our vision of "All means *all*" was reflected in the evaluation notes of the staff and parents.

Changing Beliefs—Changing Practice

As a result of our work together in one year, the beliefs of adults and children have shifted at Garfield. Teachers have begun to connect their practices with student outcomes because of an in-depth understanding of data. They see more clearly now the importance of accountability for all students and pose the question, "Is this happening because of race?" as a part of their assessment and planning. We have a more balanced representation of students in all programs, from Title I to Gifted and Talented Education. Students see themselves as able to reach for leadership positions that they had not previously sought. Parents ask more specific questions about their students' work and attend meetings to talk about instruction, both at home and at school, that is in response to their students' performance. In 2001, our test scores on four different measures, including the SAT-9, continued to rise in over half of all areas. We had paused to become thoughtful about our work and to plumb deeply into our values and our academic achievement as measured by traditional assessments, which continued to grow as well. The most significant exception is the reading performance of Latino students. They have become our new target for improvement.

In retrospect, I suspect that I learned most about constructing an equitable learning environment in our school for children and adults by opening up the opportunities to learn for others, rather than embracing a top-down leadership style. How could I know how to create the best system of instructing a majority population of children of color without embracing and engaging experts in the field to weave the tapestry of learning? Those experts at Garfield have become the staff, the community, the families, and the children themselves.

WINTERBURN SCHOOL (K–8)
by Del Bouck

AUTHOR'S NOTE. As a new principal, I was uncomfortable with the expectations that I placed upon myself. I expected to be the problem-solver and to be involved in every aspect of school life. My belief was that if I could do all of this, I would be a successful leader. I realized that I could not do it alone. I knew it would take a team to do the job, and the notion of sharing this responsibility was of prime importance to me in order to succeed.

As I look back now, I can see that what I thought initially to be "shared leadership" was very different than what we see evidenced at Winterburn School today. My original assumptions were quite naive in that I saw shared leadership as a vehicle used solely for the delegation of responsibility to staff members. However, through the process of working together, staff members developed a sense of "I can do this." As this story is told, these same individuals actively seek responsibility for initiatives within the school.

Our School
Today, Winterburn School is a healthy, thriving, and successful school. The inadequacies that were once felt have been replaced with feelings of success and assurance, all as a result of those that share in the leadership process. We believed we could change and, through the course of time, we did.

When I first received the news of my appointment to the principalship of Winterburn School, I felt both the excitement and apprehension that comes with the challenge of a somewhat complex and diverse school. Having been the assistant principal for the previous 2 years, I thought that I had developed a realistic insight into the culture of the school.

Winterburn School, however, was annexed into the Edmonton Public School system during a major city expansion. Overnight, Winterburn became a "city school in a country setting" and found itself struggling to make the transition into the culture of Edmonton Public Schools. As a result of its lacklustre reputation, many families in the closest neighborhoods did not consider sending their children to the school.

A great majority of the students were bused to this educational site due to its remote location. They came from all socioeconomic backgrounds, extending from the unfortunate to the wealthy, an interesting mix that provides many opportunities for learning from one another. Our school struggled with finding its new cultural identity. At times, this frustration would evidence itself in the form of defiant students, angry parents, and disillusioned teachers.

While our school's mission was "to develop each student into a responsible, knowledgeable, and successful citizen through a partnership involving staff, parents, community, and the students themselves," it was really no different from such statements in other schools. We needed to face the challenge of creating and implementing a mission that all stakeholders would embrace.

Our Journey

The journey began as a process of trial and error that involved building, tearing down, and rebuilding. We now see it as a journey of introspective change that instilled the need for transparency and trust. This process allowed all of us to observe, interact, and experiment with each other's vulnerability. This period of reformation was about learning how to give up power in order to empower.

To this very day, we can still visualize ourselves during our first staff conversations in which we acknowledged the fact that we really didn't totally understand all of the ramifications of shared leadership but felt that it was something that we needed to explore in order to improve student achievement. We would need to lean on one another and learn from each other. At times the reaction was mixed, with the more pessimistic teachers stating that they "had enough work to do" and that they didn't need to waste their time in study groups learning about all of this "philosophical stuff."

Through these frank discussions, it became apparent that much of the discontent felt by the staff was due to a lack of understanding of their role as a staff member and a lack of responsibility for mentoring one another. We came to the conclusion that it was certainly time to renovate our relationships by tearing down these relational walls. What we thought were walls built up due to the personal egos of individual teachers was really a unified wall of frustration built upon the consistent challenges of student behavior that teachers faced. It was through this thinking process that we came to the understanding that collective success would require collective responsibility.

Constructing Change

The way we worked as a staff needed to change. In an attempt to break down barriers of mistrust and blame, we began our team meetings by giving "kudos" to one another, a process in which teachers took turns giving praise to one another for jobs well done. Within one month, evidences of this exercise could be seen infiltrating classrooms. Teachers began to feel more comfortable talking about instructional practices.

In the beginning, we saw a great need for teachers to get together and talk about general practices in teaching, school and district practices, and classroom discipline in order to foster collegial relationships. Formally, we established a basis for safe discussion through studying Fullan and Hargreaves's book, *What's Worth Fighting for in Your School* (1996) during our monthly study groups. These study groups gave way to research and conversations on topics such as continuity in school discipline, dealing with difficult students, and developing skill, in working with parents.

Monthly study-group sessions moved to weekly sessions centering on a schoolwide instructional focus. Teachers began to change the way they related to one another. Strong collegial relationships developed that supported teachers in focusing on high student achievement. Action research became the avenue for developing "group-centered" leadership. Teachers reviewed student work and researched related topics. Study groups, action research, reflection, and dialogue enabled us to stop doing some of the things that we were doing, continue doing others things, and start doing some new things.

The Leadership Team

A significant change in the way we operated would be the implementation of a leadership team. We saw this as an opportunity to engage teachers in the leadership process who already were positive relationship builders, used innovative teaching practices, and demonstrated an ability to engage others in collaboration.

One of the major struggles encountered when setting up the "Lead Team" was our own perceptions of what leadership is. This Lead Team became another avenue for us to be transparent in the process of building leadership capacity in the rest of the Winterburn teaching team. The Lead Team met weekly and assumed specific "portfolios" or responsibilities.

Lead Team members modeled these five assumptions:

- Leadership is the reciprocal learning processes that enable participants in community to construct meaning leading toward a shared purpose.
- Leading is about learning.
- Everyone has the potential and the right to serve as a leader.
- Leading is a shared endeavor.
- Leadership requires the redistribution of power and authority. (Lambert, 1998b, pp. 8–9)

Members challenged ineffective practices and inquired into more effective ways of meeting students' academic needs. They played an integral role in mentoring and facilitating staff discussions and writing about the successes of the whole school.

New Beliefs

While there were still some teachers who struggled with relinquishing the old hierarchical order of leadership and the perceived convenience it brought, beliefs began to change. Staff began to see themselves as teachers to all students. They gave up the convenience of handing over discipline problems to administration and began dealing with them personally. No longer was collaboration seen as sharing lesson plans, photocopying for one another, and working together with a buddy class; action research was no longer seen as taking away time from classroom planning and preparation; and feelings of responsibility to share in the leadership process increased.

Not only do teachers and staff members truly share the leadership, they also see themselves as responsible for building and extending leadership capacity in one another. Notably, our relationships are now based on communication that can be described as a continuous process of professional development. Team members have become highly motivated to take on innovations as a result of a new perspective they have gained or a new skill learned for the purpose of enhancing student achievement. As a result of the commitment that team members now feel, we thought it necessary to develop a set of guiding principles. These responsibility statements set the course for new teachers joining our staff and are used as a tool for dialogue in encouraging continued commitment from all team members to the shared leadership process.

CREATING POSITIVE TEAM RELATIONSHIPS
As a Team Member, I am responsible for:
1. Recognizing that we are a learning community in which all Team Members are leaders
2. Communicating, dispensing knowledge, asking for clarification and unknown information, listening to other team members with interest, reading all e-mails and written notices
3. Developing and supporting a culture for self-reflection that may include collaborative planning, peer coaching, study groups, action research, and reflective writing
4. Enabling other team members to be self-evaluative and introspective, leading toward self- and shared responsibility

5. Promoting open-mindedness and flexibility in others; inviting multiple perspectives and interpretations as a means of challenging all assumptions and forming new actions
6. Promoting collaborative decision making that provides options to meet the diverse individual and group needs of the school community
7. Engaging colleagues in identifying and acknowledging problems; acting with others to frame problems and seek resolutions; anticipating situations that may cause recurrent problems
8. Supporting new and student teachers
9. Working with colleagues to develop programs and policies that take a holistic view of children's development. This developmental view translates into concern for all children in the school.

Success at Winterburn

As a result of continuous dialogue, teachers saw the need for changing their approaches and practices. The Winterburn teaching team worked together to create a schoolwide instructional focus:

> Through the use of a variety of teaching strategies, Winterburn School will continue a schoolwide effort to increase student comprehension across the curriculum. Comprehension will be measured by the 3, 6, 9 Provincial Achievement Exams, District Highest Level of Achievement Tests, and daily dynamic assessment using the six strands (listen, speak, read, write, view, represent) of the Language Arts curriculum.

This schoolwide instructional focus gave a purpose for all teachers to ensure that they were focusing on comprehension in all curriculum areas. We observed a schoolwide increase among all students in the numbers reaching the acceptable level in language arts achievement tests. Most growth took place in our schoolwide area of focus. Each teacher and support staff member has become focused on his or her own responsibility for "sharing in the caring" and performing as an active member of the team.

Evidence of staff satisfaction is documented in an Edmonton Public Schools district survey wherein Winterburn staff indicated one hundred percent satisfaction with the learning experience provided for all students, with the focus on student achievement.

We now realize that everyone has the potential and the right to work as a leader. Parents now see themselves as partners in a trust relationship with all team members. This is evident in the 300 plus volunteers that assist our teachers throughout the school year. Parents know, understand, and support our vision to assist their children in developing to their fullest potential. The school's broad base of leadership also extends to business partners who have taken up our cause for ensuring the "best educational experience possible for our kids." Together with our parents they have created a strong financial support base allowing for value-added programming.

Winterburn is a "happening school" these days. We see ourselves as fulfilling our mission "to develop each student into a responsible, knowledgeable, and successful citizen." Now we are challenged by a lack of space due to increasing enrollment. A school that was once held ransom by ongoing struggles now stands as a true testimony to what can happen when a group of professionals choose to exercise their right to perform as a *team*.

WYANDOTTE HIGH SCHOOL
by Arthur "Gus" Jacobs

Background

Wyandotte High School is housed in a building that is a historical and community landmark built in 1936. Walking into the front hall of this stately building, one is greeted by two large stone fireplaces that stand as a monument to the era in which this masterpiece was constructed. On the second floor, the ornate library, crafted out of the finest wood by master craftsmen of the day, has the ambiance of an exclusive university.

While the university-like setting promised a great hall of learning, the reality in the late 1980s through the mid-90s was actually something quite different. What had stood as a lighthouse of academic and athletic success had become an urban high school that had lost its focus. Student achievement and graduation rates had declined dramatically. Adults in the building were either longtime veterans near retirement or new teachers who received their first job offer and didn't know the full story. The attitude of many teachers was hoping most of their students didn't show up for class, which made their job easier and "besides, they were the troublemakers anyway."

Since this was an urban high school with a very high minority population—mostly African Americans with a growing Latino population—many in the school thought that "these students" not only wouldn't learn, but also couldn't learn.

One teacher reflected on his more than 20 years at Wyandotte and spoke of how he was experiencing a growing absentee rate of his own, not coming to work because of his cynicism and disengagement. This teacher says that he "just had to get away from such a negative and dys-functional environment." This type of teacher behavior manifested itself in different ways throughout the lives of the adults at Wyandotte. The school had become too hard to deal with at the building or district level.

As in any school, there were a few bright spots created by faculty members who had unique and special talents, but the bright spots were fading as the environment deteriorated. These talented individuals were also finding it difficult to continue in such an environment, and if they had the option to leave, they would exercise that option.

The New Principal

Upon his appointment in 1997, the new principal, Walt Thompson, quickly assessed the school as being "in crisis." The crisis was the num-ber of students not achieving and literally not being there. The dropout rate measured from 9th grade through 12th grade was over 50 percent. Students were simply not completing school. Expectations for students who stayed were very low. Walt remembers when he made his first visit to meet the faculty and staff:

> My first impression was that this was a beaten down staff. It was
> one hot day. They were tired. They didn't trust anyone. Yet I
> thought I saw a glimmer of hope. But, there was doom and gloom
> from the longtimers. They looked like warmed-over soup. I talked
> about hope, reform, and restructuring. They thought I looked like
> the last two guys. I left them with a question: "How would you
> like to have a school that you would be proud to send your chil-
> dren to?"

When school started that year, Walt realized that curriculum and instruction was not a part of what assistant principals—or anyone else—did. Administrators stayed in their offices. Teachers stayed in their rooms. The students had the halls.

After meeting with department chairs, assistant principals, other teach-ers, and some parents, Walt learned that the biggest concern from all sources was the same: attendance and tardies. With an enrollment of 1,270 students, the office was logging an average of 1,000 tardies per day. Walt observed, "Kids came to school when they damn well pleased."

Walt asked the metal shop teacher to pull together a discipline com-mittee and come up with a plan of action. The committee worked with the National Education Association to waive contract agreements by find-ing time to enact the plan. In the meantime, teachers were at their doors, assistant principals were in the halls, and Walt was "all over the place." Announcements over the school intercom continued to ask for student support. Walt summarized the effort this way:

> It was significant that we took on one thing and that we were successful. We were very focused. End of the first year we reduced tardies from 1000 per day to an average of 29 per day. Teachers felt pretty good about it. We worked the sweeps of the hallways, and the teachers worked hard. First success we had. We celebrated.

As the tardy and absentee rate improved, and students were in class, how to teach them effectively became the next hurdle. Teaching throughout the building was mediocre, highlighted by what might be called "survival strategies" on how to keep a group of unmotivated, potentially unruly students under control without a major incident. Opportunities had to be developed for learning teaching strategies that focused on engaging students in their work and making that work meaningful.

As grants were being written to gain resources for professional development, the principal was now keeping two conversations alive: one on teaching and learning and one on attendance. "We had to learn how to teach all of our kids," declared Walt.

First Things First

Near the end of Walt's first year at Wyandotte, the district (with 22,000 students in 43 schools) announced that it had embraced a districtwide reform initiative called "First Things First." First Things First is a framework for school improvement developed by Jim Connell, director of the Institute for Research and Reform in Education. It focuses school improvement on seven critical features.

For students:
- Lower student-to-adult ratios
- Provide continuity of care (sustainable relationships)
- Set high, clear, and fair academic and conduct standards
- Provide enriched and diverse opportunities to learn, to perform, and to be recognized

For adults:
- Assure collective responsibility
- Provide instructional autonomy and supports
- Allow for flexible allocation of available resources

The district planned to phase in the renewal framework of First Things First over a period of 3 years, with the Wyandotte cluster (one high school, two middle schools, and seven elementary schools) being the first cluster.

The commitment to this new initiative at the district level resulted in early dismissal every Wednesday afternoon to provide 3 hours of professional development and conversation about teaching and learning. A School Improvement Facilitator would be assigned to each school (funded with foundation monies). Small learning communities were being developed.

Continued Progress at Wyandotte

With the challenge of the first year ending in a celebration of focused success around improved class attendance and a renewed focus on instruction and student engagement, trust among the staff was beginning to grow. The feeling of hope was being rekindled. Some teachers were feeling that what they said and did was starting to make a difference and was influencing the direction of the school. At the end of Walt's first year, 2 teachers left due to retirement and 2 others left due to a spouse's job change. The year before, 20 teachers had left.

The second year focused on involvement and the continued building of trust that had started the first year. Walt's role was about sustaining the conversation on what the school believed and what the core values were or were going to be. A plan for implementing the seven critical features of First Things First had to be developed.

Although progress was being made, there continued to be a lack of trust. As the focus on major reforms grew this became an even more difficult task. Walt described the task he faced:

> We had to decide what we believed. It was about our core values. There was little trust left in the district. I had to show my core values. . . . Instead of leading from the top, I led from the rear. . . . We kept our core values as a constant part of the conversation. With the victories that we were having, we patted backs a lot as a whole group; group celebrations, ice cream socials, putting accomplishments up at faculty meetings—people stood and cheered.

The School Improvement Facilitator, Mary Stewart, became a quasi member of the faculty. Her specific role was to assist with the school improvement activities around First Things First. She became part of the culture. Mary talks about how both she and Walt embraced and honored people. She planned stakeholder meetings, with Walt attending some-times. Both Walt and Mary asked strategic questions that kept the con-versation alive. But more important, the conversations were being taken seriously, and Wyandotte staff had seized the opportunity to implement First Things First in their own way.

Small Learning Communities

After the second year, Wyandotte became eight small learning commu-nities (SLC), a decision developed and supported by the majority of the staff. Students stay in their SLC through their high school experience, thus remaining with a limited number of teachers over the 4 years. Schedules are designed to allow core teachers to have common planning on a regular basis so that issues of the SLC and specific students can be discussed and planned for. The SLC has become the main unit of contact for each student at Wyandotte. The effectiveness of this plan to provide a caring place for students is illustrated by the following experience:

> A visitor to the building was discussing the restructuring of the school with a group of teachers from one of the SLCs during their collaborative planning time. A secretary from the school office came on the intercom in the planning room asking what class one of their students would be in during 4th period. Five teachers responded in unison, all knowing where the particular student was during a time when he was not in any of their own classrooms.

This is a clear demonstration of collective responsibility and a commen-tary on continuity of care for students being served.

School committees of staffing, budgeting, programs, facilities, and discipline are charged with meeting on their own to do the work of the school. The committees have representatives from each of the eight SLCs and do business by a majority vote. However, very little voting is needed as a result of full and thorough discussion of issues. In addition, each assistant principal has two SLCs with whom they work closely. Assistant principals no longer have offices in the main office area but are now located in the area of the building where their SLCs reside.

The small learning communities have taken their role of being respon-sible for the education of 160–180 students seriously. At the end of the first year of the new SLC structure, one group asked to meet with the principal about a concern they had for one of their own members, a new teacher. The ineffectiveness of this member was having an adverse effect on their community. It was clearly not a good fit for the community or the teacher. The SLC members asked to have the teacher removed and reassigned to nonteaching duties for the remainder of the year. The SLC developed a plan to teach the classes without adding additional staff until they had the opportunity to hire a new member. SLCs were experiencing the opportunity, and the responsibility, of improving what they do for their students. They also had the authority to do it.

Evidence that the learning communities are working includes the fact that it is now the primary structure of the school (instead of departments), authority and responsibility have been devolved into the community, faculty are located in the same area of the school so communication is easier, scheduling and planning is based upon this structure, and consistent cultural messages declare that "Wyandotte works."

Even though Walt would say that the process of improvement had already started at Wyandotte, he feels the school is supported by the district's focus on school improvement through First Things First. The district gave clear-cut features of school improvement as goals to drive actions. The key to the continued growth at the school is the web of trust that Walt has promoted and encouraged to grow and flourish.

> Everyone has to win. The kid has to win. The parent has to win. The teacher has to win. The system has to win. Parents in the 1950s trusted the system. Somehow the system did not treat these people right. The system was designed to teach 10–20 percent of the people. The parents we have now are the 85+ percent that the system was not kind to. We had to win that trust.

Celebrations

Trust does exist today at Wyandotte among parents, students, and staff. It's not a finished agenda, and it never will be. But it is the issue that is a primary agenda, first of the principal and now of the many leaders in the school. The power of promoting an issue, like trust, is much greater when many fill the role of leader.

From 1997 to 2001, the dropout rate at Wyandotte dropped from 28.8 percent to 7.3 percent. In 1997, 44 percent of entering 9th graders stayed to graduate; in 2001, 70.4 percent graduated. The percentage of students earning passing grades in all subjects has risen from 66.2 percent to 82.8 percent. And on the MAT-7 the 10th- to 11th-grade cohort made a 2.4 point NCE gain in reading (while other high schools in the district experienced a decline). The district has moved reforms to the next clusters, hopeful of improving results for all schools.

By the way, the teacher mentioned earlier who had growing cynicism and disengagement has crafted a different route in his work. He now has hope. He believes in the children the school serves. He became a small learning community coordinator and this past year was appointed to the position of assistant principal. He's an assistant who focuses on teaching and learning and caring for the children in the two communities that he serves. Wyandotte is about changing the lives of young people and giving them hope for the future. The adults there have also found hope for the future.

SCHOOL STORY ANALYSIS

The stories reported by principals and professors give hope that schools can reinvent themselves in ways that positively affect student learning and teacher practice. While still on a journey, each school has made significant progress and, even more important, has a clear sense of purpose and efficacy about future improvements. Because each school is unique in terms of its history, culture, and context, the paths taken vary. Yet there are some commonalities worth noting.

Each author referred to constructivist theory as an aid in deriving meaning from the work of school improvement. The case study principals seemed purposeful about sharing leadership, developing a common vision, and generating collective responsibility for solving tough problems. Conversation, professional learning, and reflection were key strategies in helping faculties coalesce and grow.

In low-achieving schools, adult relationships can become fractured and dysfunctional, so that insufficient will and skill exist to improve learning conditions. While each case study touched on the need to create a climate of trust within the school for teachers, students, and the larger parent community, Glenlawn elevated the need for building positive relationships, adopting it as part of its motto of "relationships and relevant learning." Employing another approach, Wyandotte created Small Learning Communities that fostered both trust and cohesion, creating a more personal learning environment for students and a vehicle for teacher collaboration. The various cases illustrated that relationship building takes time, is labor intensive, and derives from shared experiences that cannot be rushed or simulated. Real work on improving teacher practice and increasing student learning led to more healthy and productive relationships.

At the same time as faculty and students were engaged in the difficult work of creating new relationships, these schools placed a high premium on professional learning for teachers and staff. The processes they use differed, and in fact much can be learned from the ways each school approached adult learning. Garfield's Cycle of Inquiry, characterized by collecting data, developing a plan, enacting the plan, and assessing effectiveness, empowered teachers to take an active role in their own development and the development of the school. In addition, the quilt activity they engaged in helped colleagues understand what it meant to be a person of color and what happened if students of color did not see their history represented in the curriculum. Finally, their analysis of school-wide data gave them insights into instruction, equity issues, and student needs that they could not have gained in other ways. Each of the schools used evidence as a centerpiece for improvement.

Another common feature was the schools' use of committee structure to achieve their improvement goals. Most schools have committees as an organizational feature, but these committees were different. The Dreamkeepers at Garfield kept issues of equity and achievement before the faculty and imbued committee meetings with meaning and knowledge so that the lines between meetings and professional development became blurred. The Advocacy Committee at Glenlawn kept the needs of students at the forefront and allowed for new programmatic designs to emerge. And the Lead Team at Winterburn, through the development of a set of guiding principles, enabled the faculty to establish new, more productive norms at the school. These norms engaged the faculty in reciprocal processes for learning, decision making, and action.

Finally, the importance of inquiry and reflection cannot be overstated. For most of the schools, the asking of complex, self-reflective questions became the vehicle for renewing a commitment to student learning and equity. Engelhard Elementary School advanced a set of framing questions to guide its work and improve its practice. Those questions did not allow for superficial answers but rather prompted faculty and their parent partners to examine problems deeply and to stretch themselves, to reach for more than they thought they could accomplish. Garfield also used essential questions to guide its journey, as did Glenlawn. Their use of inquiry stands in stark contrast to the norm among educators and policymakers to jump to a solution before truly understanding the problem.

In each of the cases the principals set a remarkable example for sharing leadership, developing leadership in others, and trusting their teacher colleagues to make decisions based on what is best for students. All maintained a sense of optimism and efficacy, and none doubted that once they embarked on a journey, they would succeed. Principal Peggy Bryan at Sherman Oaks Charter School said it this way:

> Passion and commitment, if cultivated and nurtured, will ultimately override exhaustion, confusion, and inertia. A journey that energizes and empowers every single staff member and maintains every single student in our line of sight will endure.

What have these stories told us about constructivist change? We would suggest the following points:

- Someone (usually the principal) or ones (an improvement facilitator, consultant, teacher-leader, assistant principal) need to provoke a system to initiate change.
- When we learn ourselves through change, we commit to the outcomes.
- Such learning is constructivist in nature, involving reflection, dialogue and conversation, inquiry, and action.
- Learning communities among adults are prerequisite to deep learning experiences and equitable outcomes for children.
- Vision and values are the compasses of change.
- Critical incidents, turning points or fluctuations in the system (e.g., provocative data, school reorganization, declining enrollment) can be used to initiate self-organizing behaviors in an organization. That is, people begin to entertain new ways of doing things.
- Self-organizing behaviors evoke acts of leadership throughout the system.
- And, as Bryan suggests above, "A journey that energizes and empowers every single staff member and maintains every single student in our line of sight will endure."

The role played by the district or system in the cases described in this chapter varied significantly. Support ranged from excellent conceptual leadership and support in Kansas City to regional network support in Winnipeg, value-based leadership in San Leandro, and benign neglect in Campbell. As we will see in Chapter 7 as we examine the larger context, a constructivist district can provide a positive multiplier effect on school improvement.

THE SCHOOL DISTRICT AS INTERDEPENDENT LEARNING COMMUNITY

MORGAN DALE LAMBERT
MARY E. GARDNER

Why doesn't the district move out of our way so we can get on with our restructuring work?

They block everything we try to do . . . because it might rock the boat for other schools.

We feel like we'd like to build a moat around our school! [but . . .]We need their help!

> *Feedback comments by participants in a*
> *statewide symposium for restructuring school teams*
> *Anaheim, California, May 1994*

The main challenge of our time is to create and nurture sustainable communities.

> *Fritjof Capra*
> From the Parts to the Whole: Systems Thinking in
> Ecology and Education *(1994, p. 31)*

You think because you understand one, you understand two, because one and one make two. But you must also understand "and."

> *Ancient Sufi teaching, quoted by Margaret Wheatley*
> Leadership and the New Science *(1992, p. 7)*

None of us is as smart as all of us. [There is] not enough side-by-side accountability. Team members have to be accountable to one another, not just to the boss.

> *Ken Blanchard*
> *Herbst Theater, San Francisco,*
> *March 21, 2001*

Schoolhouse by schoolhouse reform just isn't going to do the job. Until you've got district capacity, you really can't pull off sustainable school-wide reforms.

> *Phil Schlechty (1998)*

Until recently, scenes in the long-running drama of school reform in the United States have tended to focus mainly on the individual school as the locus of change, with the principal and teachers as the lead actors. School districts (and states) have generally played mixed roles, retaining many traditional command and control "director" functions but relegated to the control booth and behind-the-scenes parts in the reform action on stage.

But the script is being rewritten, because there is a larger audience now (education is a high-profile national issue) and it includes a broader array of critics who are not satisfied with the performance. New directors and producers have volunteered to compose the lines and prescribe the roles, many of them from state capitols and from the White House.

The newly dramatized themes are "high standards for student achievement," "rigorous standards and accountability," "competition for recognition of success," and somewhat contradictory demands for both "coherence" and "choice among options (vouchers, charters)." The impetus for shaping standards and accountability systems and reform policies has tended to be at state levels, although the rhetoric at the federal level has also been impassioned and influential (e.g., the 2000 presidential race and the Bush administration policies). The reform mandates from all levels above the school have stressed standardized testing (mainly in "basic skills" areas), public display of results, and incentives and rewards, censure and sanctions for results.

Mandates . . . tight scripting . . . autocratic directing . . . these props don't create a hospitable context for the constructivist leader at either school or district level. Implied district roles in mandated reform of this kind are generally of a hierarchical character (directing, monitoring, accounting), but they also stress support responsibilities, options for implementation, and selective "local control."

Fortunately, there are other themes, story lines, and venues for the drama of school change, and they are attracting critical as well as popular attention on the action stage. Research on brain function and adult as well as child learning, on authentic assessment and feedback systems, on how complex social organizations (such as schools and districts) effect sustained change, and on the nature of effective leadership—insights from these sources have complicated the lives of the "producers" of simplistic one-act school reform plays.

This book concerns the leadership system needed for school and school-system change that is more complex but much more likely to produce reform and renewal that is powerful and sustainable. Other chapters deal with the underlying theory and with practice at the school and university levels; this chapter applies constructivist leadership principles to the broader school district learning community.

THE SCHOOL DISTRICT AS ECOSYSTEM

Recognition of the importance of district support linkages and the systemic nature of school change is an important strategic insight; it is also essential that the context for local school renewal be made even broader and deeper and that the linkages be seen as reciprocal. We develop in this chapter the thesis that the fully functioning school district must become a learning community in the same sense that each school must form its own learning community culture. The district is a larger entity (ecosystem) than the individual schools, but it is also interconnected in that same "web of relationships in which all life processes depend on one another" (Capra, 1993, p. 24). And that web includes each of the individual schools and school communities in the district—all connected and interdependent, whether or not they explicitly recognize it.

The ecological principles enunciated by Capra (described and expanded in more detail in Chapter 2) can be adapted to virtually all forms of collaborative learning group interaction—cooperative learning teams, collaborative teaching groups, and schools and school districts as congruent learning communities. Rephrased to fit the school district when it is viewed as a constructivist learning community, Capra's principles might look like this:

Members of a dynamic school district are interconnected in a web of relationships in which all interactive processes depend on one another. The success of the whole school district depends on the success of its individual schools and participants, while the success of each individual person and unit depends on the success of the broader community (district) as a whole. Individuals and groups, schools and the district environment in which they operate adapt to one another—they coevolve.

From this perspective, schools are not seen as dependent on benevolent district support but as interconnected in a web of reciprocally supportive relationships with not only the district but also with other schools, networks, the community, and so forth. The web has a fractal-like character, with the relationships among student learners, adult learners, school communities, and district communities all sharing many qualities. And those qualities bear a very close resemblance to the principles of ecology—interdependence, network patterns, feedback loops, cooperation, partnerships, and flexibility.

As this ecological orientation to school change grows in its influence on practitioners, it will become increasingly clear that the way the school district operates must also change in congruent ways. Site-based management, shared leadership, teacher empowerment, and the evolving commitment to equitable whole-school and whole-system change—all of these promising innovations make urgent the need to rethink the traditional hierarchical organization structure. It is our hope that constructivist leadership principles will inform the new possibilities—that the old hierarchies will be replaced by more flexible structures, by interdependent networks that rest on reciprocal relationships, by enabling processes.

It is important to note that there is rigor and a form of pragmatism built into any self-organizing system. Results drive the process of change and evolution in schools as well as in biological systems.

THE TRADITIONAL PARADIGM

Before starting construction of a new set of approaches, it will be helpful to remind ourselves of traditional school district structures and operations. Most district functions are currently drawn from the managerial and bureaucratic domains—allocation and management of resources (money, materials, and personnel); collection and dissemination of information; monitoring, evaluation, and accountability; strategic planning; development of policies and regulations; and coordination of departments, sites, and programs (viewed primarily as discrete components, all arrayed in boxes in a vertically aligned "table of organization"). In many enlightened districts, there may be substantive provision for community and school involvement in strategic planning and decision making, but the participant role is still seen as that of contributor rather than reciprocal partner in a collaborative endeavor. Even in districts in which the "decentralized decision making, site-based management" model has been embraced, there is the tendency to assign functions to discrete elements—textbook budgets to schools, monitoring and accounting to district departments, goal setting and policy making to school boards. School boards may suggest in their superintendent search brochures that they are looking for an "instruction-oriented systemic change agent," but résumés that boast of business management experience, fiscal skills, and a commitment to tough-minded accountability still float to the top.

In contrast, let us now envision what roles, structures, and processes would look like in a community that is animated by constructivist thinking.

THE SUPERINTENDENT AS CONSTRUCTIVIST LEADER

When asked who the school district's "leader" is, most people would identify the superintendent, even in a constructivist district. But they would probably add caveats about the role being shared and might submit descriptors to clarify the role. In addition to the usual managerial leadership functions, the shrewd observer might stress these five functions (the first three adapted from Senge's *The Fifth Discipline*, 1990):

> *Steward* of the vision, values, and purpose of the district. This requires that the superintendent be focused, curious, and courageous. He or she is continually ready to ask the essential questions and to resist political agendas that would divert attention from teaching and learning.
>
> *Designer* of the enabling structures and processes that support dialogic, inquiring, sustaining, and partnering conversations.
>
> *Teacher* of the board, community, district staff, principals, and leadership teams about teaching and learning and dimensions of community.

And, we would add:

> *Learner* with the board, community, district and school staff, and students. He or she listens, converses, reflects, and makes sense of the world in interaction with new ideas, information and evidence,

and other people—and strives consistently to model this learning orientation.

Participant in the array of reciprocal processes that give texture to the culture of collaborative inquiry that is growing in the school, district, and community. He or she recognizes that roles such as steward, designer, and teacher are shared by many co-leaders and that they are multidimensional.

The new roles expected of superintendents are complex and challenging, and they will not necessarily be embraced by incumbents who are comfortable in an older hierarchical tradition nor by constituents who need someone to blame when things are not "right." Murphy (1994) studied the reactions of Kentucky superintendents who had a decentralized school-restructuring program imposed on them by state law. Most felt that authority had been removed from their office, but responsibility and accountability were left behind. Even those who supported the changes reported that much more systematic support and a longer time-line of preparation and implementation were needed.

A fairly common strategy for new superintendents moving into districts that have an evident need for restructuring is to take strong, directive leadership action initially and then to transition into a more collaborative decentralized mode at a later date. In an October 2000 interview, Superintendent Jim Sweeney explained with satisfaction that he and his Sacramento, California, City School District Board were at that point ready to move into Phase II of their strategic reform plan. Much more authority and responsibility were to be moved to the site level, with variable amounts of district supervision (what he calls "differentiated autonomy"), dependent on the demonstrated "readiness" to operate independently. Peter Negroni, school superintendent in Springfield, Massachusetts, writes in *Schools That Learn* (Senge et al., 2000, pp. 425–432) about a similar "pilgrimage." The title for Negroni's story encapsulates the whole message: "The Superintendent's Progress: Moving from 'Lone Ranger' to Lead Learner in an Urban School District." The district stories that appear in this chapter describe other strategies, styles, and timetables.

Regardless of short-term implementation tactics, it is imperative that the district's superintendent believe in, promote, and model the reciprocal processes that are at the core of constructivism. But it is equally clear that the role changes may come slowly and encounter resistance, that these changes will evolve within the context of shared participation with other constructivist leaders.

THE DISTRICT AS INTERDEPENDENT COMMUNITY

The basic characteristics of participantship and leadership described in Chapters 2–6 in reference to schools apply as well to the whole set of people who provide district office services, not just the superintendent. Following a study entitled "The Role of the School District in School Improvement," Louis (1989) identified two correlates of productive support—"high engagement" (frequent interaction and communication, mutual coordination and reciprocal influence, and some shared goals and objectives) and "low bureaucratization" (absence of extensive rules and regulations governing the relationship).

In order to achieve that kind of supportive relationship, it is our thesis that the district organization must be redesigned to become the same kind of self-organizing, self-renewing system that is being proposed for schools, one that imports free energy from the environment and exports entropy, providing both "positive feedback and disequilibrium" (Wheatley, 1992, p. 78). Its primary service would be to support the needs of schools and the formation of connections among schools and with the community, providing whatever guidance, resources, and expertise it can to meet those needs—with both the needs and the strategies to meet them being collaboratively determined and carried out by collegial partners. The district must assist in facilitating the appropriate mix of freedom, dissonance, guidance, resources, opportunity, and support needed by schools to grow and evolve. And the support must be delivered in the spirit of reciprocity, for the schools and district are coevolving. The school stories in Chapter 6 and the district stories and vignettes that follow in this chapter are exemplars of such constructive partnerships.

In describing traditional district functions and current political pressures, we identified accountability as a high priority—one about which schools often feel anxiety and resentment. Paradoxically, the commitment to a particular approach to "accountability" could possibly provide a thread that can help pull together the traditional and the constructivist patterns of successful school districts. But it would not be the old model of centralized and standardized "bean-counting." Accountability in the constructivist glossary has much more to do with responsibility, self-monitoring, critical reflection on data (especially dissonant data), dialogue with "critical friends," other forms of reciprocal feedback, collaborative action research, and the internalization of evaluative criteria—the kinds of processes that sustain a healthy, self-renewing organization.

In "Reframing the School Reform Agenda: Developing Capacity for School Transformation," Darling-Hammond (1993) declares:

> The foundation of genuine accountability . . . is the capacity of individual schools: (1) to organize themselves to prevent students from falling through the cracks; (2) to create means for continual collegial inquiry (in which hard questions are posed regarding what needs to change in order for individuals and groups of students to succeed); (3) to use authority responsibly to make the changes necessary. . . . It will occur only if we build an inquiry ethic, a community of discourse in the school that is focused on students and their needs rather than on the implementation of rules and procedures. (p. 760)

The responsibility for building that kind of capacity for self-monitoring and an ethic of student-centered inquiry represents perhaps the greatest challenge for school districts today—one that warrants a fresh, deeper look at assessment and accountability.

A CONSTRUCTIVIST PERSPECTIVE ON STANDARDS, ASSESSMENT, AND ACCOUNTABILITY

> All schools for miles and miles around must take a special test,
> To see who's such and such, to see which school's the best
> If our small school does not do well, then it will be torn down,
> And you will have to go to school in dreary Flobbertown.
> Not Flobbertown! we shouted, and we shuddered at the name
> For everyone in Flobbertown does everything the same.
>
> *Dr. Suess,*
> Hooray for Diffendoofer Day, *1998*

For both better and worse, the "Standards and Accountability" themes are central to almost all of the current major educational reform and improvement initiatives. Horror stories abound about the hazards associated with narrow-minded, quick-fix, homogenizing approaches to accountability "systems." Educators and students around the country are indeed dreading the prospect of learning in a "dreary Flobbertown." If Flobbertown Elementary School were located in California, for example, they would be overwhelmed by hundreds of standards and over 9,000 benchmarks! Even the strong advocate of rigorous assessment, James Popham, was moved to issue a call to action on that topic at the 2001 conference of the American Educational Research Association (AERA). His clarion call, *Dereliction Discontinued: How AERA Can Help Deter Today's Misuse of High-Stakes Testing,* was for researchers to attempt to influence policy makers to reshape the accountability movement.

In the spirit of constructivism, this section of the book reinforces the effort to make the accountability movement more "accountable" for its impact on authentic learning of all students and on sustainable and equitable school/district reform. We add our voice to Fullan and Hargreaves's proposal that "It is time we had a new kind of accountability in education—one that gets back to the moral basics of caring, serving, empowering and learning" (1998, p. 46).

Current norms of practice seem to rest on the assumption that meaning and knowledge are defined by external policy, to be implemented in a compliant fashion at the local level. In contrast, promising practices from a constructivist point of view proclaim that meaning and knowledge are best generated through reciprocal processes that engage the learners themselves as well as their teachers. Figure 7.1 portrays this contrast in more detail. The column on the right identifies practices, tools, and strategies that "enable participants in a community to construct meaning that leads toward a shared purpose of schooling." And the district has special responsibility for promoting and modeling those "promising practices."

The constructivist district's roles include helping to expand what is assessed, what assessment strategies are used to document learning goals, and what is defined as achievement. Eisner suggests that "It is what students do with what they learn when they can do what they want to do that is the real measure of educational achievement" (2000).

Despite the pressure to dictate assessment and accountability policy that satisfies state and federal mandates and to distribute rewards and issue sanctions, superintendents and boards must ensure that the district strives to function consistently as a "congruent, interdependent learning community." That means including teachers, students, and the community in the conversations to "make meaning" of state and federal mandates. It entails working collaboratively to develop policy and actions that support student learning and connect assessment to instruction. They must resist the press to reduce measures of student success or achievement to standardized tests. Because teachers can be seduced into teaching just what is tested in high-stakes assessments, the district team must join with school-level advocates in the fight to keep the curriculum rich—and the assessment system authentic. As Lorrie Shepard (2000) points out persuasively, measuring student achievement includes, "observation, clinical interviews, reflective journals, projects, demonstrations, collections of student work" (p. 8). Districts need to join in the effort to develop a new "constructivist paradigm in which teachers' close assessment of students' understandings, feedback from peers, and student self-assessments are a central part of the social processes that mediate the development of

FIGURE 7.1

Assessment and Accountability

DIMENSIONS	CURRENT NORMS	PROMISING PRACTICES
DESIGN RESPONSIBILITY	• Schools and districts • State and federal agencies • Publishers	• Collegial groups • Teachers as primary designers
BELIEF SYSTEM	• Competition spurs achievement • The right answer can be easily measured • Learning is linear and sequential	• Learning is complex, co-created • Learner makes meaning, seeks understanding, reflects on own learning experiences • Culture of inquiry is vital • All students have access to high-quality curriculum and instruction
OUTCOMES ARE	• Static • Prescriptive • Narrow	• Evolving • Dynamic • Used to improve instruction • All students learning • Varied
RESULTS USED TO	• Sort and select • Blame schools, teachers, and students • Give sanctions and awards • Track students • Promote and retain	• Assess and chart learning progress • Inform decisions about curriculum and instruction • Diagnose and intervene • Initiate cycle of inquiry • Strengthen learner's reflection
EFFECT ON INSTRUCTION	• Extrinsic motivation • Teach to the test • Direct instruction	• Intrinsic motivation for teachers and students • All students engaged in learning challenging content • Differentiated teaching

(continued)

Figure 7.1 (Continued)

Dimensions	Current Norms	Promising Practices
Report to	• State and federal agencies • School board • Newspaper • Parents	• Students, parents, and teachers • School board • Community and educational partners
Types of Test Measurement Tools	• State competency tests (high stakes) • Nationally normed reference tests • High school exit exam • Text book test	• Published criterion referenced tests based on standards • Teacher makes formative and summative assessments • Rubrics • Exhibitions • Portfolios of work, products, and performances • Self-assessment tools and strategies
Role of Teacher	• Passive • Compliant • Acts as a monitor	• Active • Develops tools and approaches • Shares responsibilities with other teachers and students
Role of Key Site and District Administrators	• Assure compliance • Assure security of test items • Distribute and collect test materials • Execute state and national mandates • Identify practice and procedures to improve test scores • Disaggregate and analyze data	• Build a collaborative community to study student performance on tests and their work • Initiate a shared vision about all student learning • Develop policies that ensure equity in access and results • Search out best practice and new research on learning and teaching (i.e., looping, multiage classrooms, choice, and intervention) • Mediate mandates with shared vision of community about learning and assessment

- Report to state, newspaper, and community
- Reward success and sanction failure

- Seek waivers when state and national mandates do not match district shared vision
- Be willing to put forth problems and figure out, "What we don't know."
- Establish norms that expect all learners to self assess, reflect on learning, and pose own questions, maintaining openness to new ways
- Make a commitment to reciprocal accountability among all parts of the organization
- Provide resources and opportunity for continuous professional development for all adults
- Invite inquiry at all levels of the organization
- Sustain conversations using student work, embedding constructivist language, and using reciprocal processes

intellectual abilities, construction of knowledge, and formation of student identities" (p. 4). And that paradigm must take into account the moral imperative of an "opportunity to learn" for each and every student.

Fortunately, the crusade to rationalize and humanize the accountability/standards movement is not a solitary journey. Individual researchers and writers such as those cited above are supported by a growing number of professional associations, organizations, and commercial publishers, including the following:

- The National School Boards Association's chapter, "Raising the Bar: A School Board Primer on Student Achievement," in Goodman and Zimmerman (2000) identifies higher order thinking skills, intellectual curiosity, creativity, citizenship, appreciation of the arts, and development of character as critical areas of achievement and curriculum.
- Dr. James Popham's (2001) appeal to AERA is noted above.
- The Consortium for Policy Research in Education (CPRE) is working to refine a set of "Standards of Educational Accountability" that are based on a rigorous analysis of "research knowledge, practical experience and ethical considerations."
- LearnCity (Dietz, 2000) is a new organization based on constructivist learning theory that is working with many districts to help them make sense of standards and to form coalitions in that work. This Web-based approach to standards-based instruction combines the principles of seeking and valuing students' points of view, posing problems of emerging relevance to students, supporting the design of lessons around "Big Ideas," adapting curriculum to address students' suppositions, and assessing student learning in the context of teaching.
- Harcourt Brace's *New Standards Test* (Learning Research & Development Center, 1998) is an example of commercially produced assessment tools that reflect constructivist values and national standards that call for more complex performance. Further, the New Standards work represents what can be produced by broad and deep collaboration among key stakeholders—in this case, the Learning Research Center of the University of Pittsburgh and the National Center on Education and the Economy, in partnership with a number of states and urban school districts.

The responsibility for building a complex and authentic accountability system is perhaps the most significant challenge for school districts today. Capacity building and accountability are not, of course, exclusive district or school functions. They are significant examples of roles and responsibilities that must be "owned" fully but also shared at each level of the school/district learning community—in each classroom and school, at the district office, and in the spaces in between individual units in this complex and interconnected web of relationships in which all interactive processes depend on one another. Only then will the "system" become adaptive, responsive, and capable of growth and renewal—organically accountable.

CHOICE, VOUCHERS, CHARTER SCHOOLS

There are many subplots in the drama of school change and improvement. While the accountability melodrama highlights summative test scores and competitive rankings and tends to encourage consistency and even conformity in many venues, other themes have to do with diversity, variety, and choice among options, especially at the classroom and school levels.

Most schools and districts have offered some kinds of alternatives and choices for many years. Magnet schools, independent study, home schooling, continuation high schools—these are familiar forms. Relatively new on the scene (and most relevant to the themes in this chapter) are the semiautonomous charter schools that have proliferated rapidly in recent years for an intriguing mix of reasons. Some of those reasons are essentially defensive in character—a strategy to counter the threats to democracy and public education perceived to come from any increase in enrollment in private, parochial, and other forms of nonpublic independent education. That competitive threat has been exaggerated and dramatized, of course, by political initiatives in a number of states and at the highest federal levels aimed at offering vouchers (or "opportunity scholarships") to parents who are convinced that their public schools are failing to meet the needs of their children. Some districts are creating semiautonomous charter schools under the public school umbrella but with some of the character of private schools to compete and, in a sense, "co-opt" the voucher threat.

Other more substantive motives for creating charter schools are reflective of the broad-based engagement in meaning-making and decision making about teaching and learning that is advocated in this book. When a significant critical mass of members of the educational community have concluded in a deliberative fashion that an approach to education that is different from the current "standard" form makes constructive sense, it seems appropriate for alternative forms (such as charter schools) to be given serious consideration. Those alternatives vary radically in their character, from a new military charter and five very different "small autonomous schools" opening in Oakland, California, to Open Classroom and Public Montessori Programs in Lagunitas, California, to a Muslim Independent School in Edmonton, Canada. The Sherman Oaks Charter School story in Chapter 6 gives a more complete picture of one such initiative.

How school districts should respond to the press for choice and options is a sensitive and significant policy issue. The values, goals, and mission statements adopted by the school board must be kept in mind—and the need for some coherence and congruence in the district's operation. But so, too, broader values concerning democracy, equitable access, and meeting the varied needs of individuals as well as groups must be considered. One of those values addressed in the previous section on accountability suggests that whatever alternative forms of education are offered should be expected to be accountable for learning results, in some fashion that is at least as rigorous as that in other schools of the district, but not necessarily using the same tools and methods. In fact, alternative programs offer a unique opportunity to experiment in a responsible way with different forms of assessment and program evaluation—a real life example of the "organic accountability" that is being advocated.

STORIES AND VIGNETTES

Organic accountability, reciprocal relationships, shared responsibilities, dynamic learning organization—these esoteric-sounding terms relate to complex interactions that are often negotiated through conversations and stories. Accordingly, some actual stories may help clarify meaning and to form the foundation for the constructivist approaches we are advocating.

THE SARATOGA SCHOOL DISTRICT STORY
by Mary Gardner, superintendent

Saratoga is a small, suburban, San Francisco Bay Area school district of 2,400 students, serving a predominantly upper-middle-class population. The community is becoming increasingly diverse, with 37 percent first- or second-generation from Japan, Korea, Taiwan, China, India, and the Middle East. Some of the roles and strategies I report will not fit the circumstances faced by superintendents of large districts. But the collaborative, co-learner interactions and reciprocal processes can and should be modeled and promoted by district staff even in large, urban communities.

Along with others, I strive to be the steward of the district vision, purpose, values, and goals that are manifest in our strategic plan. Because I am an avid reader of educational research, legislation, and policy, I see many documents that have relevance in our dialogues and discussions. I share readings with others, although I am not the only one who brings readings to a study group. I also invite teachers to talk about their best practice in relationship to what we are reading or studying.

The story of how Saratoga became a more constructivist district began in 1988 when I was the assistant superintendent. The critical event that led over time to a fundamental shift in leadership philosophy was concern about our Gifted and Talented Education (GATE) program. We had many complaints from parents about the identification process, the quality of the program, and the fact that their children "were gifted all day every day, not just when they were in a 3-hour pull-out GATE program." Teachers complained about large numbers of children leaving their classrooms during the pull-out program, reducing the time they had for instruction. They didn't have much interaction with GATE staff; and since they were hearing about the "fun and exciting activities" the GATE teachers were providing, they felt they were in competition for students' and parents' praise. When California broadened the criteria for inclusion in the program, we knew this could only contribute more frustration about how we were serving GATE students.

A task force was formed that included parents of children in the GATE program and parents whose children qualified but who had decided not to enroll them. There were site and district administrators, board members, a teacher from every grade level and from special education, and several GATE teachers.

Over the next year everyone on the committee read the newest research about gifted instruction, multiple intelligences, instructional strategies, and inclusion and equity issues. They collected stories from students who were tested and did not qualify and their parents. They also gathered information from participating students and their parents about the quality of the program and what kept them in the program, or, if they had withdrawn, why. Members of the committee visited both our own GATE classrooms and exemplary GATE programs in our area as identified by the state.

At the end of a year's study, this committee recommended to the school board that we identify all of our students as gifted and talented, stop the pull-out program based on an IQ measure of academic ability, and expand the identification process for all students, using Howard Gardner's theory of multiple intelligences. Waivers were secured from the California

Department of Education. We established an ongoing advisory committee, began a professional development program focused on identifying best teaching practices for a video library, and sent teachers to workshops on teaching gifted students and identifying multiple intelligences. A group of teachers also began to write sample lessons directed toward cooperative learning, creative and critical thinking, and problem solving—for all students. The professional development was organized and provided predominantly by teachers teaching teachers.

Over these last 12 years, Saratoga Union School District has continued to use this basic collaborative process for struggling with major changes and significant issues (e.g., middle school structure, kindergarten program, revision of curriculum, adoption of textbooks, restructuring special education to strengthen inclusion, and differentiated instruction). The process has included well-advertised public meetings, inviting all parents and some community members to hear about the assumptions and rationale behind changes. Workshops have been provided for parents, teachers, administrators, board members, and middle school students about constructivist leadership, how to facilitate effective meetings, how to participate in dialogue and conversation honoring multiple points of view, how to make informed decisions, how to work with difficult people, and the process of change.

A similar inclusive process was used 8 years ago when we articulated a vision and purpose and composed value statements that guide our yearly goal setting. Every 3 years we formally review these statements and make changes to keep them relevant and authentic. Our purpose, "to engage hearts and minds in learning both now and in the future," has become our district logo and can be seen and heard as a beginning assumption for all studies and planning.

We are working to make our personnel policies and practices more collaborative and decentralized. The board, administration, and teachers continue to strengthen their interest-based bargaining skills through ongoing workshops with consultants who help them refine their abilities to find common ground and to respect each other as professionals. We have worked together to develop a beginning-teacher support program and an evaluation system that emphasizes self-assessment, reflection on work, and dialogue with peers at the heart of the process.

The same inclusive decision-making processes have been used to select instructional programs that are congruent with our values. For example, LearnCity was chosen to help us make meaning out of California's rigorous standards/assessment/accountability requirements because that comprehensive support program promotes critical and creative thinking, problem solving, and cooperative learning strategies that we value. For similar reasons we have selected the New Standards Math Test (Harcourt Brace) to evaluate our math curriculum and instruction.

As much as has been done, there is still much to do. Conflicts at all levels of the organization still occur; there are times when someone short-cuts the processes because of time or behaves in an autocratic way, causing a loss of trust. We are just beginning to bring students into the conversations. While more diverse voices are being heard, there is still not full representation. There is difficulty in repeating workshops often enough to sustain the leadership growth and include more people in the work. We know the benefits for students of including more voices, of involving everyone in meaningful conversations, and of continuing our odyssey as a constructivist school district.

STORIES FROM PRACTICE: A 35-YEAR PERSPECTIVE
by Morgan Dale Lambert

My first major experience as a change agent was 35 years ago as principal of an innovative high school in which many of the currently resurgent reform strategies were being pioneered—modular/flexible scheduling, collaborative planning and team teaching, self-directed (independent) study, small-group instruction, integrated guidance curriculum, and community-based learning. Exciting successes were experienced at Canyon High School (Castro Valley, California), many of them foreshadowing the cooperative learning and collaborative teaching practices currently in vogue. But the negative lessons were just as instructive—and are especially relevant to the themes of this chapter.

District office involvement and support were conspicuously and painfully absent, and this proved to be the fatal flaw that led to the eventual abandonment of the modular/flexible scheduling program. The maverick school was isolated and suffered particularly from an absence of articulation ties with feeder schools; students arrived with no real preparation for the responsibilities entailed in self-directed study.

We learned two other important lessons. First, the developmental needs of *all* students must be kept as a central focus for instructional change initiatives—not just those who respond eagerly and responsibly to new and exciting learning opportunities. Second, parents must be involved as fully participating and informed partners; and the involvement must come early, be continuous, and be perceived as substantive and respectful. The minority of parents whose children were floundering ultimately sealed the fate of this noble early experiment in "restructuring" (M. Lambert, 1993).

Lack of district office support was key to the failure to reach potential at our innovative high school. Curiously, my second story reveals the other side of that same coin—and also has both positive and negative lessons from which to learn. Later in my career, I responded to a job announcement that used the title "Assistant Superintendent for Instruction and School Improvement." Recognizing a school district that would support innovation and change, I leapt at the chance. Again, many satisfying ventures and successes grew out of this opportunity to function as school-oriented district office change agent, and I still heartily endorse this posture. But my experiences also revealed the power of what has been called "systemic inertia" (Szabo, 1995) and the limitations on the effectiveness of a central office change agent (particularly an outsider brought in to "reform" schools), especially when the school board is in a hurry to get the job done quickly and massively. In spite of the press for quick change, perhaps even because of it, I learned to value complex collaborative processes that build respectfully on local school strengths, on analyzed "readiness" and capacity, and on relationships that strengthen over time.

These insights were of great value when I later became superintendent of a school district that was already highly innovative and where the culture supported collaborative leadership among teachers and parents. In that setting, the superintendent's roles were largely those of facilitative leader, problem-solver, and mediator among empowered initiators. A pioneer in the school choice movement, Lagunitas School District (Marin County, California) offered to parents and students options among a Public School Montessori Program, a "Summerhill-ian" Open Classroom Program, and a more traditional Academics and Enrichment curriculum. Learning challenges for me included how to build more collaborative relationships with other districts and with the county and state and how to maintain harmony and coherence among sometimes highly competitive ideologues.

My next learning experience was as facilitator and school/district coach for a major statewide reform project in California, coordinated by the California Center for School Restructuring (CCSR). In that role, I had the rare opportunity to use the lessons learned in all of my change agent roles. As in my own personal early experience as a high school principal, California's restructuring program began with a heavy emphasis on local school initiation and only token regard for district involvement. Entering its third year in 1994, much more interest developed around the broader context, particularly in the strategies for engaging the district office as collaborative partner. And the statewide leaders recognized the need to build cultures of inquiry and reflective learning communities—in each school but also in the district and broader community as well.

The orientation of CCSR leaders and the design of the state restructuring program itself were distinctly constructivist in character. This orientation was evident in the commitment to plan and implement programs collaboratively, to focus on equitable student learner outcomes, and to learn by reflecting on authentic experience and engaging in carefully designed "cycles of inquiry" (Shawn, 1994). The design of a research and development initiative in the district office role in facilitating school restructuring was formed largely by this kind of reflection on experience and promising practices. An early lesson in the CCSR initiative was that there must be an underlying support system that has two interrelated dimensions—one that provides for monitoring and public accounting and a second that emphasizes the collective organizational learning that sustains systemic change. The Accountability/Learning Support System (Shawn, 1994) that resulted was designed and constructed by the actual participants—a set of teachers and administrators working collaboratively with CCSR staff. Participant reflection and feedback after a year's experience with A/LSS produced a new understanding—that the support network must include the district office as a fully participating partner. Accordingly, the revised CCSR format called for district representatives to join school teams in all major network functions—including an ongoing District Cycle of Inquiry on the effectiveness of district support strategies.

When state funding for CCSR's approach to school restructuring ended, many of the collaborative and constructivist strategies were adapted and extended in new initiatives, notably the Bay Area School Reform Collaborative (BASRC), a major Annenberg-funded network of schools and districts. Researchers have carefully tracked the BASRC reform efforts and results and are reaffirming the conclusion that sensitive but substantive district engagement is of vital importance in achieving and sustaining schoolwide change.

In recent years, my circle of reflection and inquiry about school district roles in deep and sustainable educational reform has enlarged. It has incorporated insights from reading and from interviewing superintendents, change facilitators, and researchers from all kinds of school districts in the United States, Canada, and Australia. Those insights are reflected in the "Guiding Principles" section that concludes this chapter.

A TALE OF THREE CITIES

Many of the dramas of successful school change take place in smaller suburban communities. A greater and more complex challenge is faced by leaders of large, diverse, urban school districts. Two such districts that serve more than 20,000 students each have demonstrated improvement strategies with impressive results that make them instructive exemplars.

COMMUNITY SCHOOL DISTRICT TWO, NEW YORK CITY

Superintendent Elaine Fink and researcher Lauren Resnick describe a set of comprehensive instructional leadership strategies at the heart of a school improvement program that has produced elevated student learning results sustained over a 12-year period. There is evidence that the district is building "a culture of learning and mutual dependency among staff at all levels: people expect support in solving problems of instructional practice from their peers and supervisors, and problems in design or implementation of instruction are shared and discussed (even with supervisors) rather than hidden from view" (Fink and Resnick, 2001, p. 4).

Among the distinguishing features that contribute to teaching and learning successes are the following:

- The district "reorganized to move most resources and decision making to the schools" (p. 5), but there is clear evidence of strong central leadership in forming, implementing, and monitoring a coherent plan and system. Most conspicuous is an unrelenting, uncompromising focus on instructional issues such as "balanced literacy"—in all staff meetings at all levels of the district.
- The design concept of "nested learning communities" contributes to congruence in teaching and learning strategies and relationships at all levels of the district—from the core communities in the classrooms up through schools, support and study groups, mentorships, and in the coaching behaviors of the top-level district leaders.
- A strong emphasis is placed on job-embedded and continuous professional development at all levels. There is a focus on principals, for whom monthly conferences, institutes, mentoring, and coaching provide the "intellectual glue for system-wide improvement" (p. 8).
- Partnerships with Bank Street and other local colleges ensure a steady flow of qualified teachers. This is a luxury that many urban districts do not share.
- A reciprocal two-way accountability program is in place, featuring collegial analysis of problems and evidence and supervisory "walkthroughs." Student achievement results are highlighted, always "in the context of collegial discussions about approaches to improving learning ... the district's message is not one of meeting test score goals but rather as a guide to the effectiveness of practice" (p. 10).

The indications of sustained change and improvement in New York City District #2 schools are significant enough that many of their strategies have been adapted in other communities. In particular, the supervisory "walk-through" has been introduced in many other settings. It entails a visit to every classroom in a school, with systematic observation of teaching and learning, followed by collegial analysis—a valuable context for district and school interaction.

Kansas City School District, Kansas City, Kansas

As in the New York City district, there is a strong instructional focus in the Kansas City, Kansas, community of schools and a comparable whole-district commitment to implement a reform program in a deliberate, systematic, and sustainable way. The major component of the reform and continuous improvement program is appropriately called "First Things First." The Wyandotte High School story in Chapter 6 gives the perspective of a school in the first cluster to implement the First Things First initiative. That story should be read in tandem with this district vignette to appreciate the larger picture.

While the district was centrally involved in selecting the reform program and identifying goals, there is strong emphasis on teacher leadership and local school/cluster autonomy in designing strategies for making progress toward goals. Significant features of this initiative include

- A full-time School Improvement Facilitator (teacher) assigned to each high school, to a pair of middle schools, and to each trio of elementary schools (facilitation functions are described in Chapter 6)
- "Continuity of Care" provided in part by looping in elementary and secondary schools and by forming small vertical learning communities (in the high school, sets of teachers and students who stay together for 4 years)
- Weekly 2-hour released time for collegial interaction among faculty at every school
- Partnerships with a university (University of Missouri, Kansas City), a foundation (Kauffman), school improvement consultants (Institute for Research and Reform in Education), and stakeholder community groups
- Strong commitment to building organizational leadership capacity as well as leadership among teachers and administrators

Superintendent Ray Daniels brings a history of more than 2 decades with the district and personal qualities that contribute significantly to the district's continuing improvement. Daniels is tenacious, committed to staying the course and working through rough spots without abandoning promising practices. Further, his inclusiveness means that planning and problem-solving processes engage union and community representatives so that they too can commit to the outcomes. A supportive board speaks powerfully to the quality of his leadership. He points with pride to evidence that student achievement is rising as a direct result of this initiative and declares, "This is our reform effort and we're going to stay with it!"

SOUTH PASADENA UNIFIED SCHOOL DISTRICT, PASADENA, CALIFORNIA

During his entire 12 years in this diverse district (6 as superintendent), Les Adelson has worked at restructuring the system, decentralizing and building what he calls a "community of practitioners" in each school and the whole "family of schools." In recent years those efforts have been reinforced and expanded through partnerships with the University of California, Los Angeles (UCLA) Advanced Management Program and with a major school reform initiative, the Los Angeles Annenberg Metropolitan Project (LAAMP).

- There is a 12-year history of increasing use of "interest-based bargaining" in relating to the teachers association. A 1996 training session for all district staff and interested parents was facilitated by professionals from the California Foundation for the Improvement of Employee/Employer Relations (CFIER).
- All school staff and teachers have participated in professional development sessions on shared decision making; and a guide for that process has been published and is being used in all schools.
- With help from LAAMP facilitators, a Critical Friends Group is functioning in every school as a "forum for teachers to improve their practice."
- Data Teams also function in every school, and "The South Pasadena Family believes that data collection and use has been institutionalized and is part of the district culture . . . for the purpose of moving closer to ensuring equity and access to the academic culture for all our students" (Adelson, personal communication, August 2001).
- The responsibility for selecting new administrators has moved to the site level. Interestingly, the superintendent is frequently an observer during the process and reserves the right to question recommendations but has never exercised that option.

- Block scheduling and a once-a-week block of collaboration time have helped to strengthen a commitment to ongoing professional development.

The 5-year LAAMP funding has ended, but the district is redirecting regular resources to continue to build their "community of (skilled and informed) practitioners."

GUIDING PRINCIPLES FOR CONSTRUCTIVIST SCHOOL DISTRICTS

The stories and vignettes throughout this chapter and book depict changing schools and districts that are moving in the direction of the interdependent learning communities that we are advocating. While promoting this change, the district must also maintain "global stability in the presence of many fluctuations and instabilities occurring at the local level throughout the system (Wheatley, 1992, p. 94). In the final analysis, a district that is constructivist in nature will be open to change and be involved with school and other partners in designing the processes that build resiliency into a system.

The stories of school and district change are encouraging, and practitioners need also to see a more comprehensive set of guidelines and recommendations as principles to keep in mind on their journey. Those guidelines and principles must in themselves be "enablers" in the sense described in Chapter 2—facilitating the reciprocal processes that evoke potential, construct meaning, reconstruct assumptions, and frame actions. The last part of this chapter suggests such a set of principles, summarized in Figure 7.2.

1. Promote and model the behavior and informed decision-making processes that contribute to students and adults participating effectively in an equitable democracy.
A major theme throughout this book is the renewing of the mission of public schools to prepare learners for life in an equitable democracy. Every district policy and process needs to contribute to the accomplishment of that mission—directly and by serving as catalyst, model, promoter, and accountability partner. The constructivist processes espoused here serve to engage both adults and students in problem analysis and problem solving, in deep conversations leading to shared meaning, and in the informed and responsible decision making that is at the heart of democracy.

FIGURE 7.2

Guiding Principles for Constructivist School Districts

1. Promote and model the behavior and informed decision-making processes that contribute to students and adults participating effectively in an equitable democracy.

2. Provide resources and collaborate with schools and the community to identify shared values and create compelling visions, mission statements, and unifying purposes.

3. Engage in equitable large-scale devolution of authority, resources, and responsibilities—all within a coherent district context.

4. Buffer, navigate, and mediate between state and national mandates and constructivist principles of learning and leading—advocating for policy change and waivers when needed.

5. Design policies, procedures, and structures that pass the "enabler test" (being congruent with shared values and consistently supportive of teaching and learning.

6. Create personnel policies and practices that nurture the continuous development of all personnel, from recruitment and induction through engagement in varied leadership roles.

7. Collaborate with schools in creating and protecting prime time for professional development and other forms of collaborative and collegial interaction.

8. Develop information and technology systems that support administrative and accountability functions but are designed primarily to facilitate instruction, communication, and decision making.

9. Model and support the collaborative strategies of a learning organization at all levels (classroom, school, district, school board, community).

10. Move beyond condescension and confrontation toward interest-based collaboration in relationships with unions and associations.

11. Establish a comprehensive guidance system that attends to the "protective factors" needed to build resiliency as well as the academic needs of all students.

12. Use assessment and accountability tools and approaches that are congruent with constructivist learning.

13. Encourage well-designed classroom and school-level innovation, collaborate in program assessment, and systematically facilitate the scaling-up of promising practices.

It is our contention that these reciprocal processes will facilitate growth and development of organizations (schools and districts) as well as individuals and that they improve the learning experiences of students. Longitudinal evidence of this growth and improvement is accumulating in initiatives such as those described in this text and in the League of Professional Schools (Glickman, 1998).

This principle is fundamental to all the other guidelines that follow.

2. Provide resources and collaborate with schools and the community to identify shared values and create compelling visions, mission statements, and unifying purposes.

One of the first actions for a constructivist school district is to engage all members of the educational community in creating visions and mission statements that clarify purpose and lead to coherent action. The processes that produce such statements must be inclusive and collaborative, taking place in individual schools as well as the district. District responsibilities include assisting in providing resources for this time-consuming process, monitoring for congruence among varied visions, and ensuring that usable data are accessible that reflect the needs of students and the expectations of the broader community. The superintendent is centrally involved as "steward of the vision, values, and purpose of the district," but the stewardship must be shared to have sustainable impact. Three vignettes will help make these design principles real:

- Alameda Unified School District, in a diverse community next door to urban Oakland, California, took imaginative advantage of business and community partnerships in developing strategic plans for the whole district, for each school, and for the community itself. The whole process was inclusive and collaborative in character, with more than 2,000 people directly involved (teachers, parents, students, business-people, and civic officials). The student outcomes that emerged are at the core of school restructuring initiatives; and the linkages and processes are still being used as the district and community engage with new crises and opportunities, namely, the impact of closure of a large U.S. Navy base and a major grant to pilot collaborative district leadership strategies.
- Superintendent Daniel Callahan has guided the educational community of Martinez, California, in a 2-year effort to renew their District Strategic Plan and to make it comprehensive, functional, and congruent. His goal was to move the district toward Extraordinary Purpose, which was not achieved by the organization in its previous

configuration. In a personal communication (September 2001), Callahan describes how Administrative Domains were identified that parallel Teaching Domains. Utilizing the Mutual Commitments template from the Cambridge Group (strategic planning consultants), "we have established the essential links between administrative evaluation, locally developed standards and rubrics for administrative performance, Site and District Strategic Plans, and the explicit expectations for system support to help all the elements move forward. The process has emerged within the context of constructivist, distributed leadership and emphasizes support for continual administrative learning, with associated risk-taking, rather than autocratic 'accountability.'" In that spirit of reciprocity and mutuality, all administrators are expected to include in their professional development plans at least one "stretch goal" that they may not reach, and the entire system accepts responsibility for providing support for the effort to live "at risk"—so necessary if one is to achieve Extraordinary Purpose.

• The Calgary Board of Education (Canada) is an urban school district of more than 100,000 students. Former superintendent Donna Michaels led the system to organize into eight vertical learning communities based on a collaboratively developed visionary description of Quality Learning for students. The district has become a purposeful learning organization. As expressions of their shared vision, the system for leadership evaluation as well as student learning have been based on constructivist assumptions and principles, with a strong emphasis on self-reflection, continuous growth, respect for diversity, and personal planning. With those values as the foundation, recent school closures and consolidations have been conducted through an engagement of all stakeholders (Michaels, interview, January 2001).

3. Engage in equitable large-scale devolution of authority, resources, and responsibilities—all within a coherent district context.
This devolution affects classrooms, teams of teachers, schools, and school clusters—and it must occur in a systemic way that also provides for capacity building and accountability.

The decentralization show has played to mixed reviews in a number of large urban districts over the past decade (New York and Chicago are two notable examples), but it has not often been accompanied by the needed professional development, the radical redistribution of resources, the assumption of responsibility for quality teaching and learning in every school and classroom, or the systemic policy changes that would support and protect the distribution of leadership and authority. There is the danger that the locus of coercive or authoritarian power may simply move from the center to neighborhoods unless a culture that supports a more collaborative form of leadership is carefully nurtured.

The Sherman Oaks Charter School story about creating a 90-minute daily time block for teachers to work together is a promising example of prioritized collective decision making. Another encouraging example of decentralization can be found in the Glenlawn High School story, where the Winnipeg, Canada, district dispersed resources and gave schools authority to contract for services from the central office or other sources.

4. Buffer, navigate, and mediate between state and national mandates and constructivist principles of learning and leading—advocating for policy change and waivers when needed.

Even when federal and state mandates have elements of democratic purpose (i.e., equal access for all students), they are typically insufficiently sensitive to the diverse contexts and needs of local communities. Very little room is provided for flexibility or for local adaptation of the conditions of the mandate. Once the mandates become compliance issues, they diminish the power of communities to work together to develop a shared vision and mission around the intended purpose. Conversations shift from generative decision making to compliant implementation ("What do we value? vs. "How will we comply?"), taking away authority but leaving responsibility.

We have earlier made the statement that we "hope to persuade educators and those who influence educational policy to choose integrity over urgency, autonomy and discretion over control." When mandates come "down from above," the constructivist district has the responsibility to work collectively at making meaning of the mandates within the context of its own shared vision and purpose. If it violates the vision and purpose of the community, then the district must seek legislative change or waivers in order to maintain the integrity, discretion, and complexity of its vision and work. Another sometimes defensible strategy is, of course, "benign neglect."

5. Design policies, procedures, and structures that pass the "enabler test" (being congruent with shared values and consistently supportive of teaching and learning).

This redesign must support the decentralization essential to a system of interdependent learning communities. Policies can be designed to satisfy legislative or school board intent without getting in the way of new ideas and well-planned change initiatives. The policies and practices must be made compatible with a commitment to informed innovation, risk taking, results-oriented accountability and continuous growth, and change. Involvement of school representatives at the developmental stage of a policy is an obvious first step on this path. Readiness to revise policies and procedures, negotiate waivers and exemptions, decentralize budget and personnel decisions, and seek changes in laws are signs that the system is becoming responsive in the policy arena. A few enlightened districts (such as Kansas City, Kansas) are auditing old policies to make sure they are congruent with current decentralization and school-restructuring goals. Clearly, skill and sensitivity will be required in balancing the paradoxical district roles of creating dissonance and providing support.

6. Create personnel policies and practices that nurture the continuous development of all personnel, from recruitment and induction through engagement in varied leadership roles.

Recommended personnel policies and practices that contrast with those in more traditional school district cultures are highlighted separately in Figure 7.3. The figure outlines selection and induction practices that are more collaborative, systematic, and school based. A much more comprehensive professional development program starts with selection and incorporates professional development, supervision, evaluation, and movement into leadership roles in a seamless process. Activities and strategies have a more collegial character, but they also promote more autonomy through self-analysis and self-direction, encouraging pervasive reflection on practice.

A rich array of teacher leadership roles continues to develop as schools and districts restructure. Teachers on special assignment, peer coaches and mentors, lead teachers, consulting teachers, teacher researchers, adjunct professors (e.g., professional development schools), as well as the traditional administrative positions are all part of the context for professionalism. Teachers in these roles develop a more mature learning relationship with their colleagues as they engage together in continuous growth, inquiry, and collaborative leadership.

As Barth (2001b) points out,

> teachers who choose the path of teacher leadership experience a reduction of isolation, which comes from frequent companionship and collegiality among other adults; the personal and professional satisfaction that comes from improving their schools; a sense of instrumentality, investment, and membership in the school community; new learning about the schools, the process of change and about themselves, which accompanies being a leader; and professional invigoration and replenishment, which spill over into their classroom teaching. These teachers become owners and investors in their schools, rather than mere tenants.

FIGURE 7.3

Personnel Practices and Policies

TRADITIONAL/HIERARCHICAL CENTRALIZED	COLLABORATIVE/CONSTRUCTIVIST DECENTRALIZED
	RECRUITMENT
Districts offer bonuses and other financial incentives, lower standards and qualifications, offer emergency and intern credentials, provide assurance of intensive but short-term on-the-job basic skill training, college Job Fairs.	Districts work to enhance teacher professionalism (including salary schedule improvement); assure access to mentoring and other forms of long-term professional development and leadership opportunities; aggressively recruit among under-represented groups and through nonconventional channels.
	SELECTION OF PERSONNEL
Application documents seldom include much more than letters of recommendation, credentials, and transcripts. Paper screening is followed by individual or panel interview; occasional teaching/supervision sample or observed performance; site visitations for administrative position finalists. Final selection is by central authority.	Preparation programs assist in development of portfolios that may include assessment center results (including simulations, interactive role playing, problem-solving exercises). There is increasing reliance on assessment of videotaped or live performance samples, and broad-based local site engagement in selection.
	ORIENTATION OF NEW PERSONNEL
Formal orientation activities are followed by standardized staff development programs. They may include access to a mentor; usually they are self-contained and not sustained.	Orientation and enculturation processes for both teachers and administrators include formal and informal activities that are part of a complex professional development program. Strong links are developed with local universities, regional and county offices, other districts, professional networks. Professional Development Schools and California's Beginning Teachers Support Assessment Program (BTSA) State Task Force are exemplary models.

(continued)

193

FIGURE 7.3 (CONTINUED)

TRADITIONAL/HIERARCHICAL CENTRALIZED	COLLABORATIVE/CONSTRUCTIVIST DECENTRALIZED
PROFESSIONAL DEVELOPMENT	
Emphasis is on skill development, knowledge acquisition, training by prescription. Delivery is through formal workshops, courses.	Emphasis is on professional development through multiple learning opportunities embedded in authentic tasks such as collaborative action research, study groups, participation in decision making, co-planning, mentoring of new educators.
Individual professional development plans, where they exist, are objectives based in relation to teacher evaluation criteria and are determined by evaluator.	Professional development plans are personal, collegial, and school based, with room for choice, sustained commitment, and multiple forms of learning.
The majority of professional development days are scheduled and structured by the district and/or board and reflect primarily district/state/federal mandates.	The majority of professional development days are designed by local staff who are also involved in determining district priorities that shape the common days and programs. Programs feature work in reciprocal processes, action research, teaching and learning from student work, leadership team development, protocols, reciprocal team coaching, collaborative planning.
District goals dominate the design of local school improvement plans. School plans are viewed primarily as instrumental in moving toward district goals.	Local school improvement plans have ongoing professional development at the center. School plans inform and are informed by district goals and vision.
SUPERVISION AND EVALUATION	
Supervision is performed by administrators and quasi-administrators such as department chairs. Peer coaching and informal supervision may be encouraged, but the enabling structures for sustained collegial work seldom exist.	Critical self-analysis, peer observation and feedback, cognitive coaching, critical friendship, engagement in collaborative action research—these norms constitute the core of collegial supervision and evaluation practice.

Evaluation is essentially an administrative function, performed in strict compliance with contract and district regulations.	Administrators play central roles, but not exclusive, in evaluation (especially with new teachers and those experiencing difficulty). Their assessments add to a performance portfolio that also includes self and peer assessment reports, student and parent feedback and other performance artifacts.
Contracts often prohibit or expressly constrain involvement of peers in evaluation activities.	Various initiatives (such as California's Peer Assistance & Review Program) engage peers systematically in assessment, performance review, and support.

REASSIGNMENT AND TRANSFER

Contract provisions and the "needs of the district" control matters of assignment and transfer. Often, poorly performing staff are transferred from school to school with minimal or no school control.	Reassignment is requested by an educator attracted to the program and philosophy of another school; educator is invited to another school because of needed skills and perspective. Explicit and equitable criteria for involuntary transfer are developed collaboratively.

CONTRACTS, REGULATIONS, AND WAIVERS

Adversarial contract negotiations and centrally designed policies and regulations are the norm.	Nonconfrontational, interest-based bargaining produces contracts that are congruent with flexible district policies. As these collaborative processes mature, district and union leaders become more confident in confronting issues such as collective responsibility for dismissal of ineffective personnel.
Emphasis is placed on developing clear, detailed, and replicable clauses, regulations, and procedures for compliance.	Policies and procedures parameters serve emerging goals; flexible policies grow out of change efforts and respond to needs identified by school site leadership teams.
Exemptions and waiver procedures may be made available but they are viewed as evidences of weakness or failure.	Waivers to state department and legal regulations are framed and supported by district as such waivers respond to local needs.

Many progressive districts now expect each teacher and administrator to create and maintain a portfolio that contains products and artifacts that sketch a profile of professional development, self-assessment, and leadership involvement. Such evidence can chronicle the path of development that Barth describes. Universities are beginning to incorporate this strategy into their leadership preparation programs as well (see Chapter 8).

7. Collaborate with schools in creating and protecting prime time for professional development and other forms of collaboration and collegial interaction
These are complex, skillful, and intensive group processes that require much more time than the typical teacher's school day and year can provide. Moving major authority for scheduling and conducting staff development activities to the school level and encouraging weekly late-start or early-dismissal days (by lengthening the other days) are two rather simple tactics, but more substantive adjustments are needed. Block scheduling and other strategies for making schedules more flexible are coming back into favor, but they too are limited in impact because the time "container" is still too limited. The Sherman Oaks Charter School story of using parent volunteers and paraprofessionals to free teachers for daily collaborative time is a creative exemplar.

Through special project funding or legislation, collaborative time is sometimes created, but such budget line items are vulnerable—likely to be cut when special funding ends or the economy takes a downturn. An instructive example of the latter is a 2001 proposal by California's governor to allocate state money to lengthen the instructional year for all middle school students. A top-down proposal that didn't have substantial grass-roots support, it quickly dropped out of the legislative agenda when the energy crisis topped the political agenda.

Longer term and basic structural changes in the support for extending the work year for most teachers are clearly needed. Districts and teachers associations need to take an aggressive leadership role in seeking the additional funding that will be needed to support fundamental redesign of school schedules, including the incorporation of planning, collaboration, and staff development time in an extended work/study year.

8. Develop information and technology systems that support administrative and accountability functions but are designed primarily to facilitate instruction, communication, and decision making.
Many school districts are taking the lead in developing comprehensive

technology/information systems, usually with a primary emphasis on business, administrative, and accountability (reporting) functions. In second priority position are usually found pupil personnel services and direct instructional applications. Seldom is much attention given to the vital dimension of communication networking among teachers; teams of teachers, principals and other school leaders; and school networks. The district must reorder priorities to make certain that the systems serve effectively to support informed decision making, to build a culture of inquiry that is informed by data as well as driven by values (LearnCity, cited in the Saratoga story above, provides a system for this kind of integration). The self-organizing system that we are advocating requires/demands a continuing inflow of information—reinventing the way things are perceived, the way things are done.

Access to the world of information through technology has changed and increased dramatically in recent years, and progressive districts are ensuring that enrichment of teaching and learning is the guiding purpose. In the state of Victoria, Australia, every public school teacher has a laptop, and there is at least one computer for every three students. In San Lorenzo, a low-wealth California district, special project funds are delivering a laptop to every student in Grades 4–12. Business partnerships are collaborating in this arena at an unprecedented rate. Most school districts and many schools have some kind of technology plan that includes staff development, curriculum, and instructional components. Constructivist leaders are monitoring and refining those plans to make sure that they are sensitive to issues such as equity of access, variable needs and learning styles, and other human values.

If teachers are to become full participants in a technology-enriched culture of inquiry, along with their school and district administrator colleagues, they must have easy and direct access to the channels and tools of communication. In today's school, that means access not just to a telephone, but to a fax machine, modem, e-mail, electronic bulletin board, Web pages, and so forth. And the content that goes through those channels will be varied—ideas, questions, suggestions, critiques, feedback, of course, but also data. Schools, districts, networks, counties, universities, publishers, consultants, and other service providers all need to be linked by technology that makes accessible multiple forms of data about students (attendance, test scores, performances), family, graduates, the community, and career needs and requirements.

While technology is an increasingly vital information vehicle, the most significant communication channels in a constructivist culture will still be personal and relational—conversations, peer coaching, study groups, protocol sessions, reciprocal team coaching. The inquiring school will take nourishment out of a rich stream of data and other forms of information and evidence.

It is a shared school and district responsibility to generate and discover information and then to use it to make connections, to find and analyze problems, to disclose and process dissonant information, and to link information and evidence to action-oriented decision making. One of the most promising strategies for achieving the desired critical discourse and inquiry ethic is through engagement in collaborative action research, which has been described in Chapters 3 and 4—much of it at the school level but some in cross-school and district inquiry teams. The Leadership Academy in the Surrey School District of British Columbia, Canada, uses the Internet extensively to support the conduct of action research projects and the broad dissemination of both formative learnings and summative findings.

9. Model and support the collaborative strategies of a learning organization at all levels (classroom, school, district, school board, community). Cooperative learning, collaborative planning and teaching, peer coaching, collegial observation and feedback, study teams, reciprocal team coaching, results-focused inquiry, interest-based bargaining—these site-level practices are all mutually reinforcing fractals of the same generative processes that sustain a constructivist culture. The district uses the same processes in forming and facilitating its own committees and activities, modeling and creating a climate of expectancy that will influence school communities. The district stories that appear earlier in this chapter (Saratoga, Kansas City, and South Pasadena) showcase many of these strategies.

School boards also need to monitor their own work to ensure that their actions and rhetoric are congruent with and supportive of the collaborative culture that is desired. Their most appropriate focus is on policy formation, articulation of vision and goal statements, reciprocal communication with the community, facilitation of partnerships and network linkages, approval of budgets congruent with the vision and goals, and proactive interaction with regional, state, and national groups that affect or produce policy and mandates.

An example of modeling collaborative inquiry at the highest levels is provided by Missouri superintendent Jerry Cooper, who negotiated a reciprocal learning clause into his contract with school board members. They agreed to read selected books and analyze them together and to accompany the superintendent in attending all regional and national conferences.

Vibrant districts are cultivating the "spaces" among schools and between schools and the community, helping to make the web of relationships that connect individuals and make groups strong and productive. The artificial lines that traditionally separate schools are made permeable; the border areas form the context for cross-school dialogue, for the exchange of energy between subsystems in a larger ecosystem.

10. Move beyond condescension and confrontation toward interest-based collaboration in relationships with unions and associations.

Once achieved, a culture of collaboration, reciprocity, and critical friendship will not survive long if administrator and teacher colleagues abandon these relationships periodically to engage in adversarial bargaining. A growing number of school districts are moving toward quite a different approach, toward negotiations that emphasize beginning with the identification of common or overlapping interests and then engaging in joint problem solving, working hard to build and maintain trust and mutual respect (Butler, 1995). The 12-year history of "interest-based bargaining" noted in the South Pasadena story undoubtedly laid the foundation for the school improvement initiatives in that district. It also led to a standards-based teacher evaluation system in the Martinez School District cited above.

An example of the potential power of administrators and teachers acting together to influence and change policy comes recently from the province of Alberta, Canada. Provincial officials had issued an accountability mandate that was perceived at the local level as unconstructive, too much of a "carrot and stick" approach. Superintendents and teachers from around the province engaged in collaborative dialogue and agreed to lobby collectively for withdrawal and reformulation of the mandate; and it came to pass.

11. Establish a comprehensive guidance system that attends to the "protective factors" needed to build resiliency as well as the academic needs of all students.

A sadly common practice in districts that encounter budget problems is to reduce or eliminate counselors and transfer the guidance function to the administrators who also serve as disciplinarians. Much more enlightened are efforts to keep instruction and guidance functions linked and extended over periods longer than one year.

The research on resiliency has changed the face of guidance and indeed broadened the focus of student outcomes to including student development as well as achievement. *Resiliency* means the capacity to bounce back regardless of difficult situations and relationships. Resilient children possess social competence, problem-solving skills, autonomy, and a sense of purpose and future. Organizations can establish what are known as "protective factors," those factors closely identified with student resiliency. The protective factors include a caring environment, high and positive expectations, and opportunities for meaningful participation and contributions (Krovetz, 1999). Further, active participation is directly linked to attitudes about and performance in school and high self-confidence and esteem, especially among children of color and females (Wedding, 2001). It is the responsibility of the district to insist that protective factors be in place and that the appropriate training and resources have been made available to support resiliency.

A promising practice in elementary schools entails "looping," wherein students stay with the same teacher over 2 or 3 years. Secondary schools have had success with asking some or preferably all teachers to take on guidance responsibilities for small groups of students ("Advisory") or by forming small "learning communities" that stay together for up to 4 years.

The "continuity of care" support strategies described in the Wyandotte High School story is illustrative. So too is the testimonial from a student quoted in the Glenlawn High School story, telling of valuable learning experiences in his "student advocacy class." A major project in the state of Victoria, Australia, is helping transform school counseling into a similar kind of advocacy program.

Urban districts (Chicago, New York, Oakland) are increasingly using the strategy of creating small semiautonomous schools to serve the academic, guidance, and equity needs of students. Research evidence is beginning to accumulate that reinforces the notion that "small is better," especially for students of color and of poverty (Wasley, 2002).

12. Use assessment and accountability tools and approaches that are congruent with constructivist learning.
Earlier in this chapter (see Figure 7.1), we examined the role of school and district leaders in relating to pressures for standards, high-stakes assessment, and accountability systems that are sometimes at odds with constructivist learning and leading principles. Simply put, the emphasis in constructivist accountability shifts from assessment *of* learning to assessment *for* learning and informed decision making. Standards of authenticity and congruence need to be applied not just to student learning but also to teacher learning and to the monitoring and evaluation of schools, programs, and districts in a system that is holarchic, not hierarchical. The portfolio and rubric lenses for looking at student learning, for example,

can be adapted for use in assessing the performance of educational organizations at all levels (see Appendix).

When the assessment and evaluation functions are seen primarily as dynamic dimensions of a multifaceted learning and feedback system, the gathering and analysis of student, teacher, and program performance data become congruent processes that reinforce and inform each other. When these data become a part of the information system described above, and the responsibility for sharing information with all stakeholders is taken seriously, assessment becomes an enabling structure for the district.

While most assessment activity remains focused on classroom and school levels, the district has enabling functions that are vital. Because of political pressures, high stakes, and the potentially controversial nature of some forms of alternative assessment, an important district role is to serve as buffer, defender, and interpreter, especially during the early stages of innovative assessment initiatives. District endorsement for and participation in "senior exhibitions," for example, could work to broaden a community's understanding of the nature of assessment. The district can also help identify like-minded schools and districts around the globe and to use technology to create a virtual learning community among them.

13. Encourage well-designed classroom and school-level innovation, collaborate in program assessment, and systematically facilitate the scaling-up of promising practices.
The role of the school district in selecting and supporting systemwide improvement programs and strategies is commonly recognized as vital and relatively straightforward. The Kansas City story is a positive exemplar. More complex but just as important are district strategies for providing "top-down support for bottom-up change" in districts where much (not all) of the authority and responsibility for innovation and improvement have moved to the classroom and school levels. Phil Schlechty sagely reports, "The more I work, the more I'm convinced that the biggest determinant of whether or not school reform will be successful is district-level capacity to support building-level reform" (Schlechty, 1994).

Since 1996, the Consortium for Policy Research in Education (CPRE) has been examining "district capacity to focus on and sustain reforms in teaching and learning, their strategies and capacity for supporting such reforms, and their approaches to scaling them up" (Corcoran, Fuhrman, & Belcher, 2001, p. 3). Among the key strategies they have identified are those aimed at ensuring that adoption and implementation decisions are based on solid evidence and that the district's own policies and procedures also are "evidence-based." Responsibility for gathering evidence and reflecting on it is shared by local and district personnel, but the district stake in preparing for "scaling-up" of successful innovations is uniquely heavy. Scaling-up can be facilitated by disseminating evidence of success, supporting cross-school communication and visits, providing incentives and resource support for adaptation, and so forth. Another valued district function is "reducing distractions and buffering the work from competing agendas" (including incongruent political pressures!).

CONCLUSION

A school district that restructures itself to function as a constructivist learning community will look and act very differently from a traditional district. In this chapter, we have described some design principles and shared some stories about places where constructivist strategies are being used effectively. It is vital that school districts become collaborative places of learning in which adults as well as students are continuously engaged in inquiring, reflecting, conversing, changing, and growing. Some of the learning will occur in individuals who are building an increasing sense of efficacy or agency; and most of it will grow out of reciprocal relationships in interactive learning and leadership groups. Many of the adult learning groups (study teams, curriculum development councils, collaborative action research teams) will and should cross school lines; those lines among schools and between schools and the district will become more permeable, and the spaces will become more like synapses that connect than voids that separate.

With the increase in the amount of autonomy and authority assumed by schools, clusters of schools, and cross-school teams and committees, the district roles will become more complex yet equally significant. They will emphasize capacity building, creating enabling structures and processes, coordinating school and district initiatives and services, facilitating reciprocal relationships, and ensuring coherence, responsiveness, and accountability in the whole system. They will attend carefully to the admonition in the Sufi teaching "But you must also understand 'and'" as they nourish the connections in their increasingly interdependent learning community.

While the design principles for building a constructivist school district culture are getting somewhat clearer, there remain some profound unresolved issues and questions:

- Are most school boards and district offices so comfortable in their hierarchical ivory towers that it is hopeless, that it would be better to abandon the structures altogether?

- Can constructivist thinking influence the standards/accountability movement and make it more authentic and equitable? ("accountability with a constructivist face?")
- Will primary authority for educational reform move over the long term to state and federal levels or return to some balance of school/district/state control?
- Can any but small suburban school districts create community?
- What is the role in constructivist leadership for charismatic style or the capable hierarchical thinker?
- Will universities be able to play their part in preparing constructivist leaders and supporting their long-term development?

The answers to these questions are, of course, "in construction"— being explored as pioneers blaze the trail and reflect on the obstacles they encounter. In Chapter 8, Margaret Szabo and Linda Lambert respond to that last question by proposing a framework for preparing constructivist leaders, describing exemplary programs, and speculating on the future of leadership preparation.

The saga of school reform is indeed a long-running drama, and we are nowhere near the last act. The scenes described in this chapter and in Chapter 6 clearly show that there are capable and creative actors on the stage. It is the hope of the authors of this book that the concepts and strategies of constructivist leadership can help the actors to move beyond improvisation and toward the epic scale of the sustained change that is needed.

CHAPTER 8

THE PREPARATION OF NEW CONSTRUCTIVIST LEADERS

Margaret Szabo
Linda Lambert

During the last 7 years, the heightened accountability climate has drawn sharp attention to the preparation of educational leaders. The shared verdict has been troubling: Preparation programs are labeled as antiquated and out of touch with the new realities of schooling. They are decontextualized classroom experiences with little relevance to today's schools. They have failed to develop the leaders who can improve these schools. Indeed, our schools are failing because our leaders are lacking—both in number and in quality. The critique involves all aspects of such programs, including content, delivery, format, field involvement and support, and follow-up. While overstated, the criticism is not unfounded. In this chapter we will describe some remarkable exceptions: those programs that engage leaders in professional, constructivist, timely, field- and inquiry-based learning experiences within communities of learners and leaders. These programs are deeply engaged with schools as they are now, yet committed to creating the schools that should be, the schools in which each child learns well and develops a commitment to a larger life out there in society and a richer life inside each of them.

The preceding chapters seek a deepened understanding of our theoretical construct for constructivist leadership. Chapter 1 describes an evolutionary view of leadership theory into the twenty-first century, while Chapter 2 once again insists that constructivist leadership represents a leap in conceptions of who leads and how that leadership is manifested. Leadership is described as the reciprocal processes shared by many rather than a set of behaviors invested in one person. It is not role-specific but derives from a mutuality of purpose, shared values, and communities that connect teachers and administrators, parents and students who work in the same school or district and are engaged in common efforts to create professional knowledge and grow together. Such learning communities are prepared to focus on student learning as the content and goal of leading. As we witnessed through multiple examples, these communities work effectively with the technical core of knowledge about teaching and learning in today's schools: instruction and assessments, standards and data, new knowledge about how humans learn, and resource management.

What most distinquishes the theory of constructivist leadership from other theories is the emphasis on the professional growth of the faculty. The goal of leadership, then, is to enhance student learning and adult learning, based on principles of constructivism. These principles suggest the following:

1. Learning is an active rather than a passive process.
2. Learning is by nature social and is most likely to occur when learners share ideas, inquire, and problem solve together.
3. Learners, to go beyond rote learning, must have opportunities to make sense of new knowledge and create meaning for themselves based on individual and shared experiences.
4. Reflection and metacognition contribute to the construction of knowledge and the process of sense-making.
5. New learning is mediated by prior experience, values, and beliefs.

These principles inform and shape the programs described in this chapter. When applied to the leadership of schools, they call forth vivid images that challenge existing views of leadership.

Earlier chapters in this book developed these images in depth. The notion of a community designed to promote individual and collective growth has been advanced throughout this book and given life through the narrative of school and district stories. The use of a typology of conversations—personal, inquiring, partnering, and sustaining—to further the reciprocal processes of leadership moved the discussion of constructivist leadership from the theoretical to the application stage. New understandings about leadership were gained not only from the discussion of types and purposes of conversations in schools but also from the chapters that illustrated the power of language to effect change and the use of narrative, story, and personal metaphor to promote adult development. The chapter on the role of the district office stressed the importance of acquiring skill in creating enabling structures that support constructivist communities.

This chapter builds on these previous images and offers some new ones related to the preparation of constructivist leaders in university graduate programs as well as regional, district, and independent initiatives. We are encouraged as we return to two of the three programs featured in the 1995 text. The chapter presents a design for leadership preparation based on the principles of constructivism, situated learning in community and inquiry, and the theory of leadership advanced in this book. This set of design features holds great promise in a field battered by critique and challenged by new realities.

TOWARD A THEORY OF THE PREPARATION OF CONSTRUCTIVIST LEADERS

WHY AND HOW DOES LEADERSHIP PREPARATION NEED TO CHANGE?

We will not get better schools and more equitable learning results until we support leaders in new ways of thinking, acting, and leading. Chapter 2 describes a system of such new thinking—a theory of constructivist leadership—and suggests that those who perform acts of leadership need the following knowledge, skills, and dispositions:

- A sense of purpose and ethics
- Facilitation skills
- Understanding of constructivist learning for all humans
- Understanding of change and transitions
- Understanding of context so communities of memory can be built and enriched
- An intention to redistribute power and authority
- A personal identity that allows for courage, risk-taking, low ego needs, and a sense of possibilities

Among the multitude of knowledge, skills, and dispositions effective leaders must draw upon, this list distinguishes constructivist leadership from more traditional theories. It is precisely a dearth of such capacities that thwarts the good intensions, high hopes, and hard work of would-be school reformers. Until school communities are understood as organic, dynamic fields of human hope, purpose, and energy—and populated by people with the skills and capacities to harness this energy field toward common purposes—we are unlikely to see schools making a difference in the learning and life chances of our children.

In the enterprise of leadership development, then, the stakes are high. The ultimate purpose of leadership development is the creation of schools as vibrant learning communities that are led by confident, competent, and caring leaders (Norris, Barnett, Bascom, & Yerkes, 2002). Programs to develop constructivist leadership aim to support educators in the life-long process of becoming such leaders—leaders who have the knowledge, skills, and dispositions to build leadership capacity in others and with others to create learning communities that are vibrant, caring places to teach and learn.

What Matters Most in Preparing Constructivist Leaders?

In contrast to the many traditional programs which, as observed above, "have failed to develop leaders who can improve schools," formal preparation of constructivist leaders means designing programs that enable participants continuously to

- reflect upon, question, and challenge current ways of thinking, acting, and leading
- clarify, change, and/or strengthen their values, beliefs, and patterns of thinking
- work explicitly at aligning leadership behavior and school practice with these strengthened ways of thinking

Yet in most leadership development programs, scant attention is given to the role that unexamined, implicit values, beliefs, norms, and patterns of behavior play in supporting the status quo and in obstructing fresh thinking and new approaches to making schools work better for all students. Typical programs focus on the transmission of traditional knowledge and skills about management, finance, law, curriculum, teaching, assessment, governance, personnel management, and so forth. Absent deep processes for questioning the status quo, reflecting on personal beliefs, and challenging the assumptions of traditional schoolkeeping, this customary curriculum develops leaders prepared to manage schools as they currently exist rather than transform them.

Figure 8.1 presents a rationale and set of design features for leadership preparation programs that aim to change the world of schooling by changing the ways leaders think, learn, and grow as individuals and as members of dynamic, purposeful educational communities. Such leaders transform themselves, their preparation cohort community, and the educational settings in which they work. Figure 8.1 also constructs a system of thinking—a theory—about *what matters most in the preparation and development of constructivist leaders.* The elements of the theory derive from our work in constructivist leadership, personal school leadership experience, observations of constructivist leadership in action, and inquiry into what constructivist leaders say has been crucial to their own development. What follows in the remainder of this chapter is a narrative description of the theory, examples and analysis of how these program design principles come to life in four preparation programs, and, in conclusion, a discussion of the challenges and opportunities facing the field of educational leadership preparation.

Six Design Principles for Developing Constructivist Leaders

The schema in Figure 8.1 illustrates our proposed theory of leadership preparation and its logical flow and component design principles. The six design principles are expressed as broad, reciprocal processes underlying constructivist learning and leading. It is important to note that these design principles are overlapping and contain one another; they work together as an integrated, dynamic, and interconnected whole. Often the six principles are mutually reinforcing: The more one is present, the easier it is to practice another. Together, these design principles present a vision of powerful development and learning for educational leaders, one that supports sustained individual and community learning and transformation.

Figure 8.2 provides a snapshot summary of links among the design principles and the questions and needs paramount to participants. It displays examples of strategies that support participants in trusting, purposing, doing, constructing, reframing, and transforming within a community of learners. The guidelines and suggestions in Figure 8.2 might be useful for program designers and instructors as they review, revise, or build new programs of leadership preparation.

1. Trusting: Who Are We and Am I Safe Here?
Becoming a confident, capable, and caring constructivist leader is a lifelong learning process that involves taking responsibility for one's own learning within the context of a community of learners and site-based colleagues. This responsibility requires active and reflective participation

FIGURE 8.1
A Theory of Preparation of Constructivist Leaders

THEORY OF ACTION	THEORY OF ACTION TRANSLATED TO PROGRAM DESIGN PRINCIPLES
IF . . . LEADERSHIP DEVELOPMENT PROGRAMS	
SUPPORT PARTICIPANTS IN LEARNING COMMUNITIES THAT . . .	
• Meet people where they currently live in their heads and hearts; • Challenge and support self-disclosure, risk taking, and reflection; • Sustain trusting relationships throughout the development and learning process;	1 TRUSTING
WHILE ENGAGING PARTICIPANTS IN DYNAMIC, REFLECTIVE PROCESSES OF . . .	
Purposing—Learning and leading by co-designing goals and activities, including • Personalization and individualization; • Common goals and expectations;	2 PURPOSING
Doing—Learning and leading by experiencing and participating in authentic learning community activities, including • Individual-centered activities; • Community-building activities;	3 DOING
Constructing—Learning and leading to make sense of everyday practice, including • Attention to discrete topics, skills, challenges and possibilities; • Attention to real world, integrated, holistic, problem- and practice-based topics, skills, challenges, and possibilities;	4 CONSTRUCTING
Reframing—Learning and leading by transforming thinking and action, including • Self-assessment and personal accountability for growth in leadership behaviors and practice; • Participation in mutual accountability for growth, change, or improved results;	5 REFRAMING
THEN . . . AS A RESULT WE WILL SEE MORE EVOLVED • Values and commitments; • Knowledge, skills, and capacities for constructivist leadership; • Schools and educational workplaces as vital, democratic, and caring places for powerful teaching, learning, and productive work	6 TRANSFORMING
AMONG . . . • INDIVIDUAL PARTICIPANTS, • THE COHORT GROUP, • IN LOCAL EDUCATIONAL COMMUNITIES	

FIGURE 8.2

Reciprocal Processes as Design Principles for Leadership Development Programs

DESIGN PRINCIPLES	ADULT LEARNERS' CENTRAL QUESTIONS & NEEDS	EXAMPLES OF SUPPORTING PRACTICES, ACTIVITIES, AND STRUCTURES
1 TRUSTING	*Who are we and am I safe here?* A safe context for risk taking and self-disclosure	• Year-long cohort group of 20–25 participants and 2–3 partner instructors; residential retreats, whole day meetings; • A diverse group of individuals to maximize potential learning; activities to maximize understanding of differences and commonalities among participants; • Instructor, coach, and mentor relationships are personalized and contextualized through site visits, one-on-one conversations, and coaching; • Frequent socializing: meals, celebrations, games, appreciations; team building; • Taking time to elicit and address emotions, questions, concerns.
2 PURPOSING	*Where are we going?* A sense of direction for desired growth and change	• Journal keeping; writing narratives, case stories, metaphors; • Dialogue with on-site mentor, instructors, critical friends in the cohort; • Self-assessment using varied tools, criteria, perspectives; • Inquiry about and analysis of site improvement needs; and of current site leadership capacity; • Feedback from site colleagues (*Note:* See also many practices under "constructing" and "reframing").
3 DOING	*How will we get there?* A practice field for action and reflection	• Modeling and encouraging authenticity—showing up as the real you; • Involving participants in leading and facilitating learning community activities; • Varied modes of activity, learning styles, and forms of expression; (kinesthetic, visual, spatial, verbal, mathematical, interpersonal, movies, books, art, crafts, music, dance, and so forth); providing choices; • Cultivating constructive irreverence, a sense of wonder and joy, and playfulness; • Inquiry, action research, fieldwork; exhibitions, demonstrations, and presentations.

	What are we working on and learning about?	
4 **CONSTRUCTING**	Authentic content—topics and issues as grist for meaning-making and skill building	• Model, teach, and build learning activities around dialogue, conversation, and reflection processes: dyads, personal experience panels, support groups, protocols, debriefing, fishbowls; • Emphasis on integrated and holistic themes rather than single-topic or discipline-based; however, address selected topics, skills, tutorials, workshops based on need, interest, timeliness; • Practice-centered, just-in-time learning, problem-finding and defining; coaching, advising, consulting; • Workshops, inquiry, and conversations with experts and distinguished constructivist leaders; • Building a community of expertise by identifying and sharing skills, experiences, resources, knowledge.

	How else might we/I view this?	
5 **REFRAMING**	A practice field for habits of mind and metacognition	• Surfacing and questioning assumptions; considering new perspectives and possibilities; • Journal writing, reflection, story telling to reveal patterns of values, beliefs, assumptions, and thinking; • Emphasis on inquiry and systems thinking: inquiry and analysis of how seemingly discrete problems (attendance, dropout rates, teacher turnover) connect to deeper patterns, long-term processes, and cultural norms; • Visits to constructivist schools; conversations with constructivist leaders to discover alternate ways of thinking about what is desirable and possible.

	How far have we gone? What difference are we making?	
6 **TRANSFORMING**	Connecting to moral purpose; new and deepened values and commitments; learning, action, and change in the service of a greater good	• Marking growth and change in values, commitments, skills, knowledge, and action; juxtaposing espoused values and goals with evidence from practice; • Self-assessment and accountability for growth in leadership practice using case stories, portfolios, evidence, and examples from personal leadership practice; • Participation in mutual accountability for growth and change through critical friendship, feedback, cognitive coaching, and assisting one another to frame new goals and actions; • Cultivating a capacity for unflinching acknowledgement of gaps, needs, and areas for growth; relentless pursuit of personal and community development toward heartfelt values, visions, and ideals.

in open and honest self-disclosure, risk taking, and deep and meaningful dialogue with co-learners. In addition, in such an ecological community, the greater the diversity within the group—race, ethnicity, language, sexual identity, class, income, and so forth—the greater the potential for learning and the greater the need for trusting relationships among participants. And trust is a result of shared experience over time. If trusting relationships is the air that learners breathe, then a central task for program designers is to engage participants in learning communities that

- Meet people where they currently live in their heads and hearts
- Challenge and support self-disclosure, risk taking, and reflection
- Sustain trusting relationships throughout the development and learning process

The central question underlying this design principle is *how to create a context that supports the building and sustaining of trusting relationships* among diverse participants in the learning community. Our experience and research suggest that a year-long cohort group of 20–25 participants—with the greatest possible diversity among members in the group—is an ideal structure in which to nurture such relationships. Getting to know and trust people takes time, and as time goes on, people know more and more about each other and build a rich history of shared experience—all of which intensifies and accelerates self-disclosure, risk taking, and meaningful dialogue. We have often observed that such year-long cohort groups—at the conclusion of a formal preparation program—spontaneously self-organize to continue meeting and learning in community.

2. Purposing: Where Are We Going?
One of the recurring challenges of constructivist leadership is interconnecting individual strengths and needs with group strengths and needs: for example, the science teacher-wizard who is a brilliant individual practitioner, but has no influence or responsibility beyond his or her own classroom and students; or conversely, the highly skilled, tightly knit science department that assigns new teachers to the most difficult and undesirable schedule. Learning *how to facilitate a group to foster growth in the individual—and the individual to support the growth of the group*—is a crucial leadership skill. Such skill is fostered through participation with the instructor and fellow cohort members in the collaborative codesign of learning activities that serve both their own needs and goals and those of the group.

Facilitated collaboration draws forth or evokes each person's schema, or mental model, of perceptions, experiences, beliefs, and assumptions.

These rich individual tapestries contain interests and goals generated through passion and values. These individual interests and goals serve as a driving force of the learning community, yet need to be balanced and interrelated with whole-group and program goals as well.

The central program design challenge is how to support collaborative processes for generating, balancing, and interrelating concern for promoting individual goals and well-being as well as whole-group goals and well-being. Figure 8.2 includes suggestions for pursuing this balance through activities such as journal keeping, dialogue with critical friends, self-assessment, and analysis and sharing of common and diverse site improvement needs.

3. Doing: How Will We Get There?

We've laid the groundwork for working on "trusting" (who are we?) and "purposing" (where are we going). This design principle—"doing"—is concerned with how to *pursue* the goals—*how to design activities that elicit and sustain authentic interest, investment, and engagement in learning* among diverse participants who, in most instances, are juggling demanding, full-time work, families, and personal lives. In these circumstances, meaningful learning requires both personal and contextual authenticity. Contextual authenticity grows out of the concepts of "situated learning" or "situated cognition" (Brown, Collins, & Duguid, 1989; Resnick, 1987). In this line of research, the activity in which knowledge is developed or deployed is integral to learning and cognition. Situations are said to coproduce knowledge through activity. Personal authenticity requires openness and honesty—showing up as "the real me" (Barth, 2001a). In describing the Aspiring Principals' Program (see next section), Barth observes,

> the "real me" was showing up. Something about these activities allowed principals to participate fully, to reveal themselves, to disclose, and not to check that real me at the door, as the job so often demands we do (or we suppose that it does). When learners were authentic, the learning became authentic because it was self-constructed, related to practice, and accompanied by a sense of wonder. (p. 160)

This authentic and situated nature of learning suggests the importance of grounding the preparation of constructivist leaders in *three facets of authentic doing:* (1) the reality of their own practice—the complex, dynamic, context-specific demands of particular school and workplace situations; (2) the reality of participation in the emerging preparation program learning community—the messy, contingent, interactive, and reciprocal processes involved in building and sustaining a community of learners; and (3) the reality of showing up as "the real me."

The design issues here involve these questions: How will individuals be supported to be fully themselves and to pursue personal interests and needs? What will individuals do on their own and in fieldwork at the site? What content and activities are useful and important to experience in and as a group? In Figure 8.2, notice a pattern of behaviors and practices that elicit and sustain authentic engagement, including modeling authenticity; involving participants in facilitating group activities; providing choices and varied modes of activities, learning styles, and forms of expression; cultivating irreverence, wonder, and joy; inquiry and action research; fieldwork projects; exhibitions and presentations.

4. Constructing: What Are We Working on and Learning About?
People learn how to develop and lead learning communities by constructing meaning from their own experience and by bringing new knowledge, skills, perspectives, and theories to bear upon their everyday practice. This design principle concerns the issue of *what specific kinds of content should serve as the grist for constructing new meaning* and building new knowledge, skills, and dispositions. The design challenge here is how to center content on real-world, practical issues from everyday practice while creating space for considering new possibilities and ways of thinking about these pressing problems.

On the one hand, education serves up to would-be leaders a host of relatively predictable, but nonetheless knotty, problems and challenges concerning organization and management of systems: for example, communication, governance, resources and budgeting, community partnerships, testing, attendance and discipline, conflict, curriculum development, professional development, state and district policy, and so forth. Which of these—at a given time, for a given individual or group—are of highest need and merit in-depth treatment as discrete topics? On the other hand, the flurry of each individual's everyday practice also presents holistic, integrated, and context-specific challenges. How do instructors elicit these and use them as grist for shared meaning-making? What balance between topic-centered construction of knowledge and practice-centered meaning-making will maximize authentic engagement?

5. Reframing: How Else Might We View This?
As a high school vice principal once observed, in the press of everyday practice there is little opportunity or incentive to pause and consider just why we spend all day shooting alligators instead of draining the swamp. Creativity, flexibility, and nimble mindedness in meeting challenges and solving problems is a hallmark of skillful constructivist leadership. Rather than taking problems at face value, one at a time (shooting alligators),

skillful leaders help others look beneath the presenting problem to underlying patterns, practices, beliefs, and causes (draining the swamp).

In education we have been powerfully conditioned—by lack of time, huge class size, dearth of resources, and professional isolation—to ignore problems until they reach a critical threshold or to take care of them quickly and often perfunctorily. The prominence and persistence of these bad habits in problem solving have important implications for developing constructivist leaders. More than anything else, program designers need to answer the question: *What is a powerful pedagogy for thoughtfulness*—for supporting participants to shed old, vestigial habits of mind and to grow new, more functional ones. Figure 8.2 describes activities that support metacognition, mental flexibility, and reflection-before-action, such as inquiry, use of storytelling, anecdotes, case studies, and journal writing coupled with skill building in questioning and cognitive coaching. Other strategies include providing question stems ("What is that situation a case of?"; What do you think is the cause of . . . ?") and repeated coaching and practice at defining problems at causal rather than surface levels.

6. Transforming: How Far Have We Gone and What Difference Are We Making?

In the medium to long run, the desired outcomes of leadership preparation programs have to do with fostering growth and progress along several dimensions of development. In particular, we focus on *three broad domains to identify needs and directions for growth and change:*

- Values and commitments
- Knowledge, skills, and capacities for constructivist leadership
- Schools and educational workplaces as vital, democratic, and caring places for powerful teaching, learning, and productive work

For example, participants within our Professional Administrative Credential Program at California State University at Hayward (CSUH) captured some of their own personal perceptions of transformation this spring in the following excerpts:

"I think my greatest area of growth has been in the area of ethical and reflective practice. It has helped me become clearer about my values; *I have found my center.*"

"I have a heightened sense of intentionality about what I do, a clearer focus and understanding about what I am trying to accomplish. I have increased my understanding about how to move toward equity."

"As a leader I have found myself posing the difficult questions: Why do these achievement discrepancies exist? What is lacking in the services we provide? What are we going to do about it?"

"This year has allowed me to respond with confidence from who and what I am, not from what I think others want from me or for me to be."

"I can now inspire others to look beneath the surface of their own reactions as well as others'."

Peter Senge (2000) observes that growth and development involve moving from the "current state toward a more ideal state." Participants need experiences that help them see themselves and their school communities as they currently are—accurately, honestly, and often painfully. In addition, they need experiences that expand their sense of the possibilities for change and improvement—new and vivid images of themselves as effective constructivist leaders and of their schools as vibrant, caring learning communities. Among many other sources of such images, we have chosen to highlight a few as especially apt and useful tools for guiding self-assessment, identification of gaps and needs, goal setting, and developing action plans for progress toward more ideal states. Figure 8.3 summarizes these selected sources and illustrates how the ideas might be used to help participants visualize a developmental path from where they are currently to where they would like to be in relation to the three domains.

In summary, our theory of leadership development anticipates that the more programs are characterized by the design principles and learning activities summarized in Figures 8.1 and 8.2, the more progress and development we would expect to see among participants along the three kinds of developmental continua in Figure 8.3.

We now turn to four specific examples of preparation programs that provide vivid examples of how these design features translate into strategies for developing constructivist leaders.

CURRENT UNIVERSITY PRACTICE AND CONSTRUCTIVIST LEADERSHIP

Constructivist learning continues to receive a good deal of attention. The impact of constructivist approaches can be seen most clearly in K–12 education, professional literature, state curriculum frameworks, and school reform provisions. At the university level, interest in constructivist learning

FIGURE 8.3

Sources for Visualizing and Assessing Developmental Progress as a Constructivist Leader

DOMAINS OF DEVELOPMENT	SOURCES OF DESCRIPTORS FOR STAGES OR LEVELS OF DEVELOPMENT	EXAMPLES OF DEVELOPMENTAL CONTINUA
VALUES, COMMITMENTS, AND RELATIONSHIPS	Hall, B., et al. (1990) *Developing Human Values*	FROM... Safety / Survival — Belonging / Self-worth — Creative Expression / Self-actualization — Inter-relatedness / Ethical Good ...To
	Kohlberg, L. (1976) *Moral Stages and Moralization: The Cognitive Developmental Approach*	SIX STAGES OF PROGRESS TOWARD REALIZATION OF STAGE 6 IN WHICH: Right is defined by conscience according to self-choosen ethical principles such as justice, reciprocity, equality, and respect for the dignity of human beings as individuals.
	Gilligan, C. (1982) *In a Different Voice: Psychological Theory of Women's Development*	Add caring to the above ethical principles.
	Loevinger, J. (1976) *Ego Development: Conceptions and Theories*	FROM... Dependence / Stereotyping / Fear of punishment — Independence / Multiplicity / Conformity to rules — Interdependence / Complexity / Self-evaluated standards ...To
KNOWLEDGE, SKILLS, AND CAPACITIES FOR CONSTRUCTIVIST LEADERSHIP	Lambert, L. (1998b) *Building Leadership Capacity in Schools*	FROM WE DO NOT DO THIS... ...To WE ARE REFINING THIS • Broad-based participation in the work of leadership • Skillful participation in the work of leadership • Inquiry-based information informs shared decisions and practice • Roles and responsibilities reflect broad involvement and collaboration • Reflective practice and innovation are the norm

continued

FIGURE 8.3 (CONTINUED)

DOMAINS OF DEVELOPMENT	SOURCES OF DESCRIPTORS FOR STAGES OR LEVELS OF DEVELOPMENT	EXAMPLES OF DEVELOPMENTAL CONTINUA
	California Professional Standards for Educational Leaders (2001)	FROM . . . . . . To Developmental descriptors of practice are forthcoming for six broad areas of standards: stewardship of a vision; instructional leadership; efficient and effective management; collaborating with families and community; modeling ethical practice and professional growth; understanding and influencing the larger context.
SCHOOLS AND EDUCATIONAL WORKPLACES AS VITAL, DEMOCRATIC, AND CARING PLACES FOR POWERFUL TEACHING AND LEARNING	Szabo, M. et al. (2001) Five impact statements from the "Rubric for Bold, Socially Responsible Leadership" (extracted and paraphrased)	LESS TRUE . . . . . . MORE TRUE 1. Race, class, and other subgroup memberships are no longer good predictors of academic success (or failure). 2. Inquiry cycles and continuous improvement are part of the day-to-day culture of the school. 3. Values and resources align to support inter-relatedness among decision making, school programs, and outcomes for students. 4. Everyone feels cared about as an individual and feels s/he has the power to change what needs to be changed and to make a difference here. 5. Two-way learning partnerships support the creation of new knowledge and help the school community proactively meet new challenges.

Our theory of leadership development predicts that the more programs are characterized by the design features and learning activities summarized in Figures 8.1 and 8.2, the more progress and development we can expect to see among participants along the three kinds of developmental continua in Figure 8.3.

and leading appears to be increasing. When choosing the candidates to feature in this chapter, we had many more nominees.

Four programs are described here as illustrative of innovation in leadership preparation. The exemplars are the Department of Educational Leadership at California State University at Hayward (CSUH); the Department of Educational Administration and Supervision at Wichita State University, Kansas; the Division of Educational Leadership and Policy Studies at the University of Northern Colorado, Greeley; and the Principal Residency Network (Aspiring Principals Program) at The Big Picture Company in Providence, Rhode Island. Two of these programs, Hayward and Wichita, were featured in the 1995 text. All have made significant changes to their programs and teaching practices to incorporate theories of constructivist learning and leading into their preparation of school leaders or, as is the case with the Aspiring Principals program, created a new entity designed to shift significantly the focus of preparation.

CALIFORNIA STATE UNIVERSITY AT HAYWARD

In the years since we last wrote about the CSUH programs, the faculty of the Department of Educational Leadership has placed even greater emphasis on modeling constructivist leadership in its own organization, behavior, and practices. The department has engaged current participants, graduates, and employers of graduates in assessing what is working and what needs to be improved to do a better job of preparing school leaders. As a result, many of the key features that further the development of constructivist leaders described in 1995 remain in place. Other features have been added, emphasized, or revised in an effort to strengthen program coherence around a more vivid and concrete picture of the department's goal: bold, socially responsible leadership. The following "big ideas" and accompanying practices seem to be those that most powerfully support the growth and development of constructivist leaders in CSUH programs. Among many other practices, the department emphasizes these five big ideas because—done well—they provide the essential context for the varied learning activities to take hold, flourish, and make a difference in the quality of preparation.

Devoting Time to Grow Shared Beliefs
Shared—and ever-evolving—beliefs and assumptions guide program design and practice at CSUH. Two core sets of values and assumptions form the foundation of the programs offered by the department. First is a heartfelt vision of the nature of school leadership in a democratic society. The faculty continues to devote time to articulating its fundamental understandings about school leadership and the nature of powerful teaching and learning

in the preparation of school leaders. Revisiting the department mission statement each year, the faculty has refined it into its present form:

> The mission of the Department of Educational Leadership is to pre-
> pare and influence bold, socially responsible leaders who will trans-
> form the world of schooling. Our central role is to ignite the leader-
> ship capacity needed to create vital, democratic, and caring places
> for powerful teaching and learning.

Undergirding this mission is an explicit statement of department values
and beliefs, which include democratic collaboration; diversity and equity;
bold, socially responsible leadership; critical inquiry; and continuous
improvement. Flowing from and supporting this vision of schools in a
democratic society is a core set of assumptions about the constructivist
nature of learning to lead:

- Knowledge and beliefs are formed within the learner.
- Learners personally imbue experiences with meaning.
- Learning processes should cause learners to gain access to their
  experiences, knowledge, and beliefs.
- Learning is a social activity that is enhanced by shared inquiry.
- Reflection and metacognition are essential aspects of constructing
  meaning and knowledge.
- Learners must be engaged in a critical role in assessing their own
  learning.
- The outcomes of the learning process are varied and often unpre-
  dictable.

Bringing these rich sets of ideas to life across eight full-time faculty, three
adjunct faculty, six cohort groups, 200 students per year, and four different credential and degree programs requires authentic collaboration—and
significant time together as a faculty. Department members meet together
for two residential retreats each year, and for about a day and a half each
month. In addition, program colleagues meet for coplanning and sharing
ideas. These investments of time foster construction of shared understandings and commitments and result in an unusually high degree of continuity of beliefs and approaches across the department's varied programs.

Developing and Using a Rubric as a Tool for Coherence
A "Rubric for Bold, Socially Responsible Leadership" supports coherence among values, vision, goals, curricula, instruction, student assess-

ment, and program evaluation and improvement (Box 8.1). Beginning in 1999, students and faculty worked together to define more vividly what is meant by "bold, socially responsible leadership." Together, faculty and students have developed and begun to use a rubric that defines essential "mindscapes" of such leadership, how it looks in practice, and the impact such practice would have in schools. Below is a chart summarizing the five mindscapes. Along with each of the mindscapes and its desired impact is a listing of the key areas in which candidates will develop and demonstrate knowledge and skills. The Appendix provides the complete Rubric.

During the development of the Rubric, the department reviewed and revisited the faculty's knowledge base in order to clarify and align their beliefs and understandings about leadership and their expectations for aspiring leaders with those of the larger educational community, including the recently published California Professional Standards for School Leaders (CPSELs). The department Rubric incorporates the CPSELs and, further, makes the role of the department's beliefs and values more explicit, extending them by describing developmental levels of practice. Instructors and participants use the Rubric in a variety of ways as a tool for constructivist learning and leading. It supports continuous self-assessment, reflection, and goal setting, and, as one faculty member observed, "the Rubric lends itself to an endless variety of activities that promote dialogue, build common meaning, and support groups to collaborate their way toward continuous improvement."

Organizing Relationships and Curricula Around a Cohort Structure

Department programs are organized around cohorts of one professor and 20 to 24 students who work intensively together for three quarters. This structure supports the relationships needed to model how to develop a learning community and to experience the power of generative dialogue, shared experience, and emotional support. Continuity of time and relationships builds mutual trust and enables reflective participation, honest self-disclosure, critique of one another's thinking and actions, and the opportunity to bring different lenses to bear on problems in practice as they change in substance and complexity over the year.

Such continuity also fosters a truly practice-based integration of the curriculum as common challenges, needs, and themes emerge from participants' day-to-day experiences. For example, participants in one cohort were having difficulty dealing with conflict. Beginning with cases from their own experience, the group identified readings, theory, guest experts, and inquiry questions to pursue in constructing new knowledge together.

BOX 8.1

*Summary of the Five Mindscapes from the Rubric for
Bold, Socially Responsible Leadership*

MINDSCAPE 1: Teaching and learning for equity and high achievement.

Essential questions: What difference are we making and for which students? From whose perspective? What skills and support do I need to take risks and lead for equity?

Desired impact: Race, class, language, culture, income, gender and sexual identity are no longer good predictors of academic success (or failure). All students are producing high-quality work and achieving at high levels.

Key knowledge and skill Areas include understanding of and strategies for ensuring equitable learning outcomes; student/teacher relationships; teaching, including subject matter expertise, best practices and exemplary instruction; inquiry and adjustment of curriculum, pedagogy, and assessment; and cultural competence.

MINDSCAPE 2: Systems thinking and strategic approaches to developing a learning community.

Essential questions: What are powerful ways to include and energize everyone to share responsibility for equity and better results for all students?

Desired impact: All members of the school community (students, parents, teachers, administrators, district staff, school board, and community members) are pulling together in a constant direction toward achieving a shared vision. The norms, beliefs, structures, and skills for inquiry, innovation, and continuous improvement are part of the day-to-day culture of the school.

Key knowledge and skill areas include understanding of and strategies for ensuring diversity and inclusion; democratic processes and collaboration; systems thinking; and a culture of inquiry and continuous improvement.

MINDSCAPE 3: Building organizational capacity through resource coherence.

Essential questions: How are we doing at focusing resources and energy where they will make the most difference to the quality of teaching and learning?

Desired impact: There is a constancy of effort and progress and a sense of efficacy and accomplishment in the midst of the flurry of daily activity. Values and resources align to support inter-relatedness among decision making, school programs, the school community, improvement efforts, and outcomes for students.

Key knowledge and skill areas include understanding of and strategies for ensuring organizing and managing effectively; building infrastructure including systems, processes, and practices; planning backwards; and integrating and using technology.

BOX 8.1 (CONTINUED)

MINDSCAPE 4: Ethical, caring and reflective practice.

Essential questions: Who belongs and has influence—and who doesn't? How does it feel to work, learn, participate, and live here? From whose perspective?

Desired impact: Honest, open discussion of significant—and sometimes difficult—issues and questions is valued in a supportive, caring learning community. Personal reflection results in focused, ethical behavior and practice. Everyone belongs, feels known and cared about as an individual, and feels s/he has the power and skills to change what needs to be changed and to make a difference here.

Key knowledge and skill areas include understanding of and strategies for ensuring: caring and belongingness; aligning values, behavior, and action; and critical friendship and reflection.

MINDSCAPE 5: Engaging and influencing forces within the larger community.

Essential questions: How are we engaging outside resources, forces, and relationships to help us learn and change what needs to change to get the results we want?

Desired impact: The school actively engages and influences the context to generate the knowledge, resources, and support needed for continuous improvement of teaching and learning. Two-way learning relationships and partnerships support the creation of new knowledge and help the school community proactively meet new challenges.

Key knowledge and skill areas include understanding of and strategies for ensuring: balancing organizational integrity and adaptation; inside/outside: mutual influence; inside/outside: building learning relationships.

Emphasizing Connections among Constructivist Leading, Learning, and Assessment

Department programs explicitly focus on the theory of constructivist leadership and leadership capacity as "the reciprocal processes that enable participants in an educational community to construct meanings that lead toward a shared purpose of schooling" (Lambert, 1998a). The department believes that schools should work as democratic institutions, including the recognition that all people associated with schools (teachers, administrators, students, staff, parents, and other community members) possess leadership qualities directly related to achieving school goals. Educational leaders must learn how to work effectively with the processes that bring these qualities to the fore among all those in their school community. So, to a large degree, the curriculum, pedagogy, and assessment resemble "a play within a play" in which process is content and content is process. Students participate in coconstructing and coleading their cohort learning community by engaging in the very same kinds of learning and assessment processes that they need to use at their work sites to build skillful, broad-based leadership capacity (see, for example, activities and practices described in Figure 8.2).

Further, programs emphasize that assessment activities are themselves forms and tools of constructivist leadership. Varied assessment practices—self-assessment, written reflections, feedback from peers and supervisors, portfolios, in-basket activities, oral and written presentations, culminating portfolio presentations, and conversations—elicit and model commitment to continuous growth and development, inquiry, collaborative action research, and processes for continuous improvement. Participants frame personal and collective goals based on varied self-assessments; design and engage in authentic work, site-based practice, and scholarship to pursue these goals; collect, analyze, and present data about changes and growth; engage in dialogue and feedback sessions about their work; and reflect on lessons and implications for reframing their leadership actions. The Rubric will be increasingly used to guide the various phases of these dynamic, nonlinear leadership and assessment processes.

Valuing Partnerships and Reciprocal Relationships in the Broader Context

Significant and ongoing partnerships and relationships with schools, districts, and other educational entities in the broader region help the department stay grounded, get feedback, and improve the quality of its programs. In addition, the faculty believes that the systems and policies that surround schools and school leaders must place greater value on constructivist leadership and create more friendly and supportive conditions for the practice of such leadership. Consequently, building and sustaining partnerships—with districts, policy-making entities, community organizations, professional organizations, and sister institutions of higher education—is an integral part of the department's theory of leadership development. In varied ways, the department actively engages and influences the context to generate the knowledge, resources, and support needed to *make the educational world a safer place for constructivist leadership*. Four prominent examples of such efforts include

- *The Leadership Academy:* A partnership with 17 school districts, the county office of education, and the Association of California School

Administrators to design and run a Preliminary Administrative Credential cohort.

- *Leading for Equity, Achievement, and Democracy (LEAD):* A collaboration with the Bay Area Coalition for Equitable Schools, the Oakland Unified School District, and other participating districts to design and run a Preliminary Administrative Credential cohort with an emphasis on leadership and design of small schools.
- *Joint Doctoral Program in Urban District Leadership:* A partnership with San Jose State University, San Francisco State University, and the University of California at Berkeley has developed a Joint Doctorate in Urban District Leadership based upon the agreement that it is with districts that the success or failure of urban education lies.
- *The California Professional Standards for School Leaders:* Department members participated in a 2-year collaboration with statewide professional organizations, districts, and universities to develop this set of standards to guide preparation, induction, professional development, and support over the span of administrators' careers.

WICHITA STATE UNIVERSITY, KANSAS

Early in 2001, Linda Lambert and Kent Peterson were invited to review the educational administration programs at Wichita State University, Wichita, Kansas. Since we had both written previously about the innovative nature of the program (Lambert et al., 1995; Kelley & Peterson, 2000), we welcomed an opportunity to take a closer look at the programs. We were curious whether the intentions of the program were maintained 8 years after it started and 7 years after it had been featured in *The Constructivist Leader.* And, we wanted to know whether any program could be as good as it looked on paper. The answer to both questions is "yes."

The program is designed to provide in-depth, field-based inquiry as a major strategy to achieve situated cognition, enabling participants to construct knowledge through social interaction within a meaningful context. This context, the school district, serves as the field for inquiry for teams of candidates. The conception of leadership assumes that certain capabilities, or areas of expertise, are essential to this form of adult learning: working with dynamic, contextual complexity; needing few or no prompts to conceptualize and perform the work; demonstrating and teaching strategic thinking and action; valuing others as assets; and inquiring into practice. These leadership expertise capabilities are demonstrated within selected performance standards.

Educational Administration and Supervision (EAS) offers a particularly successful and high-profile doctoral program as well as a master's program that seek to carry out a similar philosophy and approach. We found these features to include:

- Philosophical congruency and currency
- Field-based, authentic inquiry
- Team approach, including team teaching
- Cohesive faculty who share common understandings of the program, philosophy, curriculum, and delivery strategies
- Significant service to students in the form of advising, coaching, supporting, providing feedback on work, and acting as co-learners
- Program participants who develop and evidence self-direction and self-responsibility
- Curriculum based on national standards and authentic experience that is integrated with field study
- Quality field-based studies for public distribution, exhibition, and use
- Strong relationships with districts and schools, especially willingness of districts to provide substantial released time
- High completion rates (97%)

Based on program philosophy and assumptions, the curriculum at the master's and doctoral levels is inquiry-based; that is, the process is the content, and the process is the medium through which curriculum content is discovered and explored. The curriculum is coherent, integrated, and responsive. At both the master's and doctoral levels, EAS outcomes, Interstate Leadership Licensure Consortium (ISLLC) and National Council for the Accreditation of Teacher Education (NCATE) standards, and practicum and field-based inquiry experiences inform course content. At the doctoral level, content is driven by applied inquiry, state-of-the-art administrative theory, problem solving and decision making, technology, and dissertation research.

Innovative instruction within EAS master's and doctoral programs is constructivist in nature, closely aligned with program philosophy (instruction in the district certification program is more traditional). Such teaching practices include: seminar dialogues, case studies, analysis of site issues, coaching, team (including the faculty members) investigation through applied inquiry, action research, and reflective writing.

The program at the doctoral level is delivered in cohorts in all-day Wednesday seminars and field-based inquiry, team meetings in the field, and one-on-one advising (particularly during the dissertation phase), both in person and on-line. Courses or seminars are team taught at the master's and doctoral levels. Released time (one day a week) is provided by the districts for 2 years for candidates in the doctoral program. Interdependent learning communities model teamness and distributed knowledge in ways that we find increasingly duplicated in schools and districts. The assumption that faculty and participants work as peers and co-learners strengthens the team and teaches collaborative work. Classes and conversation are held on campus, in districts and schools, and on-line.

Student and Program Assessment: Current Practices

Candidate assessment values multiple forms of evidence based upon identified leadership characteristics, job-related professional criteria, and emergent criteria stemming from field practice. Multiple tools are used for assessment: Leaders Expertise Rubric (Checklist), Intern Team Member Performance Rating Sheet, portfolios, demonstrated competency on selected standards, Reflective Logs, case development as comprehensive examination, oral interviews, field study products, and the dissertation. At the master's level, assessment processes utilize all of these tools with the exception of the Leaders Expertise Rubric. Comprehensive team exams are a day long with an analysis of a case study; at the doctoral level the comprehensive team exam includes an extensive product and an individual interview. In addition, the dissertation constitutes the final product.

Program assessment also includes multiple feedback sources. Data related to program completion rates indicate nearly 100 percent. Superintendent surveys and conversations (personal communications, March 5–6, 2001) indicate that the field-based studies have been useful to districts, and the program is perceived as of high quality. Even though the 20 percent released time is a sacrifice (especially for a very small district) a commitment still exists to continue the time for the doctoral (and master's program in a more limited way). Regional leaders in the field believe that doctoral program graduates are expert leaders.

UNIVERSITY OF NORTHERN COLORADO, GREELEY

For more than a decade, the Division of Educational Leadership and Policy Studies at the University of Northern Colorado (UNC) has offered degree (master's and doctorate) and licensure programs in leadership roles in the field of education. The faculty incorporate innovative teaching practices and strong student advisement and guidance approaches, engage in inquiry about leaders and leadership, and demonstrate leadership at local through international levels.

Working with faculty from other national universities, the faculty at UNC have researched the unique nature of their programs (Norris et al., 2002). These programs are remarkably congruent with the framework for the preparation of leaders described earlier in this chapter. Further, program belief statements are consistent with constructivist leadership:

- Human growth and development are lifelong pursuits.
- Organizations are artifacts of a larger society.
- Learning, teaching, and collegiality are fundamental activities of educational organizations.
- Validated knowledge and active inquiry form the basis of practice.
- Moral and ethical imperatives drive leadership behavior.
- Leadership encompasses a learned set of knowledge, skills, and activities.
- Effective leadership in educational organizations depends on individual and team efforts.
- Leaders' behavior and actions model their belief and values.
- Leaders effect positive change in individuals and organizations.

These program beliefs are expressed through several program features, described in the following paragraphs.

Cohort Community
Based on the belief that "learning, teaching, and collegiality are fundamental activities of educational organizations," the licensure and master's program the and first year of the doctorate programs are designed as cohort communities. Communities are designed as transformative experiences for schools, districts, and the program itself. Case studies indicate a high level of transfer of these principles of action into the field. The cohort classroom experience is enriched by field-based inquiry, team building, district collaboration, and internships.

Constructivist Approaches to Pedagogy
The cohort community design is the setting for constructivist learning experiences. Attention to knowledge of self and others, an ethic of care, and a willingness to share power through collective contribution form the foundation of these communities. The model for preparation offered here suggests that through purpose, interaction, and interdependence within community, participants move through stages of development. These stages are expressed through evolving self-empowerment that leads to the empowerment of others and the community. The pursuit of self-

understanding and a clarification of core values are situated in learning communities. As participants clarify their own identities, they become more inclusive, receptive, and global in their perspectives. By retaining a habit of reflection, together with continuing conversations, these learnings and commitments become transferred to schools.

Preschool through Grade 12 Content

The preparation of administrators for P–12 schools is the major program focus. National administrative standards are integrated with social constructivist aims for inquiring, ethical, and democratic leadership. For instance, these outcome areas reveal the connections: a recognition of personal convictions and how to promote moral and ethical responsibility; knowledge of theories of leadership, change, and learning in adulthood; ability to model collegial leadership styles; and understanding of the evolving roles of the principal.

The Leadership Development Alliance, a District Partnership

The Leadership Development Alliance (LDA) is a partnership between the educational leadership program and four school districts. Based on the need of districts for a high-quality leadership pool of candidates and pervasive research on the efficacy of such programs, the program was established in 1999. LDA features are designed to benefit all partners, including the graduate students, and to incorporate the components of other successful partnerships (Whittaker & Barnett, 2000). The program is based upon mutual need and agreed-upon principles; joint planning and selection of participants; on-site delivery of the program (rotated among districts); district input into the curriculum and instruction; cohort groups; mentors; and midprogram review. This thoughtful partnership has anticipated challenges and proactively planned to meet them by attending to joint vision and goals, shared resources and roles, and the skillfulness and commitment of those involved.

Authentic Assessment

Assessment begins at the time of program selection with interviews and written products (goals and an essay on issues of significance). Curriculum-embedded assessments provide a means for candidates to demonstrate program outcomes: inventories of leadership strengths and theories; simulations, case studies, role-playing; shadowing and interviewing of administrators; and journaling and portfolios of internship artifacts. A strong emphasis is placed on formative assessment and feedback. Summative examinations, papers, and dissertations are primarily connected to the doctoral degree.

THE PRINCIPAL RESIDENCY NETWORK (BIG PICTURE COMPANY), PROVIDENCE, RHODE ISLAND

The Principal Residency Network (PRN) is a national training and certification program for school principals. Founded in 1998 as an initiative of the Big Picture Company in Providence, Rhode Island, the program was originally titled the Aspiring Principals Program. The Principal Residency Network is a leadership development and certification program that prepares aspiring principals through a full-time, school-based apprenticeship. It is a partnership among the Big Picture Company, university certification programs, regional Principal Residency Networks, local school reform organizations, local schools, and local mentors and aspiring principals. The mission of the PRN is "to develop a cadre of principals who champion educational change through leadership of innovative, personalized schools." The national PRN office is responsible for curriculum and material development, program expansion, and training and support of local project directors. Currently there are networks in Rhode Island, the greater Boston area, and southern New Hampshire, with a plan to open new sites over the next few years.

The description that follows is based on conversations with co-founder Elliot Washor and current national director Molly Schen, on anecdotes about the program from PRN Advisory Board member Roland Barth (2001a), and on phrases and passages from the program description published by the Big Picture Company on its Web site. The program flows from a clear, compelling, and explicit theory of leadership development involving connections among the following elements: the Mission Statement (see above), a Big Picture of Learning and Leadership, Design Principles, and Program Components and Requirements.

A Big Picture of Learning and Leadership

The program is based on an experiential model of learning grounded in teaching "one student at a time" while engaging each learner in a regional network and a small learning community of peers and mentors. A fundamental belief is that—at all educational levels—the best learning takes place in small communities that integrate academic and applied learning, promote collaborative work, and encourage a culture of lifelong learning. The program involves a collaboration among aspiring principals, distinguished principals, individual small schools, a regional PRN, and the National Office. The mission of PRN states:

> We cultivate reflective school leaders who demonstrate vision and moral courage; who are committed to social justice and equity; and

who understand learning, teaching, and organizational development. We believe that great principals act as change agents within the schoolhouse, in their communities, and in the larger context of educational reform. Mentor principals, participating schools, and program centers are selected for their ongoing commitment to this philosophy of learning and leadership.

Design Principles

- *The residency.* Aspiring principals learn the craft of the principalship through full-time, site-based residencies under the guidance of a mentor principal. Participants serve their school communities for 12 to 20 months and are awarded principal certification upon completion of the residency. Rigorous, individualized learning plans guide their experiential study. The program is committed to building an authentic curriculum around in-school stewardship that is relevant and responsive to the needs of the school community and the aspiring principal.
- *Learning from experience is not inevitable.* Experiential learning requires deliberation, self-awareness, and constant feedback. Aspiring principals are trained to be reflective practitioners who derive insight from their experiences and know how to modify their practice accordingly. Journal writing and regular, in-depth discussions with the mentor principal are critical, as are retreats, readings, and school visits.
- *Real-world assessment.* Participants learn through the real-world consequences of their projects. They document their efforts and results and create portfolios illustrating project work, writing, research, and reading. They give formal exhibitions through which they publicly present their work and reflect upon their learning goals and growth. One exhibition involved developing and implementing a comprehensive, long-range technology plan integrating curriculum, teaching, learning, and assessment. Participants receive ongoing written and verbal feedback from colleagues in the program cohort and from a school-based feedback circle.
- *The greater the diversity, the greater the learning.* The PRN recognizes that a respect for equal opportunity enhances learning and promotes the common good. In order to develop a cadre of leaders that reflects the diversity of our student populations, the program works directly with schools to find and recruit talented educators who have not traditionally been represented in school leadership positions.

Program Components and Requirements

INDIVIDUAL WORK

- *An Individualized Learning Plan* incorporating state standards and school needs with professional and personal learning goals.
- *Project-based Learning* addressing a challenge or need in the school; the project must involve assessing school-based data, developing and implementing strategies for change, evaluating program outcomes, and making adjustments as necessary.
- *Writing* in which participants continually reflect on their work and leadership development through formal and informal writing.

GROUP WORK

- *Team Meetings* in which the aspiring and mentor principal team meets daily for at least 30 minutes and weekly for an extended meeting.
- *Network Seminars and Institutes* that bring aspiring and mentor principals together in monthly network seminars and quarterly institutes to share best practices, provide support and critical feedback, and discuss theory and research related to educational leadership.
- *Cross-School Visits* within and outside the program network expose participants to a range of school practices, designs, and cultures and help build critical friends groups in the network.

PERFORMANCE ASSESSMENT

- *Portfolios* to illustrate learning and demonstrate readiness for leadership work.
- *Exhibitions* twice each year in which participants present their project work to a panel of participants, mentors, university faculty, and school community members.
- *Mentor Narratives* written twice yearly to assess the aspiring principal's service to the school, scholarship, growth, and leadership potential.
- *Feedback Circle* in which aspiring principals regularly enlist school community members to provide ongoing, in-house feedback and evaluation.

These elements interrelate and reinforce one another to provide a powerful leadership development experience for participants. Roland Barth (2001a) shares the reflections of one aspiring principal:

> The Aspiring Principals' Program is real-world training. Each day I have dealt with real situations, from budgeting to community relations, curriculum and

assessment issues to staffing and absent teacher coverage. I have worked to bring a diverse group of teachers together around a shared vision. I have challenged the local board of education and district-level administrators on staffing and budgeting issues. These are not textbook or case study scenarios. The people and the problems are real, and I am a direct participant with a vested interest in the outcomes. (p. 127)

COMMON ELEMENTS IN CONSTRUCTIVIST LEADERSHIP PROGRAMS

The above examples of four programs at three different universities and a private organization represent attempts to rethink the shape and texture of professional preparation. There are, however, common elements among them that provide signposts for other institutions desiring to reform their approaches so as to incorporate constructivism into their conception of leadership. These elements include the following:

1. *Conceptual congruence based on social constructivist values.* All programs are guided by clear core values that include social justice, equity, and democratic dimensions, as well as shared understandings about human learning and development. These values and understandings are expressed within a coherent conceptual framework and accompanying design features and principles.

2. *Pedagogy that emphasizes problem-based, constructivist forms of instruction.* These include team learning, shared inquiry, action research, reflective writing and dialogue, and use of narrative, story, and metaphor. Authentic work in the community of learners and in the field are generative and problem based. Generative forms of instruction enable students to construct knowledge based on their prior experience, beliefs, and values and to make meaning together.

3. *The use of cohorts to integrate the curriculum and to build among students a sense of collegiality and collaboration.* The cohort structure allows classes to function as a school faculty and to engage in goal setting, team planning, shared learning, and community building. Trust develops over time as knowledge, experience, values, and aspirations are shared. Within the Principal Residency Network, the teams are small—a candidate and his or her principal mentor; however, they become part of a larger community of learners through monthly Network seminars, quarterly residential institutes, and cross-school visits.

4. *Authentic assessment as integral to programs.* Each program uses innovative and consistent approaches to assessment. With the belief

that assessment is key to reflection, learning, and growth, curriculum-embedded assessment is the norm. Each program employs portfolios, journals, exhibitions, product development, inquiry, other projects, and multiple forms of formative feedback.

5. *Experience in changing cultural norms and fostering growth.* Because all four programs represent departures from traditional preparation programs, students and their professors or instructors assume new roles and responsibilities. Students take a more active role in their own learning and in shaping the outcomes for learning. Professors shift from center stage to a facilitation role, helping students to create meaning and apply new knowledge.

6. *Partnerships with districts and other organizations.* The LEAD Cohort at CSUH and the district partnerships at Wichita and Colorado are exemplary models of reaching out to build reciprocal relationships with a larger context. Within the network, partnerships particularly focus on securing sites with extraordinary principals who can serve as models and mentors. As we shall see, such approaches signal a major wave in the future sea change in leadership preparation.

The above program descriptions and synthesis of common elements provide only snapshots of how constructivist approaches shape the structure and content of leadership preparation programs. They do, however, reveal what is possible when constructivist theory informs the design of leadership programs. They also provide a bridge from what is to what can be.

CHALLENGES, TENSIONS, AND PROMISES

We began this chapter observing that preparation programs have fallen short, as noted in mounting evidence that too many schools are failing to serve the needs and ideals of a democratic society and that school leaders who can improve our schools are lacking in both number and quality. We then turned to exceptions to this observation, to descriptions of ideas about leadership preparation programs designed to develop leaders with the knowledge and skills to create the schools that should be. We know far more now than we did a decade ago about how to prepare constructivist leaders capable of transforming the world of schooling. And we have much yet to learn and to accomplish. The future holds many challenges, tensions, and promises as we seek to create an educational world in which constructivist leadership is widely practiced, creating more vibrant, caring, and powerful places for teaching and learning.

Redefining the Job of School Leadership

The job of the principal is widely regarded as consummately onerous: low pay, inadequate support, high stress, lack of respect, and exorbitant expectations and responsibilities. Every new policy and call for reform carries with it new roles, tasks, and demands for principals and other educational leaders who are expected to do *more work*—rather than to *work differently*. Constructivist leadership is about working differently. It is about seeing the school as an organic leadership community, one capable of living, growing, learning, and transforming itself. A major challenge for advocates of constructivist leadership is to join with district, regional, and state policy makers in identifying underlying causes for the crisis in school leadership and in codeveloping more compelling and functional visions of what leadership should be. Every pressing educational issue (e.g., testing, accountability, curriculum standards, teaching standards, professional development, resource allocation) has important implications for school leadership—and parallel opportunities for advocates of constructivist leadership to add their voice and experience to the dialogue.

The Standards Movement

First came student learning standards, then curriculum standards, teaching standards, and now standards for school administrators. The standards movement has the potential to become a juggernaut. Like most policy instruments, standards are a set of tools to serve larger ends: higher goals and expectations for all; a vision to drive change and improvement, a mechanism to focus curriculum, teaching, and assessment on what matters most; and a guide for improving instruction.

We can liken our dilemma with standards for administrators to the parallel dilemma that we've presented in this text regarding standards for children and standards-based accountability. As Reeves (1999) points out about the use of standards in "90/90/90"[1] schools, it is "not merely that they had standards, but rather, how the standards were implemented, monitored, and assessed" (p. 12).

In programs in which a more reductionist approach is applied, disparate knowledge is situated in separate courses and assessed through examination. The movement toward state uses of examinations based on national standards is undesirable to the extent that it can encourage and reinforce

[1]90/90/90 schools have 90% of their students in poverty, 90% are students of color, and 90% are above average in academic performance.

such limited approaches. Devoid of an overall theoretical framework, persistent core values, cohort communities, and authentic assessment, standards can actually handicap the work of developing effective educational leaders.

At the University of Northern Colorado, standards are an integral part of a broad-based developmental program. In the Principal Residency Network, standards are incorporated within the Individual Learning Plan. At California State University at Hayward, the integration of standards within an assessment rubric and process informs a curriculum implemented through learning communities. Such uses of standards hold great promise for a high level of performance among candidates and future administrators.

The challenge for preparation programs is to anticipate the reductionist pressures of the standards movement and find ways to use the resources and energy behind that movement in the service of deeper, more transformative learning goals.

ENHANCEMENT OF UNIVERSITY PROGRAMS THROUGH PARTNERSHIPS

Models for the reform of leadership preparation programs come from both inside and outside the university. These diverse settings hold promise for the further development of constructivist leadership and suggest that partnerships between universities and school districts can lead to new conceptions and practices in the preparation of school leaders. Such partnerships can facilitate the blending of theory and practice, providing opportunities for leadership candidates to experience the community, reciprocal processes, visioning, and mutual growth that are characteristic of constructivist leadership. University faculty must be vigilant, however, about retaining both theory and practice, articulating class and field experiences, and sustaining attention to reflection and research. These criteria create a particular sensitivity to programs that would offer one-shot or disconnected sessions.

Partnerships among universities and districts are increasing. Our examples of outstanding programs all include partnerships. Such partnerships ideally increase the relevancy and respectabiity of both partners. When they are based on shared goals, commitments, resources, and personnel, practices within and among partners become more transparent, more frequently held up to scrutiny, and more compelled to evidence success.

Other players are joining these partnerships with an array of sponsoring agents and aims. These include professional organizations such as the Association of California School Administrators and leadership academies and institutes in Missouri, Ohio, Michigan, Massachusetts, California, and elsewhere. Sponsoring agents range from private foundations and organizations, intermediate or county units, and states or provinces. These entities hold an advantage of resources and personnel for research and development as well as access to state-of-the-art literature and influential thinkers and writers in the field.

In Canada and Australia, partnerships exist among multiple agencies that are involved in the preparation and development of leaders. Excellent examples of such programs exist in Winnipeg, Calgary, and the Surrey (British Columbia) school systems, and the Australian (Melbourne) and Tasmania Principals Centres. However, since administrative credentialing is not required in these countries, participation is voluntary.

MOVING BEYOND THE UNIVERSITY FOR THE PREPARATION OF LEADERS

In some regions, we hear the cry for abandonment. There are those who have given up hope that universities can adequately respond to a demanding agenda for the preparation and credentialing of educational leaders. And, so goes the critique, they may not be equipped to do so. Charges of being ill equipped to deliver high-quality preparation have raised questions of currency of experience of faculty, outdated philosophies, relevancy of curriculum, quality of pedagogy, and inadequate field-based application and articulation.

The professional organizations, academies, centers, and institutes described above are emerging as key vendors and providers. In some areas, the field is becoming competitive; in others, these organizations are replacing the university as the center of leadership preparation.

There is less challenge to the traditional role of the university as the grantor of master's and doctoral degrees in educational leadership. The tension that exists around the issue of credentialing or initial preparation is not universal in this domain. In Canada, England, and Australia, university degrees also serve as the foundation for leadership preparation. While the university is still acknowledged as a center for research, knowledge generation, and publications, roles in preparation and credentialing are under close examination.

TEACHER LEADERSHIP DEVELOPMENT

A broader focus is emerging regarding the preparation of school leaders, and it is challenging old notions of who, in fact, leads. Throughout this text, we have advanced the thesis that leadership is best shared among faculty members who function in learning communities. In this conception of leadership, teachers share responsibility for decision making, goal setting, identifying core values, and developing processes that spur the growth of teachers, parents, students, and administrators alike. Leadership development efforts at Georgia State University, San Jose State University, Wyoming State University, the Ohio Leadership Academy, and the Australian Principals Centre in Melbourne are focusing on the preparation and development of teacher-leaders. These efforts range from workshops and conferences to special degree programs.

These efforts hold profound implications about the future of schooling and the promise of building leadership capacity. The more broad-based and skillful the participation, the more probable will be the growth of school and district capacity for sustainable development.

CONCLUSION

This text sets forth a renewed and deepened concept of constructivist leadership, the processes and strategies essential to the work, and stories and frameworks for moving forward. In order to accomplish the aims presented here, it is essential to prepare and develop the leaders who will transform—reconstruct—the world of schooling. This challenge can only be met by those who are themselves social reconstructionists, those who abhor the way things are and dream of what might be. Since preparing leaders is essentially a constructivist process, the work requires the commitment of people who are clear about their core values and the compelling need of humans and societies to transform their collective lived experiences.

Epilogue

LINDA LAMBERT

A longitudinal epiphany sounds like an oxymoron, for we are losing
our capacity for epiphanies played out through time.

Mary Catherine Bateson
Peripheral Visions *(1994, p. 113)*

As we ended the 1995 text, we challenged readers to consider two
notions essential to longitudinal epiphanies—insights that deepen over
time. One essential notion is that one of the greatest achievements of the
twentieth century has been the shift from static core metaphors to dynamic
core metaphors. By this we mean that our key concepts about the world
are no longer static. We now think of intelligence, roles, learning, gender,
even the universe, as breathing, expansive concepts that change with time
and new knowledge. Further, we noted that every conversation alters the
direction of change by deepening our understandings of our work and our
learning. We proposed that one of the major responsibilities of schooling
was to create learning opportunities through which core metaphors or
concepts evolve.

The authors of this book, as well as the readers, have had time to
delve more deeply into the meanings of the ideas we describe here. Most
notably, perhaps, we have been able to observe and converse with others
who are expressing constructivist leadership in their own practice. Those
stories appear throughout this text, especially in Chapters 6 and 7.

Sources of inspiration for our own epiphanies about learning began
early for many of us. These short vignettes tell you more about who we
are and how we initially came to understand learning for ourselves and
became intrigued with learning as a profession. When I was very small,
my mother would come to my bedside in the twilight of the morning,
wrap me in a blanket, and take me out to our sacred place on the damp
grass to watch the sunrise. She would keep saying, "Isn't that beautiful?
Look at all the colors, Linda." My mother was an artist, a poet, and a
feminist.

Mary Gardner's mother was also an artist. Her natural ability to write stories, draw landscape and flowers, and play the piano intrigued Mary as a young child. Her father was a scientist whose love of geology, chemistry, and the outdoors was generously shared on family vacations. Mary recalls, "On many family outings, I remember feeling pulled between sitting with my mother as she captured the horizon and the panoramic beauty in life with her pastel chalk or watercolors and walking with my father to find fossils, petrified wood, and geode treasures. I remember with clarity the day I discovered that I didn't have to choose between them. I could enjoy both."

Morgan Lambert's inspirations go back a generation—to a grandmother who chose "Paula Revere" as a pen name for her writing for the Womens' Christian Temperance Union. And to a grandfather who left a traditional Presbyterian ministry to travel around California in a truck with a bed and a printing press in the back—preaching, writing, and distributing revolutionary social reform tracts. Both wrote for causes they believed in; both found satisfaction influencing by the pen.

One of Joanne Cooper's earliest epiphanies came the summer of her junior year in high school. Horizon Girls, a campfire group, had been earning money for 4 years to take a trip around the United States. They ended their 19-state tour with tea at Eleanor Roosevelt's apartment in New York. "Here we were," Joanne recalls, "nineteen provincial high school girls from Forest Grove, Oregon—not a bit famous or even the least bit important on most levels. The Campfire Executives in New York asked, 'My dear, however did you get in to see Eleanor Roosevelt?' We said, 'We wrote and asked her.' I learned that often if you want something, you have merely to ask for it. The world frequently opens up to you in ways you would never have believed possible."

Diane Zimmerman came to her early epiphanies on questioning as a shy schoolgirl. A turning point in her journey away from shyness was in the seventh-grade math class with Mr. Gash. He insisted that students ask questions. He would say, "There is no such thing as a dumb question," and then he would just wait. She began to understand that asking questions was a good thing to do and to appreciate her own father's tendency to ask complex questions at home. Diane learned that asking questions was a powerful way to learn by bringing understanding, focus, and curiosity to the process.

For Deborah Walker, an epiphany about the power of language to create and communicate meaning came to her as a young student. Always an avid reader, Deborah learned early on that she had an ability to construct new learning through her writing, for herself and her intended audience. Writing became a way to organize thinking and to connect with previous experience. As a school and district leader, Deborah's longitudinal epiphany came in the knowledge that expectations and organizational norms can be shaped by use of simple yet compelling language.

In the early through mid-1990s, I worked in Egypt with Kawsar Kouchok, Director of the National Curriculum Center. She helped me, and we helped each other, to understand that the origin of learning lies in aesthetics and patterned experiences—because, she would argue, aesthetics evoke the senses, and patterns practice the senses. As we touch, see, smell, and hear, we find joy, a deep pleasure that comes from opening the imagination to new possibilities. These experiences sketch out our schemas that are the backdrop for lifelong learning. By tapping into our senses, we grow the learner.

More recently, I read Roland Barth's (2001a) description of his one-room schoolhouse experience at Puddle Dock School. I recall that my own small Kansas school (90 students in our K–8 school and another 90 in our 4-year high school) and one of those years in a one-room school nearby provided some parallel experiences. While gender difference provided a somewhat different lens (he could be "ornery," I was compelled to be a "good girl"), many lessons about smallness formed our values about schooling. In the whole of those 12 years, I learned that

- Learning is personal, yet . . .
- When every one learns together, everyone learns more.
- The more opportunities there are to learn, the more internal resources, capacities are evoked. We have little idea about what we are capable of until the opportunity presents itself. In a small school, everyone does everything.
- Organizing learning by age and grade limits our capacities to learn and ensures lower expectations for many. "Age" and "grade" are static core metaphors; they define and confine us.
- The assumptions about learning held by the teacher will determine how she communicates, organizes, and supports learning for children.

True learning grows from aesthetics and patterned experiences, imagination, investigation, relationships, and limitless opportunities. Do our standards expect enough—and do they expect those things that matter? Do our rubrics measure true learning? Amy Tan (2001) suggests a rubric for beauty that has caused us to challenge the quality of learning in our schools:

- *Competent* is the ability to draw the same thing over and over in the same strokes, with the same force, the same rhythm, the same trueness. This kind of beauty, however, is ordinary.
- *Magnificent* goes beyond skill. Its beauty is unique. It conveys both strength and solitude. The lesser painter would be able to capture one quality but not the other.
- *Divine* is a singular achievement that transcends descriptive language. The same painter could never again capture the feeling of this painting, only a shadow of a shadow.
- *Effortless* is yet possible for each mortal. We can sense it only if we do not try to sense it. It occurs without motivation or desire or knowledge of what may result. It is pure. It is what innocent children have, or masters can regain. It is the natural wonder that anything exists in relation to another. (pp. 276–278)

Learning in community becomes *effortless* when we are engaging the hearts and minds of learners. To be a constructivist leader is to be such a teacher for the whole school or district. Yes, learning does take effort, but when learning emerges in an environment of possibilities and community, effort feels rewarding and satisfying. We need to convene the conversation; to facilitate the dialogue; to evoke the spiritual and joyful sides of ourselves; to create space for reflection, discernment, and discretion; and to provide support and pressure. "Communities of practice," continues Bateson (1994), "blur the line between aspirants because both are still developing" (p. 115). To attend to the learning of each other is to become an eloquent participant. Such an adult community is capable of profound accomplishments.

At this point in our learning journey we offer a few longitudinal epiphanies. The perspective of this text envisions the following:

- Leadership as manifest throughout the community, thereby separating the opportunities for leadership work from role, person, a specific set of skills, and positional authority
- Leadership as expressed through the stories that we live and the lives that we story
- Purposeful learning and leading as embued with core values that ultimately include social justice, equity, and caring
- The engagement of children and adults in congruent learning communities that serve as a context for growth and development
- Constructivism at the heart of the concept of community, establishing meaning as the energy source that facilitates learning

- The preparation of educational leaders who can understand and undertake such challenges because they have been there, because they have experienced the mutual creation of meaning and knowledge in a purposeful community

We continue to be persuaded that work in constructivist leadership and learning can reconstruct our most fundamental perceptions of the concepts that define us: community, learning, and democracy. And we continue to be hopeful that schools can lead the reconstruction of society toward interdependence.

Constructing these meanings out of our lives and the lives of children is a complex undertaking, yet we are witness to the daily achievements in schools that are succeeding in these ways. Constructing a future of schooling is synonymous with constructing the everyday lives of people living in our institutions and our society, a process of learning together over time, a longitudinal epiphany. We pursue such epiphanies in order to "weave whole cloth from multiple strands."

Appendix

Mindscape Element 1: Bold, Socially Responsible Leaders Focus on . . .

Teaching and Learning for Equity and High Achievement

Desired Impact of the Leadership work: Race, class, language, culture, income, gender, and sexual identity are no longer good predictors of academic success (or failure). All students are producing high-quality work and achieving at high levels.

EMERGING LEADERS	PRACTICING LEADERS	INTEGRATING LEADERS
Equitable learning outcomes • Define equity as equality of opportunities; • Value a fairness interpretation of resource allocation (same amounts); • Use informal data to assess needs.	*Equitable learning outcomes* • Strengthen equity through providing additional program access; seek programs and practices supportive of students of color—often programs that assume that fixing the student is the remedy; • Disaggregate data to find achievement gaps.	*Equitable learning outcomes* • Define educational equity as equitable learning results; • Act on achieving equity and closing the achievement gap between white students and students of color by allocating resources in ways that ensure that historically underserved groups of students have whatever support they need to succeed—both within the regular classroom and through personalized support strategies.
Student/teacher relationships • Use traditional structures (counselors, student services, special programs) to support students; • Intensify behavioral codes in response to high numbers of referrals of students of color.	*Student/teacher relationships* • Begin to view behavioral issues as a teaching and relationship issue; • Support community building in classes; • Engage parents in conversations to bring some clarity and support for improving classroom strategies for students; • Initiate programs designed to connect students and teachers (e.g., mentoring).	*Student/teacher relationships* • Support teachers in continuously learning about their students' individual learning styles, home culture, interests, and strengths—and in using this knowledge to build caring, personalized relationships with each student; • Value and model interacting with students, parents, and teachers as caring, respectful partners in authentic learning work; • Develop and carryout strategies that build the school's resiliency "protective factors" (e.g., advisory).

(continued)

245

EMERGING LEADERS	PRACTICING LEADERS	INTEGRATING LEADERS
Teaching: subject matter expertise, best practices, and exemplary instruction	*Teaching: subject matter expertise, best practices, and exemplary instruction*	*Teaching: subject matter expertise, best practices, and exemplary instruction*
• View best practices as generic—that is, relatively fixed across differences in learning styles, cultures, and subject areas;	• Begin to focus on best practices for diverse student needs taking into account learning styles and varying subject strategies;	• Support teachers in researching, adapting, and implementing diverse practices that support each student's learning and success;
• Support uniform professional development—one-size-fits-all—both in content and strategies;	• Support colleagues working together to plan lessons, share ideas;	• Model and support working collaboratively to take personal responsibility for classroom results—and collective responsibility for the quality, coherence, and effectiveness of schoolwide practices;
• Support voluntary teacher planning; help organize staff development days around teacher concerns (e.g., discipline);	• Assist in the facilitation of faculty meetings and professional development discussions about teaching and learning on an ongoing basis;	• Model asking hard questions, reflecting, and engaging in critique of both individual and collective practice.
• Use identified resources in school plan to support staff to attend staff development.	• Secure school and district resources to support professional development.	• Devote significant time to deepening subject matter expertise;
		• Proactively align resources and structures to support professional growth;
		• Build and work toward a shared vision of learning, teaching, and best practices;
		• Expand and deepen a range of teaching strategies that engage every student in working hard at important things.
Inquiry and adjustment of curriculum, pedagogy, and assessment	*Inquiry and adjustment of curriculum, pedagogy and assessment*	*Inquiry and adjustment of curriculum, pedagogy, and assessment*
• Focus on efficient management;	• Support the use of multiple forms of evidence to develop school plans;	Initiate, facilitate, and support teachers as they:
• Make curriculum refinements based on experience, personal judgment, and standardized test scores;	• Disaggregate and review data to identify which students are succeeding and use findings to shape school action plans;	• Pose questions of practice about the learning of all students through examining student work and inquiry;
• Rely on the district for data;		• Use data/evidence from multiple sources about the quality of learning to document patterns of equity and inequity over time;

• Make little use of inquiry beyond that required for formal evaluation processes.

Cultural competence
• Focus on similarities more than dealing with controversial or provocative issues; hesitant to acknowledge or surface conflict;
• Share quotes or articles for consideration, but provide little time or few processes for thoughtful, in-depth dialogue about equity;
• Encourage teachers to take district and regional workshops on diversity; provide little follow-up within the school;
• Work with parents of students of color on a one-to-one basis.

• Build intervention strategies into the school plan.

Cultural competence
• Empower a team or committee to look at equity issues;
• Support limited full staff discussions about equity;
• Inform parents of students of color about new school practices;
• Facilitate shared meeting times to include information, program requirements, or issues of urgency.

• Use findings to address achievement gaps by strengthening and adjusting curricula, instruction, assessment, and services to students;
• Establish accountability criteria for self-monitoring of learning outcomes.

Cultural competence
• Provide time, incentives, and resources for teachers to engage in dialogue about equity, race, racism, bias, and institutional racism;
• Build partnerships with students and parents of color through active outreach, inclusion, and two-way communication; ensure that perspectives and experiences of underserved students appropriately influence changes in teaching and school practices;
• Engage in dialogue about relationships and connections among the ideals, goals, and conditions needed to promote equity, democracy, and social justice.

MINDSCAPE ELEMENT 2: BOLD, SOCIALLY RESPONSIBLE LEADERS FOCUS ON . . .

SYSTEMS THINKING AND STRATEGIC APPROACHES TO DEVELOPING A LEARNING COMMUNITY

DESIRED IMPACT OF THE LEADERSHIP WORK: All members of the school community—students, parents, teachers, administrators, district staff, school board, and community members—are pulling together in a constant direction toward achieving a shared vision. The norms, beliefs, structures, and skills for inquiry, innovation, and continuous improvement are part of the day-to-day culture of the school.

EMERGING LEADERS	PRACTICING LEADERS	INTEGRATING LEADERS . . .
Diversity and inclusion	*Diversity and inclusion*	*Diversity and inclusion*
• Participate in parent and community groups to represent the school and communicate its needs;	• Cultivate and maintain varied connections and relationships to parents, community members, and agencies to assure support of school goals and activities;	• Understand the subtleties of the school and community context and the centrality of inclusion, relationships, and diversity to a healthy community culture;
• Seek and elicit support from parents and community members who voluntarily respond and participate in school groups, meetings, and activities;	• Welcome and respect diverse perspectives as input in decision making; take needs and concerns of underserved students into account in decision making;	• Proactively elicit and include diverse perspectives; ensure that underserved students and parents are participating and influencing decisions;
• Smooth over and work around disagreements and conflicts to maintain a calm, professional atmosphere.	• Manage conflict to solve problems that arise.	• Surface disagreement, conflict, and gaps and use these as opportunities to change the status quo.
Democratic processes and collaboration	*Democratic processes and collaboration*	*Democratic processes and collaboration*
• Delegate selected responsibilities and tasks to committees and task groups facilitated by administrators;	• Support groups with time and resources to work on a problem or task;	• Value collaboration and build trust through shared experience and work;
• Seek discussion, input, or voting processes for selected issues and decisions;	• Encourage collaboration among teachers on curriculum and teaching issues they care about;	• Enable the community to use democratic processes to create meaning and a shared sense of purpose;
• Organize, prepare agendas, and lead effective meetings that accomplish the agenda goals;	• Begin to develop and employ new skills for facilitating collaborative and democratic processes;	• Consistently develop and hone skills for effective collaborative group work (e.g., inquiry, dialogue, facilitation, meeting design);
• Ask others to lead or share leadership of gatherings.	• Begin to support others to identify issues, take initiative, and collaborate on improvement work.	• Model resourcefulness, risk-taking, and empathy; empower teams/colleagues to create long-term change.

Systems thinking
- Begin to understand that important issues and problems cannot be solved in isolation from a larger context;
- Address teacher learning needs through individual training or whole school in-service;
- Identify promising strategies and provide time for teachers to learn to implement them effectively.

Culture of inquiry and continuous improvement
- Rely on personal problem-solving skills to identify problems and to suggest programs and solutions;
- Enlist others in implementing promising improvement programs;
- Communicate clearly what everyone is expected to do; provide resources; monitor progress.

Systems thinking
- Sometimes work on issues as connected to larger systems and contexts;
- Begin to connect student results to improving the quality of teaching and classroom experience;
- Begin to support teachers to identify their own learning needs (substantiated by data and data analysis) and to collaborate to find and apply promising strategies.

Culture of inquiry and continuous improvement
- Begin to engage the school community in inquiry;
- Understand and support individual and schoolwide change processes in relation to new programs and efforts;
- Begin to model asking questions and looking for fundamental causes and assumptions.

Systems thinking
- See any given strand of work as part of a larger system;
- Create systems (structures, processes, time, resources, and forums) to create shared commitments and to support learning and professional community;
- Seek and build upon connections, teachable moments, strategic approaches, and opportunities to lead.

Culture of inquiry and continuous improvement
- Understand and support the change process and change agentry in the context of dynamic systems;
- Build and support an inquiry culture to generate shared knowledge and commitment for action regarding gaps in student learning and achievement; equity; the quality of student experience, engagement, and belongingness;
- Facilitate purposeful inquiry, reflection, and continuous improvement;
- Ask questions, surface assumptions, and challenge the status quo.

MINDSCAPE ELEMENT 3: BOLD, SOCIALLY RESPONSIBLE LEADERS FOCUS ON . . .
BUILDING ORGANIZATIONAL CAPACITY THROUGH RESOURCE COHERENCE

DESIRED IMPACT OF THE LEADERSHIP WORK: There is a constancy of effort and progress and a sense of efficacy and accomplishment in the midst of the flurry of daily activity. Values and resources align to support interrelatedness among decision making, school programs, the school community, improvement efforts, and outcomes for students.

EMERGING LEADERS	PRACTICING LEADERS	INTEGRATING LEADERS
Organizing and managing effectively • Are practical; use tools to self-organize and support school management and organization; • Make use of resources from a sense of urgency; • Make resource decisions for existing or add-on programs.	*Organizing and managing effectively* • Are practical, efficient, and organized; manage and act using discussions and input of others; • Use resources with student achievement in mind; • Align resources to support improvement efforts; • Are aware of and use available resources to support existing programs as well as new ideas.	*Organizing and managing effectively* • Are practical, efficient, and organized; balance management and action with dialogue and reflection; • Act from a clear understanding of the cause-effect relationship between resource use and student achievement; • Align resources and systems to provide coherent support for innovation and continuous improvement of teaching and learning; • Garner resources through innovative thinking and flexibility; find ways to do more with current resources.
Building infrastructure: systems, processes, practices • Work from implicit values and beliefs to continue existing practices and resource allocation patterns; • Think about ideas, resources, and actions as discrete, concrete, and linear—and so, discrete programs come and go while deep structures remain the same;	*Building infrastructure: systems, processes, practices* • Facilitate development and alignment of vision, values, goals, resources, and practice; • Begin to align resources in support of change and improvement efforts; • Begin to understand and grapple with systems and contexts; develop skills for change management;	*Building infrastructure: systems, processes, practices* • Explicitly think in terms of systems and infrastructure (a complete picture); • Constantly check for alignment of vision, values, goals, resources, and practice; • Build leadership capacity by developing broad-based, skillful participation in leadership;

- Are constrained by externally defined policies, programs, and practices;
- See traditional practices and systems (attendance, behavior, schedules, grouping policies) as discrete and relatively fixed activities that are assumed to facilitate teaching and learning (a smattering of individual puzzle pieces).

Planning backwards
- Modify school plans annually to adjust for population and staffing shifts;
- Use SAT 9 data to plan and determine resource needs.

Integrating and using technology
- Respond to individual teacher needs and requests related to upgrading technology;
- Support current technology users and encourage others to begin using technology;
- View integration of technology into teaching and learning as optional—a matter of preference in style of teaching.

- Allocate some time for building and maintaining professional relationships that support discussion and collaborative work on teaching and school practice;
- Begin to relate (and adjust) systems to support student engagement in a rigorous and challenging learning community (an emerging picture).

Planning backwards
- Begin to engage in planning/inquiry/action cycles;
- Use strategic planning tools to develop a student need-based plan;
- Use multiple measures of student achievement to assign resources to meet student needs.

Integrating and using technology
- Expect teachers and students to integrate technology into teaching and learning;
- Provide time, resources, training, and coaching;
- Use technology to support core educational systems: classroom teaching and learning; curriculum development; communication; data and records; assessment and grade reporting.

- Allocate generous time to build and maintain professional relationships that support deepening dialogue and reflection on practice;
- Understand that systems and context are dynamic; facilitate adaptivity and transitions in order to meet the needs of all learners and achieve equity;
- Design and create systems (e.g., attendance and behavior policies, schedules, grouping policies) in ways that support personalization and engagement in a rigorous, challenging learning community.

Planning backwards
- Draw from a broad and ever-deepening knowledge base about learning communities; management; organizations; strategic planning; systems thinking; dynamics of change; collaborative inquiry; budgeting; law;
- Practice "forward-looking and backwards planning"; clarify and set goals and build action plans that move from the current state toward the desired goals;
- Understand and use evidence and other information to assess student and organizational learning needs and secure and align resources to meet those needs.

Integrating and using technology
- Model lifelong learning for technological literacy;
- Use varied technologies and technological applications to support core educational systems: classroom teaching and learning; curriculum development; communication; data and records; assessment and grade reporting;
- Support everyone in developing skills to participate in electronic learning communities;
- Plan, seek, and acquire resources to support ongoing infusion and widespread use of up-to-date technology.

MINDSCAPE ELEMENT 4: BOLD, SOCIALLY RESPONSIBLE LEADERS FOCUS ON . . .
ETHICAL, CARING, AND REFLECTIVE PRACTICE

DESIRED IMPACT OF THE LEADERSHIP WORK: Honest, open discussion of significant—and sometimes difficult—issues and questions is valued in a supportive, caring learning community. Personal reflection results in focused, ethical behavior and practice. Everyone belongs, feels known and cared about as an individual, and feels s/he has the power and skills to change what needs to be changed and to make a difference here.

EMERGING LEADERS	PRACTICING LEADERS	INTEGRATING LEADERS
Caring and belongingness • Act from a need to control situations and decisions; • Strive to think and act with regard for people; • Act cautiously to avoid mistakes; • Allow concern about perceptions of self sometimes to drive actions; • Display enthusiasm and a positive attitude to soothe problems and maintain stability.	*Caring and belongingness* • Consistently think and act with regard for people; • Willingly show vulnerability and lack of knowledge; • Encourage passion and enthusiasm on behalf of shared purposes; • Use authority to create voice for those willing to speak up; • Begin to apply cultural competence and emotional intelligence to broaden inclusion and improve the quality of planning and decision making.	*Caring and belongingness* • Think and act first with regard for people; • Lead with the whole self; vulnerable, fallible, and humble; admit and accept mistakes; give credit to others and keep ego in check; use humor, perspective, and patience to create a climate of caring, trust, respect, and purposefulness; • Generate passion and enthusiasm, create hope, bestow praise, and encourage the heart; • Create ways for everyone to have voice and influence within a culture of peers; • Cultivate and apply cultural competence and emotional intelligence to enhance mutual understanding, inclusion, and responsiveness to diverse needs.

Aligning values, behavior, and action
- View the values, beliefs and norms of the school culture as relatively fixed and difficult to change;
- Consider school to be a community and seek to make decisions based on what is best for that community;
- Begin to understand that actions speak louder than words;
- Aware of the influence of language and behavior on members of the school community.

Critical friendship and reflection
- Recognize that introspection and reflection are desirable;
- Seek feedback on a selective basis from trusted colleagues;
- Begin to identify significant issues and questions.

Aligning values, behavior, and action
- Make decisions and initiate system change to ensure school is student centered;
- Examine personal values and beliefs in regard to the vision for the school;
- Model and cultivate being the lead teacher/student;
- Begin to investigate the influence of language and behavior on groups within the school community;
- Speak and act with a sense of purpose.

Critical friendship and reflection
- Begin to value introspection and reflection in themselves and others;
- Seek feedback from the learning community members;
- Identify issues and question assumptions.

Aligning values, behavior, and action
- Espouse and enact a philosophy putting equity and the needs of students at the center of all school processes;
- Continuously clarify personal beliefs, values and vision (e.g., democracy, equity, caring, social justice) and how these are expressed in the educational community;
- Engage in reflective practice to insure moral and spiritual congruence;
- Engage others to examine and reflect upon their own values in relation to shared vision and practice;
- Support discussions about the influence of language and behavior on all members of the school community;
- Speak and act with conviction, passion, courage, integrity, commitment, and tenacity.

Critical friendship and reflection
- Model being teachers and lifelong learners;
- Value inquiry, creativity, and diverse perspectives;
- Give and value feedback, mentoring, and critical friendship; give and value timely feedback that is honest, direct, and tactful;
- Challenge him/herself and others; surface assumptions; collaborate to find, clarify, and address issues, problems, and questions.

MINDSCAPE ELEMENT 5: BOLD, SOCIALLY RESPONSIBLE LEADERS FOCUS ON . . .
ENGAGING AND INFLUENCING FORCES WITHIN THE LARGER CONTEXT

DESIRED IMPACT OF THE LEADERSHIP WORK: The school actively engages and influences the context to generate the knowledge, resources and support needed for continuous improvement of teaching and learning. Two-way learning relationships and partnerships support the creation of new knowledge and help the school community proactively meet new challenges.

EMERGING LEADERS	PRACTICING LEADERS	INTEGRATING LEADERS . . .
Balancing organizational integrity and adaptation	*Balancing organizational integrity and adaptation*	*Balancing organizational integrity and adaptation*
• Struggle with the seeming disconnection of public policy with school community values;	• Begin to combine and connect public policy with school community values by considering the intention and purpose of policy as it relates to work at the school;	• Align public policy with school community values and purposes; proactively initiate, develop, clarify, collaborate on, interpret, influence, and implement public policy;
• React and respond to policy requirements;	• Seek to understand the connection among policy arenas and interpret policies for others in ways that make connections more clear;	• Understand the complexity and dynamic quality of the relationship among policies; apply policies that are well integrated with the school's best practices; respond both strategically and systemically;
• Assume a hierarchical relationship among policy arenas, thereby reacting to external demands in discrete, nonsystemic ways;	• Balance rules and engagement; create guidelines for policy implementation and work collaboratively to implement them.	• Ensure the presence of high engagement and low bureaucratization—more collaboration and fewer rules.
• Create and expect rule-governed policy management; spends little time in conversations aimed at making comprehensive sense of policies.		
Inside/outside: mutual influence	*Inside/outside: mutual influence*	*Inside/outside: mutual influence*
• Communicate to the community;	• Create transactional relationships with external forces which resemble an "exchange economy;" provide services/results in exchange for resources;	• Build reciprocal relationships with external partners to support mutual awareness and learning that lead to meeting the needs of all learners;
• Accept more hierarchical relationships with external forces (e.g., district);	• Work collaboratively in the external context to identify needs and concerns; seek resources for school activities without regard to priorities about learning goals.	• Actively engage and influence the external context to generate the knowledge, resources, and support needed for continuous improvement of teaching and learning.
• React to the external context in a compliant or protective mode;		
• Allow external forces to exaggerate the sense of uncertainty, instability, and urgency in the school.		

254

Inside/outside: building learning relationships
- Manage an internally directed school;
- Engage in relationships with the immediate community and district that are not predicated on a learning relationship;
- Maintain limited connections with networks, external agencies and coaches, universities, and professional organizations.

Inside/outside: building learning relationships
- Encourage individuals to attend professional association activities and to seek higher degrees or credentials;
- Apply for promising partnerships with regional agencies or reform communities that secure additional resources for the school;
- Co-develop partnership criteria/standards that define mutual goals and means;
- Provide invited feedback to external "friends" such as preparation programs or support organizations.

Inside/outside: building learning relationships
- Build and maintain relationships and partnerships with parents and community, support providers, networks, professional organizations, consultants, universities, and personnel in the district office—in order to create new knowledge and proactively meet new challenges;
- Influence the external learning communities to improve professional practice and the preparation of educators;
- Encourage staff to create knowledge and present at professional conferences and write for professional journals.

References

Ackerman, R. H., Donaldson, G. A., Jr., & Van der Bogert, R. (1996). *Making sense as a school leader*. San Francisco: Jossey-Bass.

Adler, M. (1984). *The paideia program*. New York: Macmillan.

Angelou, M. (1993). *Wouldn't take nothing for my journey now*. New York: Random House.

Avolio, B. J. (1999). *Full leadership development*. Thousand Oaks, CA: Sage.

Baker, E., & Popham, J. W. (1973). *Expanding dimensions of instructional objectives*. Englewood Cliffs, NJ: Prentice-Hall.

Baker, W., & Shalit, S. (1992). *Exploring norms and structures that enhance our working together to improve schools—A training syllabus*. Oakland, CA: Group Dynamics Associates.

Barth, R. (1988). School: A community of leaders. In A. Lieberman (Ed.), *Building a professional culture in schools* (pp. 129–147). New York: Teachers College Press.

Barth, R. (1992). *Improving schools from within*. San Francisco: Jossey-Bass.

Barth, R. S. (2001a). *Learning by heart*. San Francisco, Jossey-Bass.

Barth, R. S. (2001b). Teacher leader. *Phi Delta Kappan, 82*(6), 443–449.

Bateson, G. (1972). *Steps to an ecology of mind*. San Francisco: Ballantine.

Bateson, M.C. (1994). *Peripheral visions*. New York: HarperCollins.

Belenky, M. F., & Stanton, A. V. (2000). Inequality, development, and connected knowing. In J. Mezirow et al. (Eds.), *Learning as transformation: Critical perspectives on a theory in progress*. San Francisco: Jossey-Bass.

Bellah, R., Madsen, R., Sullivan, W., Sidler, A., & Tipton, S. (1985). *Habits of the heart*. New York: Harper & Row.

Benham, M., & Cooper, J. (1998). *Let my spirits soar: Narratives of diverse women in school leadership*. Thousand Oaks, CA: Corwin Press.

Bennis, W. (2000). *Managing the dream: Reflections on leadership and change*. Cambridge, MA: Perseus.

Big Picture Company. (2001). *The Principal Residency Network* [Program Description Booklet]. Providence, RI: Author.

Blasé, J., & Blasé, J. (2000). *Empowering teachers: What successful principals do*. Thousand Oaks, CA: Corwin Press.

Block, P. (1996). *Stewardship*. San Francisco: Berrett-Koehler.

Bloom, A. (1987). *The closing of the American mind*. New York: Simon & Schuster.

Bloom, B., Engelhart, M., Furst, E., Hill, W., & Krathwohl, D. (1956). *Taxonomy of educational objectives: Handbook I. Cognitive domain*. New York: McKay.

Bloom, L., & Munro, P. (1995). Conflicts of selves: Nonunitary subjectivity in women administrators' life history narratives. In J. A. Hatch & R. Wisniewski (Eds.), *Life history and narrative*. Washington, D.C.: Falmer Press.

Bohm, D. (1998). *On dialogue*. New York: Routledge.

Bolman, L. G., & Deal, T. E. (1994). *Becoming a teacher leader: From isolation to collaboration*. Thousand Oaks, CA: Corwin Press.

Bowers, C. A. (1969). *The progressive educator and the Depression: The radical years.* New York: Random House.

Bowers, C. A. (1991, April). *The relevance of John Dewey and Gregory Bateson for addressing the ecological crisis.* Paper presented at the annual meeting of the American Educational Research Association, Chicago.

Bowers, C. A., & Flinders, D. (1990). *Responsive teaching: An ecological approach to classroom patterns of language, culture, and thought.* New York: Teachers College Press.

Braddock, J. H., II, & McPartland, J. M. (1990). Alternatives to tracking. *Educational Leadership, 47*(7), 76–79.

Bradley, A. (2000, May 17). Rhode Island district investing in national board certification. *Education Week on the Web* [On-line]. Available: http://www.edweek.org.

Brandt, R. (1985). On teaching and supervising: A conversation with Madeline Hunter. *Educational Leadership, 42*(5), 61–66.

Brandt, R. (1987). On leadership and student achievement: A conversation with Richard Andrews. *Educational Leadership, 45*(1), 9–16.

Brandt, R. (1990). On knowledge and cognitive skills: A conversation with David Perkins. *Educational Leadership, 47*(5), 50–53.

Brandt, R. (Ed.). (2000). *Education in a new era.* ASCD Yearbook. Alexandria, VA: Association for Supervision and Curriculum Development.

Bransford, J., Goldman, S., & Pellegrino, J. (1992). Some thoughts about constructivism and instructional design. In T. M. Duffy & D. H. Jonassen (Eds.), *Constructivism and the technology of instruction: A conversation.* Hillsdale, NJ: Erlbaum.

Bridges, W. (1991). *Managing transitions: Making the most of change.* Reading, MA: Addison-Wesley.

Brody, C., & Witherell, C., with Donald, K., & Lundblad, R. (1991). Story and voice in the education of professionals. In C. Witherell & N. Noddings (Eds.), *Stories lives tell: Narrative and dialogue in education* (pp. 257–278). New York: Teachers College Press.

Brookover, W., Beamer, L., Efthim, H., Hathaway, D., Lezotte, L., Miller, S., Passalacqua, J., & Tornatzky, L. (1982). *Creating effective schools.* Holmes Beach, FL: Learning Publications.

Brooks, J. G., & Brooks, M. G. (1993). *In search of understanding: The case for the constructivist classrooms.* Alexandria, VA: Association for Supervision and Curriculum Development.

Brophy, J., & Good, T. (1986). Teacher behavior and student achievement. In M. Wittrock (Ed.), *Handbook of research on teaching* (pp. 328–375). New York: Macmillan.

Brown, J. S., Collins, A., & Duguid, P. (1989). Situated cognition and the culture of learning. *Educational Researcher, 18*(1), 32–42.

Bruner, J. (1966). *Toward a theory of instruction.* New York: Norton.

Bruner, J. (Speaker). (1994). *Four ways to make a meaning* (Cassette Recording No. RA 4-13-54). New Orleans, LA: American Educational Research Association.

Bruner, J., & Haste, H. (Eds.). (1987). *Making sense: The child's construction of the world.* New York: Methuen.

Brunner, D. (1994). *Inquiry and reflection: Framing narrative practice in education.* New York: State University of New York Press.

Burns, J. M. (1978). *Leadership.* New York: Harper & Row.

Butler, K. (1995, February). Defining the problem—An essential aspect of successful negotiation. *CFIER Viewpoints, 3*(2), 4–5, 9. Sacramento: California Foundation for Improvement of Employer-Employee Relations.

California Professional Standards for Educational Leaders. (2001). Oakland, CA: California Department of Education and the California School Leadership Academy.

Campbell, L., & Campbell, B. (1999). *Multiple intelligences and student achievement: Success stories from six schools.* Alexandria, VA: Association for Supervision and Curriculum Development.

Capra, F. (1975). *The tao of physics.* Berkeley, CA: Shambhala.

Capra, F. (1982). *The turning point.* New York: Simon & Schuster.

Capra, F. (1993). *Guide to ecoliteracy.* Berkeley, CA: Elmwood Institute.

Capra, F. (1994). From the parts to the whole: Systems thinking in ecology and education. *Elmwood Quarterly, 10*(2).

Capra, F. (1996). *Web of life.* New York: Anchor Books.

Capra, F. (1997, April 18). *Creativity and Leadership in Learning Communities.* Lecture at the Mill Valley School District, CA. Available from the Center for Ecoliteracy [On-line]: http://www.ecoliteracy.org/pages/publications.html.

Carlsen, M. B. (1988). *Meaning-making.* New York: Norton.

Carroll, L. (1996). *The complete illustrated Lewis Carroll.* Ware, Hertfordshire, England: Wordsword.

Carter, G. R., & Cunningham, W. G. (2000). *The American school superintendent.* San Francisco: Jossey-Bass.

Carter, K. (1993). The place of story in the study of teaching and teacher education. *Educational Researcher, 22*(1), 5–12, 18.

Caufield, J., Kidd, S., & Kocher, T. (2000). Brain-based instruction in action. *Educational Leadership, 58*(3), 63–65.

Chittenden, E., & Gardner, H. (1991). Authentic evaluation and documentation of student performance. In V. Perrone (Ed.), *Expanding student assessment* (pp. 22–31). Alexandria, VA: Association for Supervision and Curriculum Development.

Clandinin, D. J., & Connelly, M. F. (1991). Narrative and story in practice and research. In D. Schön (Ed.), *The reflective turn: Case studies of reflective practice* (pp. 258–283). New York: Teachers College Press.

Coleman, J., Campbell, E., Hobson, C., McPartland, J., Mood, A., Weinfeld, F., & York, R. (1966). *Equality of educational opportunity.* Supplemental Index 9.10. Washington, DC: U.S. Office of Education.

Combs, A. W., Miser, A. B., & Whitaker, K. S. (1999). *On becoming a school leader: A person-centered challenge.* Alexandria, VA: Association for Supervision and Curriculum Development.

Conzemius, A., & O'Neill, J. (2001). *Building shared responsibility for student learning.* Alexandria, VA: Association for Supervision and Curriculum Development.

Cooper, J. E. (1995). Digging, daring and discovery: Sifting the soil of professional life through journal writing. In C. Brody & J. Wallace (Eds.), *Ethical and social issues in professional education* (pp. 103–117). Albany: State University of New York Press.

Copland, M. A. (2001, March). The myth of the superprincipal. *Pi Delta Kappan, 82*(7), 528–533.

Corcoran, T., Fuhrman, S., & Belcher, C. (2001, June 5). *The struggle for rationality: The use of evidence to make decisions in urban school districts* [Review draft]. Philadelphia: Consortium for Policy Research in Education.

Costa, A. (1989). *The enabling behaviors: A course syllabus.* Sacramento: Search Models Unlimited.

Costa, A., & Garmston, R. (1992). *Cognitive coaching leadership training—A training syllabus.* Berkeley, CA: Institute for Intelligent Behavior.

Costa, A., & Garmston, R. (1994). *Cognitive coaching: A foundation for renaissance schools.* Norwood, MA: Christopher-Gordon.

Costa, A., & Kallick, B. (1993, October). Through the lens of a critical friend. *Educational Leadership, 51,* 49–51.

Costa. A. & Kallick, B. (Eds.). (1995). *Assessment in the learning organization: Shifting the paradigm.* Alexandria, VA.: Association for Supervision and Curriculum Development.

D'Arcanglo, M. (2000, September). How does the brain develop? A conversation with Steven Peterson. *Educational Leadership, 58*(3), 68–71.

Darling-Hammond, L. (1993). Reframing the school reform agenda: Developing capacity for school transformation. *Phi Delta Kappan, 74*(10), 752–761.

Darling-Hammond, L. (1997). *The right to learn.* San Francisco: Jossey-Bass.

Deal, T. E., & Peterson, K. D. (2000). *The leadership paradox.* San Francisco: Jossey-Bass.

Delpit, L. (1995). *Other people's children: Cultural conflict in the classroom.* New York: New Press.

De Vries, R., & Kohlberg, L. (1987). *Programs of early education: The constructivist view.* New York: Longman.

De Vries, R., & Kohlberg, L. (1990). *Constructivist early education: Overview and comparison with other programs.* Washington, DC: National Association for the Education of Young Children.

Dewey, J. (1916). *Democracy and education.* New York: Macmillan.

Dewey, J. (1938). *Experience and education.* New York: Macmillan.

Dietz, M. (2000). *LearnCity Standards-Based Lessons.* San Ramon, CA: LearnCity, Inc.

Diller, D. (1999, May). Opening the dialogue: Using culture as a tool in teaching young African American children. *Reading Teacher, 52*(8), 820–827.

Dominice, P. (1990). Composing education biographies: Group reflection through life histories. In J. Mezirow et al. (Eds.), *Fostering critical reflection in adulthood: A guide to transformative and emancipatory learning* (pp. 194–212). San Francisco: Jossey-Bass.

Donaldson, G. (2000). *Cultivating leadership in schools.* New York: Teachers College Press.

Donaldson, G., & Marnik, G. (Eds.). (1995). *As leaders learn: Personal stories of growth in school leadership.* Thousand Oaks, CA: Corwin Press.

Duffy, T. M., & Jonassen, D. H. (Eds.). (1992). *Constructivism and the technology of instruction: A conversation.* Hillsdale, NJ: Erlbaum.

Dunlap, D. M., & Goldman, P. (1991). Rethinking power in schools. *Educational Administration Quarterly, 27*(1), 5–29.

Edmonds, R. (1979, October). Effective schools for the urban poor. *Educational Leadership, 37*(1), 15–24.

Egan, K. (1979). *Educational development.* New York: Oxford University Press.

Eisner, E. (1988). The ecology of school improvement. *Educational Leadership, 45,* 24–29.

Eisner, E. (2000). What does it mean to say a school is doing well? *Phi Delta Kappan, 82*(5), 367–377.

Elmore, R. (2000). *Building a new structure for school leadership.* Washington, DC: Albert Shanker Institute.

Elmore, R. F., & Burney, D. (1998). *Continuous improvement in Community District #2, New York City.* Pittsburgh, PA: University of Pittsburgh, Learning Research and Development Center.

Etzioni, A. (Ed.). (1998). *The essential communitarian reader.* New York: Rowman & Littlefield.

Etzioni, A. (Ed.). (1999). *Civic repentance.* New York: Rowman & Littlefield.

Fadiman, A. (1997). *The spirit catches you and you fall down.* New York: Farrar, Straus & Giroux.

Feuerstein, R. (1990). The theory of structural cognitive modifiability. In B. Z. Presseisen (Ed.), *Learning and thinking styles: Classroom interaction* (pp. 68–134). Washington, DC: National Education Association.

Feuerstein, R., Klein, P., & Tannenbaum, A. (1991). *Mediated learning experience: Theoretical psychosocial and learning implications.* London: Freund.

Fink, D. (2000). *Good schools/real schools. Why school reform doesn't last.* New York: Teachers College Press.

Fink, E., & Resnick, L. B. (2001). Developing principals as instructional leaders. *Phi Delta Kappan, 82*(6), 598–610.

Follett, M. P. (1924). *Creative experience.* London: Longmans & Green.

Fosnot, C. (1992). Constructing constructivism. In T. M. Duffy & D. H. Jonassen (Eds.), *Constructivism and the technology of instruction: A conversation* (pp. 167–176). Hillsdale, NJ: Erlbaum.

Foster, W. F. (1989). Toward a critical practice of leadership. In J. Smyth (Ed.), *Critical perspectives on educational leadership* (pp. 39–62). London: Falmer.

Freire, P. (1973). *Education for critical consciousness.* New York: Continuum.

Frydman, B., Wilson, I., Wyer, J. (2000). *The power of collaborative leadership.* Melbourne, Australia: Butterworth & Heineman.

Fullan, M. (1999). *Change forces: the sequel.* Philadelphia: Falmer.

Fullan, M., & Hargreaves, A. (1992). *What's worth fighting for?* Andover, MA: Regional Laboratory for Educational Improvement of the Northeast and Islands.

Fullan, M., & Hargreaves, A. (1996). *What's worth fighting for in your school?* New York: Teachers College Press.

Fullan, M., & Hargreaves, A. (1998). *What's worth fighting for out there?* New York: Teachers College Press.

Furtwengler, C. (1999/2000, Fall/Winter). Foreword. . . . Learning inquiry through situated cognition. *Journal of Critical Inquiry Into Curriculum and Instruction, 2*(1), 4–5

Gardner, H. (1983). *Frames of mind.* New York: Basic Books.

Gardner, H. (1991). Moving toward more powerful assessment. In V. Perrone (Ed.), *Expanding student assessment* (pp. 164–166). Alexandria, VA: Association for Supervision and Curriculum Development.

Gardner, H. (1995). *Leading minds: An anatomy of leadership.* NY: Basic Books.

Gardner, J. W. (1990). *On leadership.* New York: Free Press.

Garmston, R., & Wellman, B. (1998, April). Teacher talk that makes a difference. *Educational Leadership, 55*(7), 30–34.

Garmston, R., & Wellman, B. (1999). *The adaptive school.* Norwood, MA: Christopher-Gordon.

Getzels, J. W., & Guba, E. G. (1957). Social behavior and the administrative process. *School Review, 65,* 323–411.

Gilligan, C. (1982). *In a different voice: Psychological theory of women's development.* Cambridge, MA: Harvard University Press.

Glatthorn, A. (1984). *Differentiated supervision.* Alexandria, VA: Association for Supervision and Curriculum Development.

Glickman, C. (1990). *Supervision of instruction: A developmental approach.* Boston: Allyn & Bacon.

Glickman, C. (1993). *Renewing America's schools: A guide for school-based action.* San Francisco: Jossey-Bass.

Glickman, C. (1998). *Revolutionizing America's schools*. San Francisco: Jossey-Bass.

Goals 2000: Educate America Act of 1994, Pub. L. No. 103-446, H.R. 1804 (1994).

Goldberg, M. C. (1998). *The art of the question*. New York: John Wiley & Sons.

Goldman, P., Dunlap, D. M., & Conley, D. T. (1993). Facilitative power and non-standardized solutions to school site restructuring. *Educational Administration Quarterly, 29*(1), 69–93.

Gonzales, S., & Lambert, L. (2001, January). Teacher leadership in professional development schools: Emerging conceptions, identities, and practices. *Journal of School Leadership, 11*(1), 6–24.

Goodlad, J. (1979). *What are schools for?* Bloomington, IN: Phi Delta Kappan Education Foundation.

Goodlad, J. (Ed.). (1987). *The ecology of school renewal*. Chicago: National Society for the Study of Education.

Goodman, R. H., & Zimmerman, W. G. (2000). *Thinking differently: Recommendations for 21st century school board/superintendent leadership, governance, and teamwork for high student achievement*. Marlborough, MA: Educational Research Service & New England School Improvement Council.

Graham, B., & Fahey, K. (March, 1999). School leaders look at student work. *Educational Leadership*, 25–27.

Grath, W. H. (1998). Approaching the future of leadership development. In C. D. McCauley, R. S. Moxley, & E. V. Van Velsor (Eds.), *The handbook of leadership development*. San Francisco: Jossey Bass.

Greene, M. (1988). *The dialectic of freedom*. New York: Teachers College Press.

Greene, M. (1995). *Releasing the imagination*. San Francisco: Jossey-Bass.

Grossman, P., Wineburg, S., & Woolworth, S. (2000, April). *In pursuit of teacher community*. Paper presented at the annual meeting of the American Educational Research Association, New Orleans.

Hale, J. (1994). *Unbank the fire*. Baltimore: Johns Hopkins University Press.

Hall, B. (1976). *The development of consciousness: A confluent theory of values*. New York: Paulist Press.

Hall, B. P., Taylor, B., Kalven, J., & Rosen, L. S. (1990). Developing human values. Fond du Lac, WI: The International Values Institute of Marian College.

Hall, G. E., & Hord, S. M. (2001). *Implementing change: Patterns, principles, and potholes*. Boston: Allyn & Bacon.

Hallinger, P., Leithwood, K., & Murphy, J. (1993). *Cognitive perspectives on educational leadership*. New York: Teachers College Press.

Hallinger, P., & Murphy, J. (1987). Instructional leadership in the school context. In W. Greenfield (Ed.), *Instructional leadership: Concepts, issues and controversies* (pp. 179–203). Boston: Allyn & Bacon.

Harri-Augstein, S., & Thomas, L. (1991). *Learning conversations*. New York: Routledge.

Hawking, S. (Speaker). (1994). *Life works: The Cambridge lectures*. (Cassette Recordings No. 80080). Beverly Hills, CA: Dove Audio.

Haycock, K. (2001, March). Closing the achievement gap. *Educational Leadership, 58*(6), 6–11.

Heifetz, R. A. (1994). *Leadership without easy answers*. Cambridge, MA: Belknap Press of Harvard University Press.

Hershey, P., & Blanchard, K. (1972). *Management of organizational behavior*, 2nd ed. Englewood Cliffs, NJ: Prentice-Hall.

Hilliard, A. (1991, September). Do we have the will to educate all children? *Educational Leadership, 51*, 31–36.

Hirsch, E. D. (1988). *Cultural literacy: What every American needs to know.* NY: Vintage Books.

Holcomb, E. L. (2000). *Asking the right questions* (2nd ed.). Thousand Oaks, CA: Corwin Press.

Hugo, V. (1978). *Notre-Dame of Paris.* New York: Penguin. [1831]

Hyerle, D. (1996). *Visual tools for constructing knowledge.* Alexandria, VA: Association for Supervision and Curriculum Development.

Institute for Educational Leadership (IEL). A report of the task force on the principalship. In Murphy, J., & Schwarz, P. (Eds.), *Reinventing the principalship.* Washington, DC: IEL.

Isaacs, W. (1999). *Dialogue and the art of thinking together.* New York: Currency.

Jalongo, M. R. (1992). Teachers' stories: Our ways of knowing. *Educational leadership, 49*(2), 68–73.

Jensen, Eric. (1998). *Teaching with the brain in mind.* Alexandria, VA.: Association for Supervision and Curriculum Development.

Johnson, R., & Johnson, D. (1988). *Circles of learning* (2nd ed.). Alexandria, VA: Association for Supervision and Curriculum Development.

Jossey-Bass Reader on Educational Leadership. (2000). San Francisco: Jossey-Bass.

Katzenmeyer, M., & Moller, G. (1996). *Awakening the sleeping giant: Leadership development for teachers.* Thousand Oaks, CA: Corwin Press.

Kegan, R. (1982). *The evolving self: Problems and process in human development.* Cambridge, MA: Harvard University Press.

Kegan, R. (1994). *In over our heads: The mental demands of modern life.* Cambridge, MA: Harvard University Press.

Kegan, R., & Lahey, L. (1984). Adult leadership and adult development: A constructivist view. In B. Kellerman (Ed.), *Leadership: Multidisciplinary perspectives* (pp. 199–230). Englewood Cliffs, NJ: Prentice-Hall.

Kellerman, B. (1999). *Reinventing leadership: Making the connection between politics and business.* Albany: State University of New York Press.

Kellerman, B. (Ed.) (1984). *Leadership: Multidisciplinary perspectives.* Englewood Cliffs, N.J.: Prentice-Hall.

Kelley, C., & Peterson, K. (2000, June 15). The work of principals and their preparation: Addressing critical needs for the 21st century. Carnegie Foundation and the National Center on Education and the Economy. Madison, WI: Wisconsin Center for Education Research.

Kentucky Department of Education. Results matter: A decade of difference. In *Kentucky's Public Schools, 1990–2000.* Author.

Kessler, R. (2000). *The soul of education.* Alexandria, VA: Association for Supervision and Curriculum Development.

Knowles, M. S. (1970). *The modern practice of adult education: Andragogy versus pedagogy.* New York: New York Association Press.

Kohlberg, L. (1976). Moral stages and moralization: The cognitive developmental approach. In T. Lickona (Ed.), *Moral development and behavior* (pp. 31–53). New York: Holt, Rinehart & Winston.

Kohn A. (1999, December). *Performance vs. learning: The costs of overemphasizing achievement.* Distinguished Lecture given at the annual conference of the National Staff Development Council, Dallas, TX.

Krovetz, M. L. (1999). *Fostering resiliency.* Thousand Oaks, CA: Corwin Press.

Laborde, G. (1988). *Fine tune your brain.* Palo Alto, CA: Syntony.

Ladson-Billings, G. (1996). *The dreamkeepers: Successful teachers of African American children.* San Francisco: Jossey-Bass.

Lakoff, G. (1987). *Women, fire, and dangerous things*. Chicago: University of Chicago Press.

Lakoff, G., & Johnson, M. (1980). *Metaphors we live by*. Chicago: University of Chicago Press.

Lakoff, G., & Johnson, M. (1999). *Philosophy in the flesh*. New York: Basic Books.

Lambert, L. (1982). *Community as cult: A study of Synanon*. Unpublished manuscript, University of San Francisco.

Lambert, L. (1986). *Communication patterning* [Training Module]. Bay Area Regional Administrative Training Center, Marin County, CA.

Lambert, L. (1988). Staff development redefined. *Phi Delta Kappan, 69*, 665–668.

Lambert, L. (1997). Constructivist leadership defined. In Louis Wildman (Ed.), *School administration: The new knowledge base*. The Fifth Yearbook of the National Council of Professors of Educational Administration. Lancaster, PA.: Technomic Publishing.

Lambert, L. (1998a, April). How to build leadership capacity. *Educational Leadership, 55*(7), 17–19.

Lambert, L. (1998b). *Building leadership capacity in schools*. Alexandria, VA: Association for Supervision and Curriculum Development.

Lambert, L., Collay, M., Dietz, M. E., Kent, K., & Richert, A. E. (1997). *Who will save our schools? Teachers as constructivist leaders*. Thousand Oaks, CA: Corwin Press.

Lambert, L., & Gardner, M. (1993, November). *Transformative leadership and language*. A presentation to the Association of California School Administrators, Burlingame, CA.

Lambert, L., Walker, D., Zimmerman, D., Cooper, J. E., Lambert, M. D., Gardner, M.E., & Ford-Slack, P. J. (1995). *The constructivist leader*. NY: Teachers College Press.

Lambert, M. (1993, October). *Back to the future: A retrospective perspective on restructuring*. Paper presented at the annual meeting of the California Association for Supervision and Curriculum, Orinda, CA.

Lambert, M. (1995, February/March). Reciprocal team coaching. *Thrust for Educational Leadership, 24*, 20–23.

Learning Research & Development Center, University of Pittsburgh, & the National Center on Education and the Economy. (1998). *New standards tests*. New York: Harcourt Brace.

Leinhardt, G. (1992, April). What research on learning tells us about teaching. *Educational Leadership, 49*(7), 20–25.

Leithwood, K. A. (1992, February). The move toward transformational leadership. *Educational Leadership, 49*(5), 8–12.

Lerner, M. (1996). *The politics of meaning: Restoring hope and possibility in an age of cynicism*. Reading, MA: Addison-Wesley.

Lewin, R., & Regine, B. (2000). *The soul at work: Listen, respond, let go*. New York: Simon & Schuster.

Lieberman, A. (1985, June). *Enhancing school improvement through collaboration*. Paper prepared for the Allerton Symposium on Illinois Educational Improvement, Chicago.

Lieberman, A. (Ed.). (1988). *Building a professional culture in schools*. New York: Teachers College Press.

Lieberman, A. (1992, April). *Presidential address*. Speech given at the annual meeting of the American Educational Research Association, San Francisco.

Lieberman, A. (1994, April). *Women, power, and the politics of educational reform: A conversation about teacher education*. Paper presented at the annual meeting of the American Educational Research Association, New Orleans.

Lieberman, A., & Wood, D. (2001). *The work of the National Writing Project: Social practices in a network context.* Palo Alto, CA: Carnegie Foundation.

Lightfoot, S. L. (1983). *The good high school.* New York: Basic Books.

Lipsitz, J. (1995). What should we care about caring? *Phi Delta Kappan, 76*(9), 665–666.

Little, J. W. (1982). Norms of collegiality and experimentation: Workplace conditions of school success. *AERA [American Educational Research Association] Journal, 19*(3), 325–340.

Little, J. W., & Bird, T. (1987). Instructional leadership: "Close to the classroom" in secondary schools. In W. Greenfield (Ed.), *Instructional leadership: Concepts, issues, and controversies* (pp. 118–138). Boston: Allyn & Bacon.

Loevinger, J. (1976). *Ego development: Conceptions and theories.* San Francisco: Jossey-Bass.

Lorsbach, A., & Tobin, K. (1992). Constructivism as a referent for science teaching. In F. Lawrenz, K. Cochran, J. Krajcik, & P. Simpson (Eds.), *Research matters . . . to the science teacher* (pp. 21–27). Manhattan, KS: The National Association for Research in Science Teaching.

Louis, K. S. (1989). The role of the school district in school improvement. In M. Holmes, K. Leithwood, & D. Musella (Eds.), *Educational policy for effective schools* (pp. 145–167). Toronto: OISE Press.

Louis, K. S. (1995). *Professionalism and community: Perspectives on reforming urban schools.* Thousand Oaks, CA: Corwin Press.

Mager, R. F. (1962). *Preparing instructional objectives.* Palo Alto, CA: Feron.

Marsh, J. A. (2000, September). *Connecting districts to the policy dialogue: A review of literature on the relationship of districts with states, schools, and communities.* Seattle: Center for the Study of Teaching and Policy, University of Washington.

Marzano, R., Pickering, D., & Pollack, J. (2001). *Classroom instruction that works.* Association for Supervision and Curriculum Development.

McDonald, J. (2000). The trouble with policy-minded school reform. In *Education Week on the Web* [On-line]. Available: http://www.edweek.org.

McEwan, H., & Egan, K. (1995). *Narrative in teaching, learning, and research.* New York: Teachers College Press.

McIntosh, P. (1999). *Unpacking the knapsack of privilege.* Wellesley, MA: Wellesley College Center for Research on Women.

Meier, D. (1995). *The power of their ideas: Lessons for America from a small school in Harlem.* Boston: Beacon Press.

Mezirow, J. et al. (Eds.). (1990). *Fostering critical reflection in adulthood: A guide to transformative and emancipatory learning.* San Francisco: Jossey-Bass.

Mezirow, J. et al. (Eds.). (2000). *Learning as transformation: Critical perspectives on a theory in progress.* San Francisco: Jossey-Bass.

Miller, L. Scott. (1995). *An American imperative: Accelerating minority educational advancement.* New Haven: Yale University Press.

Millstein, M. M., & Belasco, J. A. (1973). *Educational administration and the behavioral sciences: A systems perspective.* Boston: Allyn & Bacon.

Mitchell, D. E., & Tucker, S. (1992, February). Leadership as ways of thinking. *Educational Leadership, 47*(5), 30–35.

Mitchell, R. (1996). *Front-end alignment: Using standards to steer educational change.* New York: The Education Trust.

Morgan, G. (1997). *Images of organization.* Thousand Oaks, CA: Sage.

Murphy, J. (1994, April). *The changing role of the superintendency in restructuring districts in Kentucky.* Paper presented at the annual meeting of the American Educational Research Association, New Orleans.

National Commission on Excellence in Education. (1983). *A nation at risk: The imperative for educational reform.* A report to the Nation and the Secretary of Education. Washington, DC: U.S. Department of Education.

Newmann, F., Secada, W., & Wehlage, G. (1995). *A guide to authentic instruction and assessment: Vision, standards and scoring.* Madison: Wisconsin Center for Educational Research.

Norris, C., Barnett, B., Basom, M. R., & Yerkes, D. M. (2002). *The learning community: A model for developing transformational leaders.* New York: Teachers College Press.

Novak, J., & Gowin, D. (1984). *Learning how to learn.* New York: Cambridge University Press.

Oakes, J. (1985). *Keeping track: How schools structure inequality.* New Haven, CT: Yale University Press.

Olson, L. (2000, November 1). Principals try new styles as instructional leaders. *Education Week on the Web* [On-line]. Available: http://www.edweek.org.

O'Neil, J. (2001). *Leading with decency and caring: Creating a school culture that brings out the best in people.* Unpublished master's thesis, University of Calgary, Canada.

Osterman, K. F., & Kottkamp, R. B. (1993). *Reflective practice for educators: Improving schooling through professional development.* Newbury Park, CA: Corwin Press.

Palmer, P. (1998). *The courage to teach.* San Francisco: Jossey-Bass.

Patterson, J. (1993). *Leadership for tomorrow's schools.* Alexandria, VA: Association for Supervision and Curriculum Development.

Pellicer, L. O., & Anderson, L. W. (1995). *A handbook for teacher leaders.* Thousand Oaks, CA: Corwin Press.

Perrone, V. (Ed.). (1991). *Expanding student assessment.* Alexandria, VA: Association for Supervision and Curriculum Development.

Piaget, J. (1964). Development and learning. *Journal of Research in Science Teaching, 2*(3), 176–186.

Piaget, J. (1985). *The equilibration of cognitive structures: The central problem of intellectual development.* Chicago: University of Chicago Press.

Piaget, J., & Inhelder, B. (1971). *The psychology of the child.* New York: Basic Books.

Popham, J. (2001, April). *Dereliction discontinued: How AERA can help deter today's misuse of high-stakes testing.* Paper presented at the annual meeting of the American Educational Research Association, Seattle.

Poplin, M. (1994, November). *The restructuring movement and "Voices from the inside": Compatibilities and incompatibilities.* Seminar conducted at the meeting of the Association of California School Administrators, Palm Springs, CA.

Poplin, M., & Weeres, J. (1993, April). *Voices from the inside.* Claremont, CA: Institute for Education in Transformation at the Claremont Graduate School.

Postman, N. (1995). *The end of education: Redefining the value of school.* New York: Random House.

Ramirez, B. C. (1996). Creating a new kind of leadership for campus diversity. In L. Rendon & R. Hope (Eds.), *Educating a new majority: Transforming America's educational system for diversity* (pp. 438–455). San Francisco: Jossey-Bass

Ragland, M. A., Asera, R., & Johnson, J. F. (1999*). Urgency, responsibility, efficacy: Preliminary findings of a study of high-performing Texas school districts.* Austin: Charles A. Dana Center at the University of Texas at Austin.

Reeves, D. B. (1999). Why standards? Academic Achievement in the 90/90/90 schools. In *Accountability in action.* Denver, CO: Advanced Learning Press.

Resnick, L. (1984). *Education and learning to think.* London: Falmer.

Resnick, L. (1987). *Education and learning to think.* Washington, DC: National Academy Press.

Robbins, P., & Alvy, H. (1995). *The principal's companion.* Thousand Oaks, CA: Corwin Press.

Rogers, C. (1959). A theory of therapy, personality, and interpersonal relationships as developed in the client-centered framework. In S. Koch (Ed.), *Psychology: A study of a science: Vol. 3. Formulations of the person and the social context* (pp. 184–256). New York: McGraw-Hill.

Rosaldo, R. (1993). *Culture and imperialism.* New York: Knopf.

Rost, J. C. (1991). *Leadership for the twenty-first century.* New York: Praeger.

Salinger, J. D. (1951). *The catcher in the rye.* Boston: Little Brown & Company.

Sarbin, T. (1986). The narrative root of metaphor for psychology. In T. R. Sarbin (Ed.), *Narrative psychology: The storied nature of human conduct* (pp. 3–21). New York: Praeger.

Schaefer, R. J. (1967). *The school as a center of inquiry.* New York: Harper & Row.

Schlechty, P. C. (1990). *Schools for the 21st century.* San Francisco: Jossey-Bass.

Schlechty, P. (November, 1994). *Top-down support for bottom-up change.* Restructuring Brief, San Mateo, CA: Bay Region IV Professional Development Consortium.

Schlechty, P. C. (2000). *Shaking up the school house.* San Francisco: Jossey-Bass.

Schlechty, P. C. (2001). *Inventing better schools.* San Francisco: Jossey-Bass.

Schmoker, M., & Marzano, R. (1999, March). Standards-based education. *Educational Leadership, (56),* 17–21.

Schön, D. (1987). *Educating the reflective practitioner.* San Francisco: Jossey-Bass.

Senge, P. (1990). *The fifth discipline: The art and practice of the learning organization.* New York: Doubleday.

Senge, P., Cambron-McCabe, N., Dutton, J., & Kleiner, A. (2000). *Schools that learn.* New York: Currency.

Sergiovanni, T. (2000). *The lifeworld of leadership.* San Francisco: Jossey-Bass.

Seuss, Dr., with some help from Prelutsky, J., & Smith, L. (1998). *Hooray for Diffendoofer Day!* New York: Knopf.

Shawn, J. (1994). *Cycles of inquiry.* Unpublished manuscript, California Center for School Restructuring, San Mateo, CA.

Shelton, C. (2000, September). Portraits in emotional awareness. *Educational Leadership, 58*(1), 30–34.

Shepard, L. A. (2000, October). *The role of assessment in a learning culture. Educational Researcher, 29*(7), 4–14.

Siegel, J., & Shaughnessy, M. (1994, March). An interview with Howard Gardner: Educating for understanding. *Phi Delta Kappan, 75*(7), 563–566.

Silver, H., Strong, R., & Perine, M. (2000). *So each may learn.* Association for Supervision and Curriculum Development.

Slavin, R. (1986). *Student team learning* (3rd ed.). Baltimore: Johns Hopkins Team Learning Project.

Spillane, J. P., & Halverson, R. (1999). *Distributed leadership: Toward a theory of school leadership practice.* Paper presented at the annual meeting of the American Educational Research Association, Montreal.

Spillane, J. P., Halverson, R., & Diamond, J. B. (2000). *Towards a theory of leadership practice: A distributed perspective.* Paper presented at AERA, San Francisio. Chicago, Institute for Policy Research, Northwestern University.

Stacey, R. (1992). *Managing the unknowable.* San Francisco: Jossey-Bass.

Steinbeck, J. (1941). *Sea of Cortez, the log from the Sea of Cortez.* New York: Viking Press.

Sterman, J., Meadows, D., Kim, D., & Paul, M. (1999). Organizational learning at work. In *The Systems Thinker Newsletter.* Waltham, MA: Pegasus Communications.

Stigler, J., & Hiebert, J. (1999). *The teaching gap: Best ideas from the world's teachers for improving education in the classroom.* New York: Free Press.

Stoll, L., & Fink, D. (1996). *Changing our schools: Linking school effectiveness and school improvement.* Buckingham, UK: Open University Press.

Szabo, M. A. (1995). Rethinking restructuring: Building habits of effective inquiry. In A. Lieberman (Ed.), *Professional development in the reform era.* New York: Teachers College Press.

Szabo, M., Hoagland, G., Lambert, L., Lopez, J., Starnes, L., Stern, J., Storms, B., & Vieth, R. (April, 2001). *Developing Bold, Socially Responsible Leaders: Strategies for Administrative Preparation Programs.* Paper presented at the annual meeting of the American Educational Research Association, Seattle, WA.

Taba, H. (1957). *Teachers' handbook for elementary social studies.* Reading, MA: Addison-Wesley.

Takaki, R. (1993). *A different mirror: A history of multicultural America.* Boston: Little, Brown.

Tam, H. (1998). *Communitarianism: A new agenda for politics and citizenship.* New York: New York University Press.

Tan, A. (2001). *The bonesetter's daughter.* New York: Putnam.

Tatum, A. (2000, September). Breaking down barriers that disenfranchise African American adolescent readers in low-level tracks. *Journal of Adolescent and Adult Literacy, 44* (1), 52–64.

Tomlinson, C. (2000, September). Reconciliable differences? Standards-based teaching and differentiation. *Educational Leadership, 58*(1), 6–11.

Tyack, D. (1974). *The one best system.* Cambridge, MA: Harvard University Press.

Tyler, R. W. (1949). *Basic principles of curriculum and instruction.* Chicago: University of Chicago Press.

U.S. Department of Education. (1991). *America 2000: An education strategy.* Washington, DC: Author.

U.S. Department of Education. (January 17, 2001). Conversation on school leadership. Washington, DC: Proceedings.

Vygotsky, L. S. (1962). *Thought and language.* Cambridge, MA: MIT Press.

Vygotsky, L. S. (1978). *Mind in society.* Cambridge, MA: Harvard University Press.

Waldrop, M. M. (1992). *Complexity.* New York: Simon & Schuster.

Walker, D. (1994). Reforming assessment in school leadership preparation programs. *The CAPEA [California Association of Professors of Education Administration] Journal, 6*(2), 43–47.

Walker, V. (1996). *Their highest potential: An African American school community in the segregated south.* Chapel Hill: University of North Carolina Press.

Walker, V. S. (1998). *Their highest potential: The story of a school in the segregated south.* Chapel Hill: University of North Carolina Press.

Wasley, P. (2002). Small classes, small schools: The time is now. *Educational Leadership, 59*(5), 6–10.

Weaver, C. (1999). Field-weaving: The new science, learning organizations, and Pathfinder School. Paper submitted to the University of Washington at Bothell.

Weber, M. (1947). *The theory of economic and social organization* (A. M. Henderson & T. Parsons, Trans.). New York: Free Press.

Weber, M. (1968). *On charisma and institution building.* Chicago: University of Chicago Press.

Wedding, R. C. (2001). The influence of race and gender on school participation. State of California Commission on the Status of Women.

Wenger, E. (1998). *Communities of practice.* New York: Cambridge University Press.

Wheatley, M. J. (1992). *Leadership and the new science: Learning about organization from an orderly universe.* San Francisco: Berrett-Koehler.

Wheatley, M. J. (1999). *Leadership and the new science: Discovering order in a chaotic world* (2nd ed.). San Francisco: Berrett-Koehler.

Whittaker, K., & Barnett, B. (2000). *University Partnerships in Leadership Preparation Programs.* University of Northern Colorado, Greeley.

Whyte, D. (1994). *The heart aroused.* New York: Doubleday.

Williams, Belinda (Ed.) (1996). *Closing the achievement gap: A vision for changing beliefs and practices.* Alexandria: Association for Supervision and Curriculum Development.

Witherell, C., & Noddings, N. (Eds.). (1991). *Stories lives tell: Narrative and dialogue in education.* New York: Teachers College Press.

Wolfe, P. (2001). *Brain matters: Translating research into classroom practice.* Alexandria, VA: Association for Supervision and Curriculum Development.

Index

Note: Page numbers followed by the letter *f* indicate figures.

A/LSS. *See* Accountability/Learning Support System

Absenteeism, student, 134, 135, 156–157

Accountability
 constructivist approach to, xv, 170–171
 rise of emphasis on, 2
 school district role in, 170–177, 173*f*–175*f*, 200–201

Accountability/Learning Support System (A/LSS), 183

Achievement, student
 at Engelhard Elementary, 130–134
 gap in, 3
 instructional leadership and, 20
 school effectiveness and, 19
 at Sherman Oaks, 141–142
 teacher expectations and, 20
 testing and, 2

Ackerman, R. H., 41, 75

Action research, 70, 135, 198

Actualizing communities, 51

Adelson, Les, 186

Adler, M., 53

Adult learning
 constructivist approach to, 34–36
 vs. learning by children, xvi

Advocacy
 Glenlawn High program, 137, 138, 139
 inquiry balanced with, 91

AERA. *See* American Educational Research Association

Alameda Unified School District, 189

Alberta, Canada, 199

Alice's Adventures in Wonderland (Carroll), 63

Alvy, H., 19

America 2000 (Department of Education), 9

American Educational Research Association (AERA), 171, 176

Andrews, R., 20

Anecdotes, 114

Angelou, M., 117

Architecture, of Sherman Oaks, 140–141

Arendt, Hannah, viii, 43

Aspiring Principals' Program, 213, 230–233

Assessment, personnel, 194*f*–195*f*

Assessment, student
 authentic, 28, 229, 233–234
 in leadership preparation, 216, 217*f*–218*f*, 224, 227, 229, 231, 233–234
 learners' role in, 28
 school district role in, 171–177, 173*f*–175*f*, 200–201
 state, 2–3

Association(s), professional, 199

Association of California School Administrators, 224–225, 237

Assumptions
 reconstruction of, 45–46
 shared, in leadership preparation, 219–220

Australia, 197, 237

Authentic assessment, 28, 229, 233–234

Authentic conversation, 78

Authentic doing, 213

Authentic learning, 213

Authority, redistribution of, 60, 190–191

Avolio, Bruce J., 38, 39

Baker, Bill, 108, 109*f*

Baker, E., 17

Bargaining, adversarial *vs.* interest-based, 199

Barnett, B., 55, 207, 228, 229

Barth, Roland, 23, 40, 43, 192, 196, 213, 230, 232–233, 241

Bascom, M. R., 207, 228

BASRC. *See* Bay Area School Reform Collaborative

Bateson, G., 23, 44, 48, 49
Bateson, M. C., 239, 242
Bay Area Coalition for Equitable
    Schools, 225
Bay Area School Reform Collaborative
    (BASRC), 183, 189
Beamer, L., 19
Beauty, rubric for, 241–242
Behavioral leadership, 10, 11f, 16–17
Behavioral learning, 10, 11f, 16–17,
    20
Belasco, J. A., 17
Belcher, C., 201
Beliefs
    changes in, 66–67
    in constructivist learning, 26
    shared, in leadership preparation,
        219–220
Bell Junior High, 58
Bellah, R., 49, 51, 54, 59
Benchmarking, 6, 72–73
Benham, M., 114, 117
Bennis, Warren, 37
Big Picture Company, 230
Biology, of knowing, 7
Bird, T., 20
Blanchard, K., 19, 165
Block, P., 37, 60
Bloom, B., 105
Bloom L., 113
Bohm, D., 63, 71, 91
Bouck, Del, 79, 128, 129, 150–155
Bowers, C. A., 23, 49
Braddock, J. H., II, 18
Brain research, 24–26
Branching maps, 93
Brandt, R., 20
Bransford, J., 49, 51
Bridges, William, 80
Brody, C., 116, 118
Brookover, W., 19
Brooks, J. G., 29
Brooks, M. G., 29
Brophy, J., 19
Brown, J. S., 213
Bruner, J., xviii, 7, 20, 21, 29
Brunner, D., 113
Bryan, Peggy, 83–84, 128, 129,
    140–144, 163
Burlow, Donna, 128, 129, 137–139
Burns, J. M., 17, 23
Bush, George W., 2
Businesses, in partnership conversations,
    84–85
Butler, K., 199

Calgary Board of Education, 190
California, testing in, 2
California Center for School
    Restructuring (CCSR), 76,
    182–183
California Literature Project, 69
California Professional Standards for
    School Leaders (CPSELs), 221, 225
California Staff Development Council, 37
California State University at Hayward
    (CSUH), 215, 219–225, 236
Callahan, Daniel, 189–190
Cambron-McCabe, N., 169
Campbell, E., 19
Camus, Albert, vii
Canyon High School, 181
Capra, Fritjof, 41, 49–50, 86, 164, 166
Career Planning Meetings, 139
Carlsen, M. B., 47
Carroll, Lewis, 63
Carter, K., 113, 115
The Catcher in the Rye (Salinger),
    123–124
Categorical questions, 99
Category structures, 92
CCSR. See California Center for School
    Restructuring
Central Park East, 83
Change(s)
    in beliefs, 66–67
    phases of, 80–81
    reciprocity and, 59
    school, stories of, 127–163
    school district, stories of, 178–183
    sea, 78–79
    systemic, 79
Charter schools, 177–178
Children, vs. adults, learning patterns of,
    xvi
Choice, school, 134, 135, 177–178
Citizenship, 8, 54
Civic repentance, 56
Civil rights movement, 9
Clandinin, D. J., 115–116
Closing activities, 96, 97
Coevolution, 51, 55
Cognition, situated, 213
Cognitive coaching, 68–69, 107–108
Cognitive Coaching (Costa and
    Garmston), 107
Cognitive development, 7–8, 24–26,
    29–30
Cohorts, in leadership preparation, 212,
    221, 228, 233
Coleman, J., 19

Coleman Report, 19
Collaborative learning
  ecological principles of, 166–167
  in leadership preparation, 212–213
  school district role in, 198–199
Collaborative teaching
  in community of learners, 22
  school district role in, 198–199
Colleges, leadership preparation pro-
    grams at, 216–234
Collins, A., 213
Combs, A. W., 21
Committee structure, 162
Common school movement, 33
Community(ies)
  ecology of, xvii, 49–51, 54–55
  of leaders, 13*f*, 21–24
  of learners, 13*f*, 21–24
  linguistics and, 91
  participants in, 48–53
  partnership conversations with,
    81–82, 84–85
  school district, interdependence of,
    170–171
  stories of school as, 120–123
  stories of self in, 118–120
Community School District Two, New
    York City, 184–185
Computers, 197
Concentration camps, 31
Conceptual maps, 92–93
Conceptual thought, 92–93
Conley, D. T., 86
Connell, Jim, 157
Connelly, M. F., 115–116
Consciousness, 107–108, 109*f*
Consortium for Policy Research in
    Education (CPRE), 176, 201
Constructing, in leadership preparation,
    209*f*, 211*f*, 214
Constructivist leadership
  challenge of, 32–33
  definitions of, viii, 1, 4, 14*f*, 36
  principles of, 26–28
  purposes of, 32–33
  theoretical roots of, 28–32
Constructivist learning
  definitions of, 1, 14*f*, 24
  principles of, 26–28, 205
  theoretical roots of, 28–32
Content
  in leadership preparation, 214,
    229
  outcomes-based education and, 5
  standards for, 5

Context
  in communities, 59–60
  for leadership, changes in, 2–4
  in learning, 30
  for trust, 212
Contextual authenticity, 213
Contingency leadership, 12*f*, 17–19
Contracts, 195*f*
Conversation(s), 63–88. *See also*
    Linguistics
  agendas in, 64
  constructivist, 64–66
  definition of, 64
  inquiring, 70–75
  leadership of, 86–87, 88*f*, 89
  partnership, 81–86
  patterns of, 90
  personal, 66–70
  sustaining, 75–81
  truth-seeking, 65
  typology of, 66, 67*f*
Conzemius, Ann, 41
Cooper, J. E., 114, 117, 112–126, 198,
    240
Cooperative learning, 22, 28
Corcoran, T., 201
Costa, A., 31, 68, 70, 100, 102, 105,
    107
CPRE. *See* Consortium for Policy
    Research in Education
CPSELs. *See* California Professional
    Standards for School Leaders
Craftmanship, 108, 109*f*
Creating Equitable Bay Area Schools,
    147
CRESST/Consortium for Policy Research
    in Education (CPRE), 176
Critical friendship, 70, 137
Cross-categorical questions, 100–101,
    105–110
CSUH. *See* California State University at
    Hayward
Cubberly, Elwood, 18
Cult communities, 52–53
Culture
  and acts of leadership, 60
  effects on learning, 27
  norms of, 31, 234
Curriculum, international comparisons
    of, 4
Cycles of inquiry, 146, 162, 183

Daniels, Ray, 185–186
Darling-Hammond, L., 170–171
De Vries, R., 30

Delpit, L., 3
Democracy
  preparation for, 8, 54
  in school administration, 16
  school district role in, 187–189
Democracy and Education (Dewey), 16
Department of Education, United States,
  9, 40
Dereliction Discontinued (Popham), 171
Detachment, professional, 118–119
Dewey, John, 1, 6–7, 16, 21, 28, 54, 68
Dialogue
  definition of, 71
  functions of, 71
  in inquiring conversations, 71–75
  linguistics of, 91
  in sustaining conversations, 79–80
Diamond, John B., 41
Dietz, M., 176
A Different Mirror (Takaki), 146
Different Ways of Knowing reform
  model, 133
Direct instruction, 19–20
Districts. *See* School district(s)
Diversity
  cultivation of, xviii
  dialogue and, 71
  in educational communities, 50
  and educators, 9
  impact of, xvii–xviii, 9
  narrative and, 112, 116–123
Doctoral Program in Urban District
  Leadership, Joint, 225
Doing, in leadership preparation, 209*f*,
  210*f*, 213–214
Donaldson, G. A., Jr., 41, 75
Dr. Suess, 171
The Dreamkeepers (Ladson-Billings), 25,
  146
Dreamkeepers team, 146, 162
Dual Immersion Program, 142–143
Duffy, T. M., 7
Duguid, P., 213
Dunlap, D. M., 86
Dutton, J., 169

EAS. *See* Educational Administration
  and Supervision
Ecoliteracy, 49
Ecological cycles, 50
Ecology
  of communities, xvii, 49–51, 54–55
  of knowing, 7
  of school, 23
  of school district, 166–167

Economic status, 27
Edmonds, Ron, 19, 32
Education Trust, 3
Educational Administration and
  Supervision (EAS), 226
Effectiveness, school/learning, 12*f*–13*f*,
  19–21
Efficacy, 107–108, 109*f*
Efthim, H., 19
Egan, K., 23, 113
Eisner, E., 23, 49, 172
Empathy, 63–64
Enabler test, for district policies,
  191–192
The End of Education (Postman), 112
Energy flow, 50
Engelhard Elementary School, 128–134,
  162
Engelhart, M., 105
English fluency and literacy, 141–142
Epiphanies, longitudinal, 239–243
Equality of Educational Opportunity
  (Coleman et al.), 19
Equity
  at Garfield Elementary, 146,
    148–149
  as goal of constructivism, 33
  impact of, xvii–xviii
  and reciprocity, 44
  school district role in, 187–189
  standards and, 5
Ethnicity, sorting by, 18
Etzioni, A., 51, 56
Evaluation. *See* Assessment
Expectations, teacher, and student
  achievement, 20
Experiential learning, 231

Facilitation, 58
Factory, school as, 21, 28
Fadiman, Anne, 89
Fahey, K., 6
Federal mandates, school district
  response to, 191
Feuerstein, R., 7–8, 31
The Fifth Discipline (Senge), 23, 168
Fink, D., 38
Fink, Elaine, 184
First Things First initiative, 157–159,
  185
Flexibility, 50, 108, 109*f*
Flexible scheduling program, 181
Flinders, D., 23
Follett, Mary, 23
Fosnot, C., 7

Foster, Rosemary, 128, 134–139
Foster, William, 40–41
Found Poem exercise, 79–80
Freire, P., 44, 61, 64
Friendship, critical, 70, 137
From the Parts to the Whole: Systems Thinking in Ecology and Education (Capra), 164
Front-End Alignment (Mitchell), 5
Frydman, B., 60
Fuhrman, S., 201
Fullan, M., 55, 83, 152, 172
Fuller, Buckminster, 47
Furst, E., 105
Furtwengler, C., 8, 23

Gardner, Howard, 24–25, 41, 113, 127, 179
Gardner, John, 39
Gardner, M., 110
Gardner, Mary, 164–203, 178–181, 240
Garfield Elementary School, 128–129, 144–149, 162
Garmston, R., 68, 100, 102, 107
GATE. *See* Gifted and Talented Education
Geertz, Clifford, viii–ix
Germany, 4
Getzels, J. W., 23
Gifted and Talented Education (GATE) program, 179–180
Gilligan, C., 55, 217*f*
Glatthorn, A., 19
Glenlawn High School, 128–130, 134–139, 161, 162
Glickman, C., 16, 19, 23, 24, 38, 54, 55, 60, 189
Goals 2000, 9
Goldman, P., 86
Goldman, S., 49, 51
Gonzalez, S., 66
Good, T., 19
Goodlad, J., 23, 49, 53
Gowin, D., 93
Graham, B., 6
Granada High School, 76
Grath, W. H., 42, 49
Great man theory of leadership, 41
Greene, M., vii–ix, 43, 63, 71
Grieving, during transition phase, 80
Grossman, P., 55
Grouping, 12*f*, 17–19
Guba, E. G., 23
Guidance system, 199–200
Gutenberg printing press, 53

Hale, J., 3
Hall, B., 217*f*
Hall, Gene, 39
Hallinger, P., 20, 113
Halverson, Richard, 41
Hanna Ranch School, 71
Harcourt Brace, 176, 181
Hargreaves, A., 83, 152, 172
Harri-Augstein, S., 78
Haste, H., 7, 29, 30
Hathaway, D., 19
Haycock, Katie, 3
Hayward, Anita, 71
Healthy Start Program, 84
Heifetz, Ronald, 38, 41
Hershey, P., 19
Hiebert, J., 31
Hierarchy, in school districts, 85–86, 167
Hill, W., 105
Hilliard, Asa, 56
Hirsch, E. D., 53
Hoagland, G., 218*f*
Hobson, C., 19
Hooray for Diffendoofer Day (Dr. Suess), 171
Hugo, Victor, 53
Huls, Jan, 128, 129, 144–149
Human relations movement, 23
Humility, 123–124
Hunter, M., 20
Hyerle, David, 93

Identity, personal
  acts of leadership and, 60
  conversations and, 66
  stories of self in action and, 117–118
  stories of self in community and, 118–120
Imagination, 63–64
Imaginative rationality, 92
Immersion programs, language, 142–143
Immigrants, sorting of, 17–18
Indian Valley School, 84
Industrial leadership paradigm, 36
Industrial Revolution, 17–18
Information and technology systems, 196–198
Initiating activities, 94–95, 96–97
Innovation
  school district role in, 201–202
  in traditional learning, 15
Input-output model of behavior, 17
Inquiring conversations, 67*f*, 70–75, 88*f*

Inquiry
  advocacy balanced with, 91
  cycles of, 146, 162, 183
  shared, 27–28
Institute for Research and Reform in
    Education, 157
Instruction
  direct, 19–20
  international comparisons of, 4,
    31–32
Instructional leadership, 12*f*–13*f*, 19–21,
    40
Interagency collaboration, 84
Interdependence, 50, 108, 109*f*,
    170–171
International comparisons, 3–4, 31–32
Internet, 198
Invitational leadership, 38
Isaacs, W., 91
Israel, 31

Jacobs, Arthur, 128, 155–161
Jalongo, M. R., 113, 114, 116
Japan, 4, 31–32
Jensen, Eric, 25
Jensen, Theresa, 128, 130–134
Johnson, D., 22
Johnson, Mark, 92
Johnson, R., 22
Joint Doctoral Program in Urban
    District Leadership, 225
Jonassen, D. H., 7
Joyce, B., 23, 49

Kallick, B., 70
Kansas City School District, 185–186
Kegan, Robert, 8, 43, 44, 48, 49, 64, 65,
    71, 94, 113, 114
Kellerman, B., 24, 38
Kelley, C., 225
Kentucky, testing in, 2
Kentucky Education Reform Act, 130
Kessler, R., 45
Klein, P., 7
Kleiner, A., 169
Knowledge
  constructivist approach to, 6–8, 26,
    27, 28
  cooperative learning and, 22
  ecology of, 7
  school *vs.* practical, 25–26
  tacit, narrative and, 124–125
Kohlberg, L., 30, 55, 217*f*
Kohn, Alfie, 5
Kopshy, Stacy, 69

Kottkamp, R. B., 113
Kouchok, Kawsar, 241
Krathwohl, D., 105
Krovetz, M., 22, 200

LAAMP. *See* Los Angeles Annenberg
    Metropolitan Project
Laborde, G., 100
Ladson-Billings, Gloria, 25, 146
Lagunitas School District, 182
Lahey, L., 114
Lakoff, George, 92–93
Lambert, Linda, viii, ix, xv–xix, 34–62,
    52, 63–88, 66, 70, 107, 110,
    127–163, 152, 203, 204–238, 217*f*,
    218*f*, 223, 225, 239–243
Lambert, Morgan Dale, 164–203,
    181–183, 240
Language. *See* Linguistics
Language immersion programs,
    142–143
LDA. *See* Leadership Development
    Alliance
LEAD. *See* Leading for Equity,
    Achievement and Democracy
Leader, definitions of, 37–38, 40
Leadership
  acts of, 57–61
  behavioral, 10, 11*f*, 16–17
  capacity for, 41, 61
  changes in context for, 2–4
  constructivist. *See* Constructivist lead-
    ership
  contingency, 12*f*, 17–19
  definitions of, xviii, 36–42
  evolution of theories of, 8–10
  industrial, 36
  instructional, 12*f*–13*f*, 19–21, 40
  invitational, 38
  learning theories and, parallel develop-
    ment of, 10–15, 11*f*–14*f*
  preparation for. *See* Preparation
  shared, 139, 150, 151
  situational, 12*f*, 17–19
  traditional, 11*f*, 15–16
  transactional, 17
  transformational, 23, 38, 39–40, 110
Leadership Academy, 198, 224–225
Leadership Development Alliance (LDA),
    229
Leadership and the New Science
    (Wheatley), 164
Leading for Equity, Achievement and
    Democracy (LEAD), 225
LearnCity, 176, 180, 197

Learning patterns
  of children *vs.* adults, xvi
  constructivist, xvi–xvii
Learning theories
  evolution of, 8–10
  leading theories and, parallel development of, 10–15, 11*f*–14*f*
Legislation, on standards, 2, 5
Leithwood, K., 39, 40, 113
Lewin, Kurt, 70
Lezotte, L., 19
Lieberman, A., 43, 55
Linguistics, 89–111
  enabling structures in, 94–97
  frameworks for, 105–110
  goal of, 89–90
  paraphrasing and, 90, 91, 101–104, 106–107
  questioning and, 91, 98–101, 106–107
  reciprocity in, 90–91
  reflective pauses and, 104–105, 106–107
  self-organization of thought and, 91, 92–93
  transformative, 110
Listening, constructivist, 89
Little, J. W., 20
Loevinger, J., 217*f*
Longitudinal epiphanies, 239–243
Looping, 200
Lopez, J., 218*f*
Los Angeles Annenberg Metropolitan Project (LAAMP), 186, 187
Louis, K. S., 23, 170

Madsen, R., 51, 54, 59
Mager, R. F., 17
Making Sense (Bruner), 30
Managing Transitions (Bridges), 80
Mandates, school district response to, 165, 191
Maps
  conceptual, 92–93
  visual, 93
Martinez, California, 189–190
Maryland, testing in, 2
Marzano, R., 6, 25
McEwan, H., 113
McIntosh, Peggy, 148
McPartland, J., 19
McPartland, J. M., 18
Meaning
  constructivist approach to, 26, 28
  nature of, 8
  reciprocity in, 43–44, 46

schemas and, 7
  as synonym for pattern, 48
Mediation, zone of, 43
Meier, Deborah, 20, 83
Memories, 59
Mentoring, 69–70
Metacognition
  reflection and, 27, 104
  states-of-mind framework and, 108–110
Metaphors
  community building through, 121–122
  static *vs.* dynamic, 239
  and thought patterns, 92
Mezirow, J., 113
Michaels, Donna, 190
Miller, L., 3
Miller, S., 19
Millstein, M. M., 17
Mindscapes, 221, 222–223, 245–255
Minority leaders, 113, 117–118, 120
Minority students, 25, 27
Mission statements, creation of, 189–190
Mitchell, D. E., 16
Mitchell, Ruth, 5, 32
Modeling, constructive, 78
Modular/flexible scheduling program, 181
Mood, A., 19
Moral development
  narrative and, 123–124
  as purpose of schooling, 54–55
Morgan, G., 39
Multiple intelligences, 25, 179
Munro, P., 113
Murphy, J., 20, 113, 169
The Myth of Sisyphus (Camus), vii

Narrative(s), 112–126
  diversity and, 112, 116–123
  fluidity of, 113
  functions of, 112–116
  and moral choices, 123–124
  power of, 113
  of school as community, 120–123
  of self in action, 117–118
  of self in community, 118–120
  study of, 113
  and tacit knowledge, 124–125
A Nation at Risk (National Commission on Excellence in Education), 9
National Commission on Excellence in Education, 9

National School Boards Association, 176
National security, 9
Negroni, Peter, 169
Networks
  of concepts, 92
  vs. hierarchies, 86
New Standards Test (Harcourt Brace),
  176, 181
New York City, Community School
  District Two, 184–185
Newmann, F., 22
Noddings, N., 113, 115
Noli, Pam, 148
Norris, C., 55, 207, 228
Notre-Dame de Paris (Hugo), 53
Novak, J., 93

Oakes, J., 18
Oakland Unified School District, 225
Objectivism, 115
Olson, L., 40
On Dialogue (Bohm), 63
O'Neil, J., 41, 44
Open-ended questions, 98–99, 100
Operating Manual for Spaceship Earth
  (Fuller), 47
Organizational behavior, 17
Organizational development, 121–122
Organizational inquiry, 70
Organizational learning patterns,
  xvi–xvii, 34–36
Orientation, of personnel, 193*f*
Osterman, K. F., 113
Outcomes, student
  community-related, 84
  constructivist approach to, 28
  standards and, 5

Paideia Program (Adler), 53
Palmer, P., 24, 38, 55–56, 65, 104, 105
Paraphrases
  advanced, framework for, 102, 103*f*,
    102–104
  definition of, 101
  functions of, 90, 91, 101
  as linguistic tool, 90, 91, 98, 101–104,
    106–107
  vs. questions, 98
Parent(s)
  involvement of, 82–83
  partnership conversations with,
    81–84
  teacher conferences with, 83
Partnership(s)
  in educational community, 50

in leadership preparation, 224–225,
    234, 236–237
Partnership conversations, 67*f*, 81–86,
    88*f*
Passalacqua, J., 19
Pathfinder School, 79
Pattern(s)
  of conversation, 90
  learning, xvi–xvii, 34–36
  meaning as synonym for, 48
  relationship, xvii, 42
  thought, 92
Patwin Elementary, 106
Pauses, reflective, 104–105
Pedagogy, in leadership preparation,
    228–229, 233
Pellegrino, J., 49, 51
Performance standards, 5
Peripheral Visions (Bateson), 239
Personal authenticity, 213
Personal conversations, 66–70, 67*f*, 88*f*
Personnel policies, 192–196, 193*f*–195*f*
Peterson, Kent, 225
Pettigrew, Mary Jo, 84
Piaget, J., 7, 29
Plato, 24
Poem exercise, Found, 79–80
Policies, district
  enabler test for, 191–192
  personnel, 192–196, 193*f*–195*f*
Popham, J., 17, 171, 176
Poplin, M., 40, 55
Postman, Neil, 112
Potentials, 45
Power. *See* Authority
Preparation, leadership, 204–238
  assessment in, 216, 217*f*–218*f*, 224,
    227, 229, 231, 233–234
  challenges to, 234–238
  design principles for, 207–216, 209*f*,
    210*f*–211*f*
  examples of programs for, 216–234
  need for change in, 206–207
  traditional, 207
Principal(s)
  as initiator of change, 129
  leadership preparation for, 204–238
Principal Residency Network (PRN),
    230–233, 236
Printing press, Gutenberg, 53
PRN. *See* Principal Residency Network
Professional Administrative Credential
    Program, 215
Professional associations, 199
Professional detachment, 118–119

Professional development. *See also*
  Preparation
  school district role in, 194*f,* 196
  traditional *vs.* constructivist, 194*f*
Protective factors, 199–200
Protocol conversation, 75, 76–77
Proximal development, zone of, 7, 30, 43
Purposing, in leadership preparation,
  209*f,* 210*f,* 212–213

Questions
  categorical, 99
  cross-categorical, 100–101, 105–110
  frameworks for, 105–110
  in inquiring conversations, 74–75
  as linguistic tool, 91, 98–101, 106–107
  open-ended, 98–99, 100
  vs. paraphrases, 98
  rhetorical, 99

Race
  effects on learning, 27
  sorting by, 18
Racism, reciprocity and, 44
Radial concept maps, 92–93
Raising the Bar (National School Boards
  Association), 176
Ramirez, B., 112, 116–117
Rationality, imaginative, 92
Reading comprehension, 92–93
Reassignment, personnel, 195*f*
Reciprocity, 43–48
  capacity for, 44
  change and, 59
  in conversations, 63, 81–86
  definition of, 44, 45, 81
  in linguistics, 90–91
  in meaning making, 43–44
  narrative and, 115
  in relationship patterns, 42
Recruitment, personnel, 193*f*
Reductionist language, 110
Reeves, D. B., 235
Reflection
  definition of, 68
  metacognition and, 27, 104
  through narratives, 112, 113–114,
    124–125
  in personal conversations, 68, 69
  and tacit knowledge, 124–125
Reflective pauses, 104–105, 106–107
Reframing, in leadership preparation,
  209*f,* 211*f,* 214–215
"Reframing the School Reform Agenda"
  (Darling-Hammond), 170–171

Relationship patterns
  diversity and, xvii
  and growth and development, xvii
  as reciprocal processes, 42
Remedial classes, 18
Repentance, civic, 56
Residencies, in leadership preparation, 231
Resiliency, student
  in community of learners, 22
  definition of, 199–200
  school district role in, 199–200
Resnick, L., 8, 23, 184, 213
Resources, devolution of, school district
  role in, 190–191
Respect, 108
Responsibilities, devolution of, school
  district role in, 190–191
Rhetorical questions, 99
Robbins, P., 19
Roberts, Charlotte, 41
Rogers, Carl, 51
"The Role of the School District in
  School Improvement" (Louis), 170
Roosevelt, Eleanor, 240
Rost, J. C., 15, 36
Roszak, Theodore, 49
Rubino, Rick, 66
Rubric, for beauty, 241–242
Rubric for Bold, Socially Responsible
  Leadership, 220, 222–223, 245–255
Rusk, Benjamin, 33

Salinger, J. D., 123–124
San Francisco State University, 225
San Jose State University, 225
San Lorenzo, California, 197
Saratoga School District, 178–181
Sarbin, T., 115
Schaefer, Robert, 70
Schemas, formation and reformulation
  of, 7, 29, 30, 45–46
Schen, Molly, 230
Schlechty, P., 23, 165, 201
Schmoker, M., 6
Schön, D., 25, 68, 124
School(s)
  change in, stories of, 127–163
  choice, 134, 135, 177–178
  as community, stories of, 120–123
  as ecology, 23
  effectiveness of, 12*f*–13*f,* 19–21
  as factory *vs.* community of learners,
    21, 28
  hierarchy in, 85–86
  shared purpose of, 53–55

The School as a Center of Inquiry
    (Schaefer), 70
School district(s), 164–203
    accountability and, 170–177,
        173*f*–175*f*, 200–201
    Alameda Unified, 189
    and alternative education options,
        177–178
    assessment and, 171–177, 173*f*–175*f*,
        200–201
    as ecosystem, 166–167
    guiding principles for, 187–202, 188*f*
    hierarchy in, 85–86, 167
    as interdependent community,
        170–171
    Kansas City, 185–186
    Lagunitas, 182
    mandates and, 165, 191
    New York City, Community Two,
        184–185
    Oakland Unified, 225
    Saratoga, 178–181
    South Pasadena Unified, 186–187
    standards and, 171–177
    stories of, 178–187
    superintendent's role in, 168–169
    Surrey, 198
    traditional, 167–168, 173*f*–175*f*
    university partnerships with, 236
School stories, 127–163
    analysis of, 161–163
    Engelhard Elementary, 128–134, 162
    Garfield Elementary, 128–129,
        144–149, 162
    Glenlawn High, 128–130, 134–139,
        161, 162
    Sherman Oaks Community Charter,
        128–130, 140–144, 163
    themes of, 128–130
    Winterburn, 128–129, 150–155, 162
    Wyandotte High, 128–130, 155–161
Schools That Learn (Senge), 41, 169
Sea change, 78–79
Sea of Cortez (Steinbeck), 34
Secada, W., 22
Security, national, 9
Self-assessment, 27
Self-construction, 68
Self in action, stories of, 117–118
Self in community, stories of, 118–120
Self-modification, 8
Self-organization, 91, 92–93
Senge, P., 23, 41, 57, 91, 168, 169, 216
Sergiovanni, T., 37, 38, 40, 41, 52
Shalit, Stan, 108, 109*f*

Shared beliefs and assumptions,
    219–220
Shared inquiry, 27
Shared leadership, 139, 150, 151
Shawn, J., 183
Shepard, Lorrie, 172–176
Sherman Oaks Community Charter
    School, 83–84, 128–130, 140–144,
    163
Sidler, A., 51, 54, 59
Silences, 104–105
Silver, Harvey, 25
Singleton, Glenn, 148
Situated cognition, 213
Situated learning, 8, 213
Situational leadership, 12*f*, 17–19
Slavin, R., 22
Small learning communities (SLCs),
    159–160
Small school movement, 20
Social activity, learning as, 27
Socialization, of educators, 9
South Pasadena Unified School District,
    186–187
Space program, 9
Spanish-speaking students, 141–142
Spillane, James, 41
*The Spirit Catches You and You Fall
    Down* (Fadiman), 89
Spirituality, 55–57
Stacey, R., 91
Staff. *See* Personnel policies; Professional
    development
Standards
    benchmarks and, 6
    constructivist approach to, xv, 5–6
    content *vs.* performance, 5
    definitions of, 4–6
    dialogue on, 72–73
    implementation of, 5
    legislation on, 2, 5
    rise of, 2
    role of, 5–6
    for school administrators, 235–236
    school district and, 171–177
Starnes, L., 75, 76, 218*f*
State(s)
    assessment by, 2–3
    effectiveness theory and, 21
    mandates, school district response to,
        191
States-of-mind framework, 107–110,
    109*f*
Steele, Jane, 148
Steinbeck, John, 34

Stern, J., 218*f*
Stewardship
  definition of, 37
  vs. leadership, 37, 60
Stewart, Mary, 159
Stigler, J., 31
Stoll, L., 38
Storms, B., 218*f*
Story. *See* Narrative
Structures
  in linguistics, 94–97
  in relationships, 47
Dr. Suess, 171
Sullivan, W., 51, 54, 59
Superintendent(s)
  leadership preparation for, 204–238
  role of, 168–169
Supervision, personnel, 194*f*–195*f*
Support, by school district, 170
Surrey School District, 198
Sustainability, 50
Sustainable development, 75
Sustaining conversations, 67*f*, 75–81,
  88*f*
Sweeney, Jim, 169
Synanon (cult), 52
Synergy, 47–48
Systemic change, 79
Szabo, M., 182, 203, 204–238, 218*f*

Taba, H., 105
Takaki, R., 146
Talking Circle, 79
Tan, Amy, 241–242
Tannenbaum, A., 7
The Tao of Physics (Capra), 49
Tardies, 156–157
The Teaching Gap (Stigler and Hiebert),
  31
Technology systems, 196–198
Test(s)
  enabler, for district policies, 191–192
  standardized, 2
Texas, testing in, 2
Thinking, self-organization of, 91, 92–93
Third International Math and Science
  Study (TIMSS), 3–4, 31
Thomas, L., 78
Thompson, Walt, 84, 128, 129, 156–160
Thorarinson, Brian, 135, 136, 137
TIMSS. *See* Third International Math
  and Science Study
Tipton, S., 51, 54, 59
Tornatzky, L., 19
Total Quality notions, 23

Tracking, 12*f*, 17–19
Traditional leadership, 11*f*, 15–16
Traditional leadership preparation,
  207
Traditional learning, 11*f*, 15–16
Traditional school districts, 167–168,
  173*f*–175*f*
Trait theory, 12*f*–13*f*
Transactional leadership, 17
Transfer, personnel, 195*f*
Transformational leadership
  vs. constructivist leadership, 39–40
  definition of, 38
  goal of, 39
  human relations movement and, 23
  language of, 110
Transforming, in leadership preparation,
  209*f*, 211*f*, 215–216, 217*f*–218*f*
Transitions
  phases of, 80–81
  reciprocity and, 59
Trust
  in community building, 121
  context for, 212
  in conversation, 65
  in leadership preparation, 208–212,
    209*f*, 210*f*
  reciprocity and, 45
Truth
  definition of, 65
  search for, in conversation, 65
Tucker, S., 16
The Turning Point (Capra), 49

UNC. *See* University of Northern
  Colorado
Unions, 199
United States Department of Education,
  9, 40
Universities, leadership preparation pro-
  grams at, 216–234
University of California at Berkeley, 225
University of Northern Colorado (UNC),
  227–229, 236
Unpacking the Knapsack of Privilege
  (McIntosh), 148

Values, in leadership preparation, 233
Van der Bogert, R., 41, 75
Victoria, Australia, 197
Vieth, R., 218*f*
Vision, school district role in, 189–190
Voices from the Inside (Poplin), 55
Vouchers, 177–178
Vygotsky, L. S., 7, 21, 30–31, 43

Waivers, 195*f*

Walker, Deborah, 1–33, 127–163, 240–241

Walker, Vanessa Siddle, 25

Washor, Elliot, 230

Wasley, P., 200

Weaver, Chris, 79

The Web of Life (Capra), 49

Weber, Max, 20, 23

Wedding, R. C., 200

Wehlage, G., 22

Weinfeld, F., 19

What Are Schools For? (Goodlad), 53

What's Worth Fighting For in Your School (Fullan and Hargreaves), 152

Wheatley, M. J., 39, 44, 45, 67, 71, 164, 170, 187

Whittaker, K., 229

Whyte, D., 57

Wichita State University, 225–227

Williams, B., 3

Wilson, I., 60

Wineburg, S., 55

Winterburn School, 79, 128–129, 150–155, 162

Witherell, C., 113, 115, 116, 118

Wolfe, Pat, 25

Women leaders, 113, 117–118

Women's movement, 9

Wood, D., 55

Woolworth, S., 55

Writing, reflective, 124–125

Wyandotte High School, 84, 128–130, 155–161

Wyer, J., 60

Yerkes, D. M., 207, 228

Yerkes (in press), 55

York, R., 19

Zimmerman, Dianne, 74, 88, 89–111, 107, 240

Zone of mediation, 43

Zone of proximal development, 7, 30, 43

About the Authors

The authors of this text have served in practically all educational roles: teacher, principal and assistant principal, district director, coordinator, assistant superintendent, superintendent, county office and leadership academy directors, international consultant, and professor. We have observed and worked directly in K–12 schools in seven states, as well as consulted with schools and educational organizations nationally and internationally. The reader will understand that we share a common worldview. We thoroughly enjoy our journeys together. With each conversation, we learn more about each other, and about ourselves.

Specifically, the authors bring both common and unique qualities to this project.

Linda Lambert is Professor Emeritus in the Department of Educational Leadership at California State University, Hayward (CSUH), a role that enabled her to observe in and work with numerous Bay Area schools and districts each year. Before moving to CSUH, she worked as a teacher leader, change agent, and administrator in five middle schools and districts, two high schools, a district and county office, and regional academies. She is lead author of the 1995 text, *The Constructivist Leader*, 1997's *Who Will Save Our Schools?*, and is the author of *Building Leadership Capacity in Schools*. These writings have led to work with thousands of principals, teacher leaders, and district personnel throughout the world. Her writing interests include work with leadership and leadership capacity, professional and international development, and school and district restructuring.

Deborah Walker, formerly of California, resides in Louisville, Kentucky, where she is Senior Deputy Director of the Collaborative for Teaching and Learning. Before moving to Kentucky, Deborah served on the faculty of the Department of Educational Leadership, California State University at Hayward, where she led the development of a new master's degree program, based on the principles of constructivist leadership and learning. She has experience as a high school teacher and principal, and as an assistant superintendent for instruction in California. She holds a doctorate in educational leadership and multicultural education from the University of the Pacific, Stockton, California.

Diane P. Zimmerman is an elementary school principal in Davis, California. After completing her master of arts from the University of the Pacific in communicative disorders with an emphasis in linguistic development, she worked as a speech and language specialist, a special education teacher, and an assistant director of special education. She is a consultant to the Institute for Intelligent Behavior and a staff developer for the Association of Supervision

and Curriculum Development. Her writings are primarily in the area of educational administration. She is a doctoral student with the Fielding Institute
in Santa Barbara, working in the field of organizational development.

Joanne E. Cooper is an Assistant Professor of Educational Administration
at the University of Hawaii at Manoa. She holds a doctorate in educational
policy and management from the University of Oregon. Her current research
interests include the use of narrative and autobiography in professional life,
organizational development, and qualitative research strategies. Her most
recent publications include an article on the use of narrative in studying the
school principalship in *The International Journal of Qualitative Studies in
Education* and an article on the use of journal-keeping in the professional life
of women administrators in *Initiatives* and in *Educational Considerations.*

Morgan Dale Lambert is a former high school teacher and counselor, principal and vice-principal of four schools, and superintendent and assistant superintendent for three school districts. He has designed and implemented a broad
array of innovative educational programs in schools and districts, all with a
distinctly constructivist flavor. He is currently serving as consultant, facilitator, and coach in two California networks of restructuring schools, including
suburban and urban districts such as Oakland and San Francisco.

Mary E. Gardner began her career as an English teacher in Rochester, New
York, a large urban school district. In Rochester, she worked as a speech therapist and language development specialist in Project Follow-Through, and had
the opportunity to work with the committee reorganizing the district to achieve
equal access and quality. In California, she began her administrative career in
Saratoga as coordinator of early childhood education and assistant superintendent of curriculum and instruction. After three intervening years as a vis-
iting practitioner at the Harvard Principals' Center and teaching at California
State University, Hayward, she returned to Saratoga as superintendent.

Margaret Szabo is Associate Professor in the Department of Educational
Leadership at California State University, Hayward (CSUH) where she facilitates leadership learning cohorts and works with numerous Bay Area schools
and districts. Before coming to CSUH, she was a teacher, teacher leader, and
high school administrator. This work focused on facilitating teacher collaboration and schoolwide systems for continuous improvement in teaching and
learning. She was the founding director of the Bay Area Coalition of Essential
Schools, a role that enabled her to work with various high schools and high
school leadership teams in the region and across the country. In 1991 she
founded the California Center for School Restructuring and served as Executive
Director from 1991 to 1997. This work included design and support of regional
and statewide support networks for 180 schools engaged in restructuring of
teaching and learning. Her inquiry and writing interests include designs for
leadership development, learning communities, leadership for small schools
and, anti-racist leadership.